PARTIES, ELECTIONS AND CLEAVAGES
ISRAEL IN COMPARATIVE AND THEORETICAL PERSPECTIVE

Israeli History, Politics and Society
Series Editor: Efraim Karsh, King's College London
ISSN 1368-4795

Providing a multidisciplinary examination in all aspects, this series serves as a means of communication between the various communities interested in Israel: academics, policy-makers, practitioners, journalists and the informed public.

Other books in the series:

Peace in the Middle East: The Challenge for Israel
edited by Efraim Karsh

The Shaping of Israeli Identity: Myth, Memory and Trauma
edited by Robert Wistrich and David Ohana

Between War and Peace: Dilemmas of Israeli Security
edited by Efraim Karsh

U.S.–Israeli Relations at the Crossroads
edited by Gabriel Sheffer

From Rabin to Netanyahu: Israel's Troubled Agenda
edited by Efraim Karsh

Israel at the Polls 1996
edited by Daniel J. Elazar and Shmuel Sandler

In Search of Identity: Jewish Aspects in Israeli Culture
edited by Dan Urian and Efraim Karsh

Israel: The Dynamics of Change and Continuity
edited by David Levi-Faur, Gabriel Sheffer and David Vogel

Israel: The First Hundred Years (5 volumes)
edited by Efraim Karsh

Revisiting the Yom Kippur War
edited by P.R. Kumaraswamy

Parties, Elections and Cleavages:
Israel in Comparative and Theoretical Perspective

Edited by
Reuven Y. Hazan
and Moshe Maor

FRANK CASS
LONDON • PORTLAND, OR

First published in 2000 in Great Britain by
FRANK CASS PUBLISHERS
Newbury House, 900 Eastern Avenue
London IG2 7HH

and in the United States of America by
FRANK CASS PUBLISHERS
c/o ISBS
5804 N.E. Hassalo Street
Portland, Oregon 97213-3644

Website: www.frankcass.com

British Library Cataloguing in Publication Data

Parties, elections and cleavages: Israel in comparative and
theoretical perspective
– (Israeli history, politics and society)
1. Political parties – Israel 2. Elections – Israel 3. Israel – Politics
and government
I. Hazan, Reuven Y., 1962– ii. Maor, Moshe
320.9'5694

ISBN 0 7146 5076 5 (cloth)
ISBN 0 7146 8123 7 (paper)
ISSN 1368-4795

Library of Congress Cataloging-in-Publication Data

Parties, elections, and cleavages: Israel in comparative and theoretical perspective /
edited by Reuven Y. Hazan and Moshe Maor
    p. cm. – (Israeli history, politics, and society, ISSN 1368-4795)
  ISBN 0-7146-5076-5 (cloth) – ISBN 0-7146-8123-7 (paper)
    1. Political parties – Israel. 2. Elections – Israel. 3. Religion and state – Israel.
  4. Comparative government. I. Hazan, Reuven Y., 1962– II. Maor, Moshe.
  III. Series.

JQ1830.A979 P37 2000
324.25694 – dc21   00-023786

This group of studies first appeared in a Special Issue of *Israel Affairs* 6/2 (Winter 1999),
'Parties, Elections and Cleavages: Israel in Comparative and Theoretical Perspective'
ISSN 0954-6553 published by Frank Cass.

Printed in Great Britain by
Antony Rowe Ltd., Chippenham, Wilts.

Contents

In honour of Emanuel Gutmann

Preface

REUVEN Y. HAZAN AND MOSHE MAOR

This book brings together a set of thorough, authoritative chapters on parties, elections and cleavages that address theoretical aspects of these concepts with reference to Israel, and subject Israel to a comparative analysis. The book is comprised of three main sections. Part 1, 'Theoretical Perspective', is comprised of chapters written by the most prominent international scholars in the field, who focus on some of the core concepts currently under debate. Part 2, 'Religion and State', presents chapters from major scholars throughout Israel who address a most volatile issue that has resurfaced, one that challenges 'secular' societies in general, and Israel in particular, at the end of the twentieth century. Part 3, 'Party System Change', includes chapters from the top Israeli scholars on political parties and party systems who deal with both long- and short-term changes in the Israeli party system of the 1990s, while placing it in a comparative and historical perspective. What emerges from this book is an analysis, couched within comparative and theoretical perspectives, that sheds new light on the themes of parties, elections and cleavages in general, and on Israeli politics and society in particular.

Parties, Elections and Cleavages: Israel in Comparative and Theoretical Perspective

MOSHE MAOR AND REUVEN Y. HAZAN

The fields of political parties, electoral systems and social cleavages have recaptured much interest in political science and within this context Israel has become an indispensable case study in the developing research literature. This volume brings together a set of thorough, authoritative articles on parties, elections and cleavages that address theoretical aspects of these concepts with reference to Israel and subject Israel to a comparative analysis. The articles are revised versions of papers delivered at a Hebrew University conference in honour of Emanuel Gutmann. It is to him, therefore, that this volume is dedicated.

Written for academics, graduate students and practitioners who wish to understand Israeli politics, each of the essays embodies a major source of information on a particular subject. That is, while concentrating on developments over the past decade – and some even during earlier periods – the essays set them in the context of either a theoretical or a comparative perspective and assess their influence on contemporary politics in Israel.

The 'holy trinity' of studies dealing with party system change consists of political parties, electoral systems and societal cleavages. This volume starts from the perspective that the trigger for changes in party systems and each of their components, might come from anywhere in the political system. Methodologically, this perspective implies that each of the aforementioned parts can be treated as either dependent or independent variables, depending on the questions asked.[1]

Taken as independent variables, electoral systems and societal cleavages are assumed to affect the parties and thereby, the party system. An alternative causal chain, endorsed here, stresses the strategic aspects of party behaviour. Political parties who have a vested interest in their own survival as organizations are assumed to mould electoral opinion and affect the 'rules of the game' by interacting with other parties. The

Moshe Maor is Associate Professor of Political Science at the Hebrew University of Jerusalem.
Reuven Y. Hazan is Lecturer in Political Science at the Hebrew University of Jerusalem.

component elements of the party system may, therefore, be considered
factors that can inhibit party system change.

An alternative causal chain is that of the system influencing its
participants. From one perspective, the party system is only a 'system of
interactions',[2] while from another, it is assumed to affect parties per se
by creating a reference point in relation to which the system operates.
Modes of coalition formation and the relationship between government
and opposition suffice to emphasize this point.

Parties nowadays operate in a context wherein cleavage structures –
class in particular, but social cleavages more generally – are weakening
as determinants of party support in advanced industrial countries. At the
same time, there is a rise in issue voting.[3] This generalization is not
without its reservations. Mair's analysis shows a rather subdued picture
of electoral change, demonstrating that the extent of any de- or
realignment has been modest.[4]

The general trend of decline in the importance of social cleavages in
electoral politics is also not without exceptions.[5] Regional identity
concerns in Canada and Belgium, for example, as well as race and
ethnicity factors in the United States, exemplify this point. In Israel,
while issue voting has risen, social cleavages have maintained much of
their ability to account for voting patterns. The major source for this
continued relevance of social cleavages in Israeli politics lies in the
nature of the issues on the agenda. These issues involve identity
dilemmas that reinforce, rather than challenge, existing social cleavage
structures.[6]

The stress on the pro-active and strategic nature of party behaviour
raises a question regarding the response of political parties to the
challenges derived from the aforementioned trends and the resulting
consequences in terms of party system change. Two broad views
dominate the understanding of students of politics concerning the
stabilizing factors that inhibit change. The first sees the powerful role of
institutions in shaping behaviour.[7] The second focuses on the role of
social cleavages in freezing the structure and direction of inter-party
competition.[8] The focus favoured here stresses the ways that the 'core
parties' – usually between two and four, with around 70 per cent of the
vote[9] – are trying to adapt to the weakening of cleavages as determinants
of party support and the emergence of issues in the calculus of voters.
Emphasis is placed on the strategies employed by parties to promote
their image – and their success in doing so – which reflect on the
autonomy of the electorate.

The questions that arise from the theoretical and comparative
analyses of the Israeli case seek to clarify aspects of constitutional
reforms and issue politics in relation to both political parties and to
party system change, or a lack thereof. Five important questions are

addressed throughout this special issue:

- What happens to party systems when social cleavages lose their force?
- Why do these processes take place later in some countries than in others?
- What are the mechanisms that trigger the emergence of issue voting while maintaining the ability of social cleavages to account for voting patterns?
- Why did the weakening of the cleavage structures and the derived fluidity of party systems not lead to substantial changes in the structure of party competition?
- What strategies are employed by political parties to neutralize destabilizing effects derived from these processes?

This volume expands both the comparative and the theoretical knowledge of parties, elections and cleavages. The rationale for subjecting Israel to this examination is twofold. First, electoral politics in Israel is engendered with identity dilemmas, which intertwine with issue and social-group based voting. Second, after the 1996 institutional reform – the direct election of the Prime Minister – Israel's regime acquired a unique blend of parliamentary and presidential qualities.

The monumental reform of the 'Basic Law: The Government' – originally enacted in 1968 and amended in 1992 – changed the electoral, political and constitutional systems in Israel.[10] The new electoral law makes Israel the first country to directly and popularly elect its *Prime Minister*, concurrently with the parliamentary elections. This new system was first implemented in the 1996 elections and was recently employed for a second time in the 1999 elections. The Prime Minister was elected using the two-ballot system – similar to French and Russian Presidential elections – thus requiring an absolute majority. The Israeli parliament, the Knesset, continued to be elected by an extreme form of proportional representation, based on fixed party lists with the entire country serving as one constituency and the legal threshold set at only 1.5 per cent, on the same day as the first round of the Prime Ministerial election.

The directly-elected Prime Minister has the power to nominate the government, but a parliamentary vote of investiture is required before the government can take office and begin to function. If the Knesset does not approve the Prime Minister's government, the result is new elections for both the Knesset and the Prime Minister. At any time during the Prime Minister's tenure, he can be ousted by the Knesset through a vote of no-confidence, which requires only a bare majority of 61 out of the 120 Members of Knesset (MKs). However, such a removal of the Prime Minister brings about the dissolution of the Knesset as well,

FIGURE 1

THE OLD AND THE NEW ELECTORAL AND POLITICAL SYSTEMS IN ISRAEL

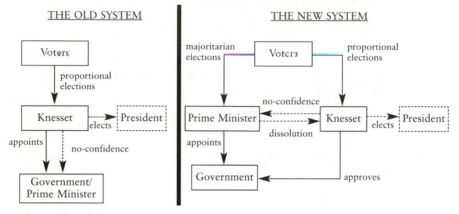

Source: Adapted from Hazan[11]

heralding new elections for both. If the Knesset votes to remove the Prime Minister from office with an extraordinary majority of 80 MKs, new elections are held for the Prime Minister only. By the same token, the Prime Minister has the power to dissolve the Knesset, which ends his tenure as well and forces new elections for both.

The main political reform that resulted from the new law is that Israel ceased to be a purely parliamentary democracy, due to its direct election of the Prime Minister. In parliamentarism, the executive emerges from and is responsible to the legislature – a fusion of powers – whereas in presidentialism, there exists a separation of executive origin and survival from the legislature. As of 1996, with the first direct election of the Prime Minister, the head of the executive branch no longer emerged from the legislature, but instead was separately elected. The direct popular election of the Prime Minister disengaged the executive branch from the legislature and hence dismantled the parliamentary system that Israel had possessed since its creation. Israel thus no longer belongs to the parliamentary regimes category. Yet, it did not cross into the presidential category, because while the Prime Minister is elected separately, he continues to be responsible to the Knesset and must be a member of it – an apparent violation of the separation of powers principle.

Israel is also not 'semi-presidential', as is the French Fifth Republic. Semi-presidentialism is a 'mixed' regime, whereby a directly-elected president coexists with a government headed by a premier who rests on parliamentary confidence.[12] Such a regime oscillates between periods of presidential dominance, where the directly-elected president is supported by the legislature, and parliamentary dominance, where the president faces a hostile legislative majority and the premier can take control of the reigns of power. The Israeli case is a synthesis of both parliamentary and presidential regime types, in which the elements are equally balanced, and not a fluctuation between the prevalence of one over the other. Israel, therefore, is no longer purely parliamentary but has not become purely presidential, or semi-presidential.

In other words, as of the 1996 elections, Israel became an institutionally unique and hybrid type of political regime. Israel now straddles the two continua that are used to distinguish different types of electoral and political systems: it has both majoritarian and proportional elections and it encompasses aspects of both presidential and parliamentary regimes. The mixed electoral system in Israel allows neither the principle of proportionality nor that of majoritarianism to dominate, but instead, allows each to operate separately, each electing a different branch of government and thereby preventing either from dominating – the results of which present a new constellation for the evolving Israeli party system. At the same time, the mixed political system allows neither the principles of parliamentarism nor those of presidentialism to dominate.

How do the Israeli parties respond to an electorate obsessively occupied with questions of identity, such as: Who are we and who do we want to be? How secure are we and how secure can we be? What boundaries do we choose for ourselves and our country? Moreover, how did the parties respond to the electoral and political reforms enacted in 1996? Was this response repeated in 1999, or did it change? How do the core parties react to newly pivotal parties they resent? In what ways does the Israeli system manifest signs of inertia or change? These questions

TABLE 1

ELECTION RESULTS FOR THE PRIME MINISTER

29 MAY 1996			17 MAY 1999		
Eligible Voters	3,933,250		Eligible Voters	4,285,428	
Voters	3,121,270	(79.4%)	Voters	3,372,952	(78.7%)
Valid votes	2,972,589	(95.2%)	Valid votes	3,193,494	(94.7%)
Invalid votes	148,681	(4.8%)	Invalid votes	179,458	(5.3%)
Candidate	Number Votes	Percent	Candidate	Number Votes	Percent
Benjamin Netanyahu	1,501,023	50.5	Ehud Barak	1,791,020	56.1
Shimon Peres	1,471,566	49.5	Benjamin Netanyahu	1,402,474	43.9

Source: Hazan and Diskin[13]

TABLE 2

ELECTION RESULTS FOR THE KNESSET

29 MAY 1996			17 MAY 1999		
Eligible Voters 3,933,250			Eligible Voters	4,285,428	
Voters	3,119,832	(79.3%)	Voters	3,373,748	(78.7%)
Valid votes	3,052,130	(97.8%)	Valid votes	3,309,416	(98.1%)
Invalid votes	67,702	(2.2%)	Invalid votes	64,332	(1.9%)
Party	**Votes**	**Seats**	**Party**	**Votes**	**Seats**
Labor	818,741 (26.8%)	34 (28.3%)	One Israel[1] ♥	670,484 (20.3%)	26 (21.7%)
Likud-Gesher-Tsomet ♣	767,401 (25.1%)	32 (26.7%)	Likud[2]	468,103 (14.2%)	19 (15.8%)
Shas ♣	259,796 (8.5%)	10 (8.3%)	Shas ♥	430,676 (13.0%)	17 (14.2%)
Meretz	226,275 (7.4%)	9 (7.5%)	Meretz ♥	253,525 (7.7%)	10 (8.3%)
Yisrael B'aliyah ♣	174,994 (5.7%)	7 (5.8%)	Yisrael B'aliyah ♥	171,705 (5.2%)	6 (5.0%)
			Shinui[3]	167,748 (5.1%)	6 (5.0%)
			Centre ♥	165,622 (5.0%)	6 (5.0%)
NRP	240,271 (7.9%)	9 (7.5%)	NRP ♥	140,307 (4.2%)	5 (4.2%)
Yahadut HaTorah	98,657 (3.2%)	4 (3.3%)	Yahadut HaTorah ♥	125,741 (3.8%)	5 (4.2%)
UAL	89,514 (2.9%)	4 (3.3%)	UAL	114,810 (3.5%)	5 (4.2%)
Moledet	72,002 (2.4%)	2 (1.7%)	National Unity[4]	100,181 (3.0%)	4 (3.3%)
			Israel Our Home	86,153 (2.6%)	4 (3.3%)
DFPE	129,455 (4.2%)	5 (4.2%)	DFPE	87,022 (2.6%)	3 (3.3%)
			NDA[5]	66,103 (2.0%)	2 (1.7%)
			One Nation	64,143 (1.9%)	2 (1.7%)
Third Way ♣	96,474 (3.2%)	4 (3.3%)	Third Way	26,290 (0.8%)	-
Others	78,550 (2.7%)	-	Others	170,803 (5.1%)	-

♣ - Parties forming the 1996 coalition government formed by Prime Minister Benjamin Netanyahu
♥ - Parties forming the 1999 coalition government formed by Prime Minister Ehud Barak
NRP - National Religious Party
UAL - United Arab List
DFPE - Democratic Front for Peace and Equality
NDA - National Democratic Alliance
1 In 1999, Labour joined with Gesher and Meimad to form a joint list called One Israel.
2 In 1996, Likud ran on a joint list with Gesher and Tsomet. In 1999, Likud ran alone.
3 In 1996, Shinui was part of the Meretz alliance.
4 In 1999, the newly formed National Unity party was based on splits from the Likud and the National Religious Party, and incorporated the Moledet party.
5 In 1996, the newly formed National Democratic Alliance ran together with the Democratic Front for Peace and Equality.
Source: Hazan and Diskin[14]

and many others that revolve around the holy triangle of party system change, are addressed in the various essays of this volume.

The volume comprises three main sections. The first part, 'Parties, Elections and Cleavages: Theoretical Perspectives', includes

contributions from the foremost international scholars in the field,
shedding fresh light on some of the core concepts currently under
debate. Part II, 'Religion and State', addresses a most volatile issue that
has resurfaced to challenge 'secular' societies in general and in Israel in
particular, at the turn of the twenty-first Century; whereas the third
part, 'Party System Change', examines the short- and long-term changes
in the 1990s Israeli party system while placing it in a comparative and
historical perspective.

The volume opens with an essay by Giovanni Sartori, refocusing the
debate on the causal chain between electoral systems and party systems.
Challenging the prevailing view that electoral systems are not a
fundamental causative factor in the development of party systems,
Sartori argues that such systems in effect 'cause' the party system. The
essay concludes with an analysis of the new electoral system in Israel and
its faults. Sartori posits that Israel constitutes the worst case of multi-
dimensional competition and cannot afford to maintain this
dysfunctional system; he then makes provocative suggestions on how to
improve the contemporary predicament in the Israeli party system.

The second essay, by Arend Lijphart, Peter Bowman and Reuven
Hazan, draws on Lijphart's previous work,[15] and that of Taagepera and
Grofman,[16] on the relationship between the degree of multi-partism and
the number of issue dimensions. It extends the analysis of Israel to 35
democracies during the period from the end of the Second World War to
the late 1990s. The authors find an extremely strong correlation between
the two variables and examine both the influence that the two variables
have on each other and their link with the electoral system. Israel turns
out to be a 'normal' case in one sense: its number of parties and the issue
dimensions of its party system are almost exactly in line with the broad
comparative pattern. But it is highly unusual in the strength and
persistence of one of the issue dimensions: foreign policy questions.

For his part, Gordon Smith addresses, on theoretical terms, aspects
of issue politics and examines Britain's New Labour as a test case – a
significant transformation that is similar to the one currently taking
place in the two major parties in Israel. Stressing the relative autonomy
of political parties, Smith sketches the forces affecting the trend toward
'issue politics' in relation to the diversity of inputs and the changing
balance among them. He then discusses the various strategies available
to parties in dealing with issues and elaborates on 'maverick issues'
which have the greatest potential for a significant transformation of a
party system. Smith argues that despite the increasing issue-basis of
politics, the core parties still retain control of political power, which at
the same time can lead to a decline in the legitimacy of the party state.

The second part addresses one of the most contentious issues in
comparative politics. Despite the significant potential for political

conflict, political systems have generally managed to resolve disputes over religious issues by peaceful means, without undermining their basic stability, unity and democratic nature. The questions that beckon are: How has this been accomplished? and What conditions and methods have made this possible?

Benjamin Neuberger delineates the main religion-state models and applies them to both Europe and Israel. He argues that there is a process of convergence of the various models. The two 'extreme' models, the 'established church' and the 'strict separation', are becoming less pure as most of Europe is edging towards the two 'moderate' models of the 'recognized communities' and the 'endorsed church'. Neuberger stresses the commonality of all four democratic models and places Israel within this comparative context.

Eliezer Don-Yehiya addresses the specific systems of conflict management in the religious area, comparing the resolution of religious conflicts in Europe, the United States and Israel. He then expands this analysis by comparing the patterns of conflict management applied to religious issues in Israel with those applied to other controversial issues.

Reuven Hazan elaborates the presence and subsequent decline of the institutional mechanisms in Israel that have helped overcome religious conflicts. His essay places Israel within a comparative theoretical construct of consociational democracies, arguing that the literature has failed to classify Israel properly because the consociational methods have transformed over time. The essay focuses on the most central aspect of consociationalism in Israel, namely, the role of the parties and the party system. Hazan discusses the impact of the recent electoral reforms in Israel on the methods of religious conflict management in the party system and examines how the reforms have undermined the ability to produce agreements and successfully manage religious issues.

The Israeli party system is frequently described as being in 'a process of change'. Attention is drawn to such diverse factors as electoral reform, changes in the number of parties, increase in electoral volatility, long-term movements in the support of individual parties, changes in social structures and an increase in the area of issue politics. All of these changes may be significant in their implications, but it is important to bear in mind that the Israeli party system may have changed far less than might have been expected and in a less fundamental way than what, at first glance, seemed to be the case. The last part of the volume examines what has exactly changed in Israel in general and in the party system in particular.

Abraham Diskin's provocative article addresses the trade-off faced by students of coalition formation, between the wish to develop simple and elegant models and the need to take into account how a few relatively weak parties can complicate their model. Diskin modifies De Swaan's famous coalition formation theory and produces a considerable improvement in the predictive power of the 'closed coalition' theory.[17] Whereas in the original model, 24 per cent of the formations examined are not closed, in the modified model, only 2.5 per cent of them remain open. In the Israeli case, the number of open coalitions drops from 44 per cent to nil. Diskin also presents a modified uni-dimensional model of the Israeli party system, with a predictive power much greater than the traditional uni-dimensional model used by De Swaan.

Gabriel Sheffer describes two systemic changes that have transformed Israeli politics since its creation. The first occurred gradually, during the late 1960s and the 1970s and was essentially a structural shift from consociational to corporatist political arrangements. This change took place despite the fact that the old social cleavages were not drastically altered. The second transformation is less clear cut and its direction is yet to be agreed upon. While traditional cleavages still linger, the waning of collective identities, on the one hand and the absence of a developed 'new politics' alternative, on the other, imply the emergence of an unstructured and almost chaotic political pluralism, the weakening of the state and a shift of power toward single-issue and special-interest groups.

Using Lijphart's models of consensus and majoritarian democracy to analyze the evolution of the Israeli political system via an analysis of changes in the pattern of party government, Peter Medding arrives at radically different conclusions. According to Lijphart's seminal analysis, during the past 50 years Israel has moved toward majoritarian democracy and has become less clearly consensual. Medding suggests that the Israeli political system has instead moved from majoritarian democracy to consensus democracy. He argues that since 1967, party government in Israel has presented a paradox: it has moved steadily in the direction of consensus democracy, approaching a situation of government without party despite, and perhaps because of, the co-existence of powerful majoritarian elements and the introduction into the system of additional majoritarian elements via electoral and regime reform.

What emerges from the aforementioned contributions is that parties, elections and cleavages in Israel have undergone a significant transformation and are currently in a state of flux. However, coupled with whatever else may be changing, some of the essential aspects of parties, elections and cleavages remain remarkably unscathed. For example, despite the significant gap between Ehud Barak and Benjamin Netanyahu in the 1999 Prime Ministerial elections, the electoral deadlock between Left and Right, characterizing Israeli parties and elections since the 1970s, has endured in the Knesset.[18] This analysis, couched within comparative and theoretical perspectives, sheds new light on the themes of parties, elections and cleavages in general and on Israeli politics and society in particular.

NOTES

1. See, for example, M. Maor, *Party and Party Systems: Comparative Approaches and the British Experience*, London: Routledge, 1997.
2. G. Sartori, *Parties and Party Systems: A Framework for Analysis*, Cambridge: Cambridge University Press, 1967, p.44.
3. R.J. Dalton, S.C. Flanagan and P.A. Beck (eds.), *Electoral Change in Advanced Industrial Democracies: Realignment or Dealignment?*, Princeton: Princeton University Press, 1984; R. J. Dalton and M.P. Wattenberg, 'The Not So Simple Act of Voting', in A.W. Finifter (ed.), *Political Science: The State of the Discipline II*, Washington: American Political Science Association, 1993, pp.193–218; M. Franklin, T. Mackie, H. Valen et al., *Electoral Change: Responses to Evolving Social and Attitudinal Structures in Western Countries*, Cambridge: Cambridge University Press, 1992; R. Rose and I. McAllister, *Voters Begin to Choose*, London: Sage, 1986.
4. P. Mair, *Party System Change*, Oxford: Oxford University Press, 1997.
5. I. Crewe and D. Denver, *Electoral Change in Western Democracies*, London: Croom Helm, 1985.
6. M. Shamir and A. Arian, 'Collective Identity and Electoral Competition in Israel', *American Political Science Review*, Vol. 93, No. 2 (1999).
7. J.G. March and J.P. Olsen, *Rediscovering Institutions*, New York: Free Press, 1989.
8. O. Kirchheimer, 'The Transformation of the Western European Party Systems', in J. LaPalombara and M. Weiner (eds.), *Political Parties and Political Development*, Princeton: Princeton University Press, 1966, pp.177–200.
9. G. Smith, 'A System Perspective on Party System Change', *Journal of Theoretical Politics*, Vol. 1, No. 3 (1989).
10. For a discussion of the politics leading to the electoral reform, see H. Diskin and A. Diskin, 'The Politics of Electoral Reform in Israel', *International Political Science Review*, Vol. 16, No. 1 (1995). For a description and analysis of the new system, see R.Y. Hazan, 'Presidential Parliamentarism: Direct Popular Election of the Prime Minister, Israel's New Electoral and Political System', *Electoral Studies*, Vol. 15, No. 1 (1996) and R.Y. Hazan, 'Executive-Legislative Relations in an Era of Accelerated Reform: Reshaping Government in Israel', *Legislative Studies Quarterly*, Vol. 22, No. 3 (1997). For contrasting opinions concerning this kind of system, see V. Bogdanor, 'The Electoral System, Government and Democracy', in L. Diamond and E. Sprinzak (eds.), *Israeli Democracy Under Stress*, Boulder: Lynne Rienner, 1993, pp.83–106; A. Lijphart, 'Israeli Democracy and Democratic Reform in Comparative Perspective', in Diamond and Sprinzak, *Israeli Democracy Under Stress*, pp.107–123; and G. Sartori, *Comparative Constitutional Engineering: An Inquiry into Structures, Incentives and Outcomes*, New York: New York University Press, 1994.
11. Hazan, 'Presidential Parliamentarism'.
12. M. Duverger, 'A New Political System Model: Semi-Presidential Government', *European Journal of Political Research*, Vol. 8, No. 2 (1980).
13. R. Y. Hazan and A. Diskin, 'The 1999 Knesset and Prime Minister Elections in Israel', *Electoral Studies*, forthcoming.
14. Hazan and Diskin, 'The 1999 Knesset and Prime Minister Elections in Israel'.
15. A. Lijphart, *Democracies: Patterns of Majoritarian and Consensus Government in Twenty-One Countries*, New Haven: Yale University Press, 1984.
16. R. Taagepera and B. Grofman, 'Rethinking Duverger's Law: Predicting the Effective Number of Parties in Plurality and PR Systems — Parties Minus Issues Equals One', *European Journal of Political Research*, Vol. 13, No. 4 (1985).
17. A. De Swaan, *Coalition Theories and Cabinet Formations*, Amsterdam: Elsevier, 1973.
18. The parties comprising the outgoing Netanyahu coalition government and their associated components, won exactly sixty of the 120 seats (Likud, National Unity, Israel Our Home, Yisrael B'aliyah, Shas, Yahadut HaTorah and the N.R.P.). See Tables 1 and 2.

PART I
THEORETICAL PERSPECTIVE

The Party-Effects of Electoral Systems

GIOVANNI SARTORI

To debate whether electoral systems are an independent or dependent variable is pointless. For we are not dealing with an intrinsic independence; we are simply asking different questions. Electoral systems are assumed to be an independent variable when the question is, What do they do? If the question is, instead, how electoral systems come about and why are they chosen, then the electoral system is treated as a dependent variable. And that is all there is to it.

Taken as an independent variable and, indeed, as a causal factor, electoral systems are assumed to affect the party *system*, not parties *per se*. Yet it stands to reason that a modification of the system of parties must also be of consequence for the component elements of the system, namely, for its parts. Note, however, that this argument goes from system to party, not from party to system. As hypothesized, the causal chain is that electoral systems cause the party system, which in turn causes parties per se to be as they are. The argument must begin, then, with the influence of the electoral system on the party system.

The first author that stated in law-like form how electoral systems 'influence' the party system was Duverger in 1950. His first law reads: 'The plurality single-ballot system tends to party dualism'. His second law reads: 'The double-ballot [plurality] system and proportional representation tend to multi-partism'.[1] These laws have been deluged with criticisms and certainly display major weaknesses. The Duverger laws posit that electoral systems affect (reduce or multiply) the number of parties; and yet Duverger never indicates how parties (their number) are to be counted. The related point is that a causal relationship is verifiable only if the effect is clearly specified, whereas the effect of the first law (party dualism) is accordion-like and the effect of the second law equally suffers from excessive imprecision. Another major and

Giovanni Sartori is Albert Schweitzer Professor Emeritus in the Humanities at Columbia University.

almost fatal weakness of Duverger's treatment is that he never states the conditions under which his laws apply or, conversely, do not apply.[2]

These weaknesses have led, unfortunately, to an outright dismissal of the nomothetic approach. When Douglas Rae took up the matter in his influential *The Political Consequences of Electoral Laws*,[3] he did not build cumulatively on Duverger but switched to a different track. Rae posits a general 'fractionalization effect' of electoral systems (whether they lead to fragmentation or not) and provides a statistical measure for it, his well known 'index of fractionalization'. Whatever the merits and shortcomings of Rae's index,[4] the point is that with Rae the political science profession enters a path of measurements whose gains in precision are outweighed by major losses of understanding.

While Duverger looked at concrete party systems (even though he did not identify them correctly), the quantitative literature that goes from Rae to Taagepera and Shugart[5] simply leaves us with arbitrary cutting points along a continuum. For example, in Rae 'two-party competition' (note, not two-partism as a system) is defined as a state of affairs in which 'the first party holds less than 70% of the legislative seats and the first two parties together hold at least 90% of the seats'.[6] Why not, instead, less than 60 per cent and 80 per cent? And what do these ratios or proportions entail in terms of systemic properties? This is what we are not told. Likewise, Taagepera and Shugart come up with what they call a 'generalized Duverger's rule' which reads as follows: 'The effective number of electoral parties is usually within ± 1 unit from $N = 1.25 (2 + \log M)$'.[7] Now and quite aside from the fact that the empirical fit of the rule is poor (as they admit), what is the explanatory value of their 'effective parties' measure? Not only are we left with a pure and simple counting of parties (of dubious empirical validity), but what is it that we have? The authors themselves ask, 'Is the new rule on the number of parties a law, a hypothesis, or an empirical data fit'? And their candid reply simply is, 'For practical matters, it really does not matter'.[8] Well, no: it matters.

The issue is whether electoral systems 'cause' something and if their effects can be rendered in terms of law-like generalizations. And 'laws' can hardly be formulated unless we are clear-headed as to how they relate to causal analysis, to condition analysis, to probability and determinism and, conclusively, to how they are confirmed or disconfirmed.[9] So, if nothing of this or the difference between law and hypothesis matters 'in practice', then the business of knowing has been put out of business. There can be no real knowing without logic, whereas what is currently considered and called 'methodology' is method without *logos*, techniques that have largely lost their logical backbone and component element.

RESTATING THE 'LAWS'

Reverting as it were to 'logical knowing', the question is: Can the impact (effect) of electoral systems be stated in terms of law-like rules that are both predictive of single events (not only of classes of events) and verifiable? But first, what do we mean by 'law'? We mean, I assume, a generalization endowed with explanatory power that detects a regularity that allows predictions. So, a law is required to assert more than a regularity and cannot consist of a mere generalization. And the point to bear in mind is that the explanatory power of a law is just as crucial as its predictive power.

Another preliminary point bears on the conditions under which a law applies or does not apply. Critics point to hundreds of occasions in which the electoral system fails to produce the predicted effects. But a law, any law, can hold only when it applies and cannot be disconfirmed by cases to which it does not apply. Water boils at 100 degrees centigrade at sea level, not at the top of Everest; bodies fall at the same acceleration, regardless of shape and size, in a void. Likewise, the laws that specify the effects of electoral systems apply only to party *systems,* that is to say, to the stage at which a loose collection of notables gives way to a structured ensemble of parties. Unstructured systems made of shapeless and volatile units escape electoral engineering and are 'lawless'.[10]

Let us come to some specifics. First of all, electoral systems affect or influence what? At first glance the direct effect of an electoral system appears to be on the voter. However, the electoral system also has a direct effect on the number of parties (the format of the party system) since it establishes how votes are translated into parliamentary seats. Other effects are instead derivative and we shall come to them in due course.

The effect of an electoral system *on the voter* can be constraining (manipulative) or unconstraining. If it is unconstraining, then an electoral system has no effect – and that is that. The effect of an electoral system *on the party system* can either be reductive (it reduces or compresses the number of parties) or not – and in the latter case we have again a non-effect. A pure system of proportional representation (PR) is ineffective in both respects: it neither has a manipulative impact on the voter nor on the format of the party system.[11] However, pure proportionality is rare. Regardless of the mathematics of proportionality, a small district (e.g., a district that elects two to five members) brings about impure proportionality. The rule of thumb here is that the smaller the district, the lesser the proportionality and, the larger the district, the greater the proportionality. Israel and the Netherlands thus rank among the pure PR systems in that they elect, respectively, 120 and 150 MPs in a single, nationwide constituency.

The bottom line is, then, that when electoral systems are effective they reduce the number of parties. This brings us back to the question of how parties are to be counted. Duverger, I have already noted, had no answer for this question and his assessment was not only impressionistic but also utterly erratic. Yet if we assume that electoral systems 'cause' the number of parties, then we must know how this number is to be determined. Clearly, parties cannot be counted at face value. In my work I have used the notion of *relevant party*, where relevance is a systemic assessment based on two criteria, namely, the coalition potential and/or blackmail potential of any given party.[12] Instead, most authors abide by measures of fragmentation (Rae's index of fractionalization and the like) and currently speak of 'effective parties'. The quantitative determinations are easy to obtain, since they are machine-made. Unfortunately, they miss *relevance* (as I define it) since they tell us just about nothing on whether, and in what manner, a party affects the party system as a whole.

At long last I can now come to the 'laws' that govern the effects of electoral systems on the number of parties. Since these rules are easily found in my book *Comparative Constitutional Engineering*,[13] they can be summarized here. The first three 'laws' deal with the conditions under which a plurality system either can or cannot produce (and/or maintain) a two-party format, whereas the fourth rule spells out the effects (and/or non-effects) of PR. In this regard, the main point is that also PR has, or may have, reductive effects on the number of parties if applied to small-sized constituencies provided that the electorates of the smaller parties are not concentrated in above-quota strongholds.

The next question is: Why are the number of relevant parties (the format of party systems) so important? Well, because the format explains and predicts the mechanics, i.e., the *systemic characteristics* of distinctive types of party systems. In my analysis, I sort out three major systemic patterns: (1) *two-party mechanics*, i.e., bipolar single-party alternation in government; (2) *moderate multi-partism*, i.e., bipolar shifts between coalition governments; (3) *polarized multi-partism*, i.e., systems characterized by multi-polar competition, centre-located coalitions with peripheral turnover and anti-system parties.[14]

I cannot explicate the above in any detail, aside from pointing out that as the analysis moves from the classification to a typology of party systems, the decisive variable turns out to be systemic *polarization*, defined as the distance (ideological or other) between the most distant relevant parties. So the question now is: Will the format be followed by the expected, corresponding mechanics (functional properties)? Given structural consolidation as a necessary condition and polarization as the intervening and/or dependent variable, I hypothesize as follows:

Hypothesis 1. When the single-member plurality formula produces a two-party format (Rules 1 and 2), the format will, in turn, produce two-party mechanics if and only if, the polarization of the polity is low. With high polarization, the two-party mechanics break down. However, since two-party mechanics implies centripetal competition, it tends to lessen systemic polarization.[15]

Hypothesis 2. Assuming a below-quota dispersion of the incoercible minorities (if any), impure PR formulas are likely to allow for one or two parties above the two-party format, that is, three-four parties. This format will, in turn, engender the mechanics of moderate multi-partism if and only if, the polity does not display high polarization.[16] However, since moderate multi-partism still is bipolar-converging (centripetal competition), it will not tend to increase systemic polarization.

Hypothesis 3. Relatively pure or pure PR systems easily allow for a five-to-seven party format. Even so, under conditions of medium-low polarization, the coalitional mechanics of moderate multi-partism is not impeded. However, under conditions of high polarization, the format will display the mechanical characteristics of polarized multi-partism, thereby including a multi-polar competition that eventually heightens systemic polarization.

Thus far, I account for just one causal factor, the electoral system. However, another causal factor at play may be the party system itself as a strongly structured and well-entrenched party system performs as a *channelling force* of its own. Thus the party system as a system of channelment may by itself 'cause' the staying power of a party configuration *as is*. Vide Austria, whose two-party format has resisted for some forty years (until the rise of Heider's Freedom Movement) the fragmenting lures of PR. But the substitution of one independent variable by another does not pose any problem to my laws, which can easily incorporate an alternative causal factor.[17] Still, I detect an incompleteness in my analysis that had long escaped me and that I must now confront.

THE NEW CASE: FROM PR BACK TO PLURALITY

My argument and my laws implicitly assume a movement from majoritarian to proportional systems, for this has been, historically, the unfailing direction of change. PR was first introduced in 1889 and no democracy switched back from proportional to plurality elections for the next seventy years until France did in 1959. In the French experience (the transition from the Fourth to the Fifth Republic), there was no apparent *resistance power* of PR, in the sense that the return to majoritarianism went smoothly and achieved (albeit slowly) its purpose. Thus the eventfulness of this unprecedented event went unnoticed. When Italy attempted a similar comeback from PR to plurality in 1994 and in 1996, the attempt miserably failed and indeed backfired. So we have a problem that has yet to be tackled.

Why has France succeeded where Italy failed? The first reason is that the two countries have followed different paths. France astutely adopted a double ballot plurality system reinforced by increasingly heightened thresholds of exclusion (today, 12.5 per cent); and the aggregative impact of this electoral arrangement was reinforced, as of 1962, by direct-majoritarian presidential elections. Italy has done nothing of that sort. It adopted a single-shot plurality system[18] with an insufficient threshold of exclusion (four per cent) and has not had, thus far, a directly elected President. The major Italian mistake was, clearly, to assume that single-ballot plurality elections would perform 'reductively'; and thus the major reason why Italians have failed to curtail the number of parties clearly lies in their failure to adopt a double ballot system. Yet the success of the French comeback has obscured the intrinsic difficulties that confront the dismantling of an entrenched pattern of party fragmentation.

Note that in Italy a single-ballot plurality system has not only failed to reduce the number of parties; it has actually produced *more parties*, causing a still higher level of fragmentation. With PR, the Italian 'relevant' parties were, until the early 1990s, six (plus or minus one); with plurality they have currently grown to twelve (plus or minus two). Why did they multiply? This question goes to the heart of the problem.

The answer lies, I suggest, in the notion (originally a Downsian notion) of a blackmail party. Remember that 'blackmail potential' is one of my two criteria for establishing party relevance. And the point now is that a switch from PR to plurality extends 'relevance', that is, *provides relevance to hitherto irrelevant parties*. The reason for this is simple. With a winner-take-all system, victory or defeat may be decided by one or two percentage points. Thus even very small parties – as long as they have a core of strongly identified voters – may display a crucial blackmail leverage. True, with plurality elections a small party cannot win; but it can easily endanger the winning chances of the major parties. Under these circumstances and given a state of entrenched fragmentation, the Italian electoral game has in fact been played by 'paying out' the minor parties (of each family), by granting them a given number of safe seats in exchange for their staying out of an agreed set of races. Paradoxically, in the case at hand it is not PR but the winner-take-all system that multiplies parties (by extending and facilitating their relevance).

Clearly, then, a return from PR to plurality requires a new engineering not covered by current know-how. The new problem is how to cope with a new kind of blackmail potential. Note that this new problem is entirely created – as all other circumstances remain equal – by the electoral system. It will have to be remedied, therefore, by electoral counter-measures. Substituting PR with a single-ballot plurality system will not, in all likelihood, reduce the number of parties. Indeed, this remedy is likely to boomerang. However, even a double-ballot system will not cure party fragmentation if it is 'closed' (i.e., if it admits to the run-off only the first two front runners), because in this case blackmail maneuvering can still be quite effective. A third warning is that electoral alliances – the French *apparentement* – should be prohibited whenever an electoral system has thresholds or premiums. For, clearly, alliances circumvent thresholds of exclusion and defy the aggregative intent of majority premiums.

Bearing these provisos in mind, in the Italian case I have proposed – at the parliamentary hearings – an 'open' double ballot system that admits to the run-off the first four runners.[19] However, one can think of other ways of disposing of extreme fragmentation. In the case of Israel, for example, I would recommend a PR system that provides substantial majority premiums for the first two parties, such as 20 per cent to the first and 15 per cent to the second.[20] We then have the solution adopted in Chile as of 1989: a two-member PR system. While this system is especially intended to reinforce the second-place finishers, the minimal size of the constituencies does not crush the smaller parties as much as one might expect because Chile permits electoral coalitions.

MISUNDERSTOOD ELECTORAL SYSTEMS

Up to this point I have dealt with the effects of electoral systems. But what about the causal factor itself? Is everything clear at this end of the argument? Not really. Also the understanding of electoral systems leaves much to be desired, for a number of voting methods are both misclassified and misunderstood. Electoral systems are fundamentally divided into majoritarian and proportional and are thus defined by reciprocal exclusion: all majoritarian systems are not proportional and, conversely, all proportional systems are not majoritarian. So far, so good. But PR systems have been devised by mathematicians and a respectable mathematician must seek perfect proportionality. Thus mathematicians have ignored ordinal proportionality and have confined PR to *equal quotas* (or quotients), that is, to systems that allocate seats to equal shares of the voting returns. Assume, however, that we encounter – as was the case in Japan until 1993 – four-member constituencies (average) that elect the first four most voted candidates. What kind of system is that?

For Lijphart and others it is a variety of the limited vote (the voter has fewer votes than there are seats) in which each voter has only one vote. Therefore, they argue, it is a single non-transferable vote system (SNTV), which is best considered 'a semi-proportional system rather than a plurality system'.[21] But the above makes little sense. First of all it makes no sense to wonder whether the Japanese system may be considered a plurality system, for that it is certainly not. Secondly, in all standard PR systems, voters have fewer votes than there are seats and with PR it is normal for voters to have just one non-transferable vote. Therefore it is superfluous to consider Japan a SNTV case. Thirdly, under what criterion is Japan best considered semi-proportional? This is a purely impressionistic assessment. PR systems have always been considered more-or-less pure (or impure). Along this continuum, is there a cut-off point for the notion of 'semi-proportional'? The answer is no and therefore this notion has no classificatory value.[22]

But why on earth have most scholars trapped themselves, in attempting to classify the Japanese case, into these tortuosities? In my opinion the Japanese system was quite simply an *ordinal proportional system* characterized by personalized voting (in lieu of list voting) and by small constituencies (and thus of the impure, least proportional variety). So, why does this straightforward understanding of the case escape us? The reason is the mathematical bias that establishes that proportionality can be achieved only via equal quotas, whereas proportionality can also be achieved – I submit – by having candidates elected in multimember constituencies on the basis of the highest portion (proportion) of the returns. Nor is it a foregone conclusion that ordinal proportionality is necessarily more imperfect (impure) than quota-based proportionality. For this matter – the degree of correspondence of votes to seats – is decided far more by the constituency size than by algorithms.

Moving on, double ballot systems (also called two round systems) represent both a neglected and highly misunderstood area of electoral systems. An expert of the stature of Richard Rose assimilates and indeed subordinates the double ballot to the alternative vote.[23] His argument is as follows: The two-ballot plurality system used in the Fifth French Republic is a *variant* of the alternative vote The difference between the Australian and French forms of alternative vote is limited, but of practical importance. Both systems heavily penalize parties that have a large vote, but more enemies than supporters. Both ask voters to state more than one preference. But the Australian system leaves it to the voter to decide his preference, ordering candidates *all at once* in a single ballot. By contrast the French system also gives an initiative to the candidates and parties after the results of the first ballot are in.[24]

With due respect, the above is a misreading. Firstly, it is the double ballot that has many variants, not the alternative vote. If anything, then, the double ballot should be the genus of which the alternative vote is a species. Anyway, the double ballot is not necessarily a single-member majoritarian-plurality system; it can also be an ordinal proportional method of electing candidates in multimember (if small) constituencies. Furthermore the similarities perceived by Rose are, if anything, dissimilarities. The alternative vote requires an absolute majority. The French parliamentary double ballot requires only a plurality; the former 'orders' the candidates, the latter does not; the former does not allow voters to change their vote, the latter does. These are hardly 'limited' differences.

So, why assimilate the double ballot to something else? In this manner, one misses that the system's unique characteristic – that the voter *re-votes* – is also its central characteristic. All other electoral systems are one-shot; the double ballot and the double ballot only, is a two-shot system. With one shot the voter shoots very much in the dark; with two shots he or she shoots, the second time, in full daylight. This entails, among other things, that in the first round the voter is free to express his first preference, i.e., to engage in 'sincere voting'. It is only at the second round that he is subjected to the constraints of the electoral system. Note, moreover, that when the voter is pressured in the run-off to vote for less preferred candidates, this constraint largely becomes the constraint of actual voting distributions (not, as in the single-ballot plurality system, of the electoral system).[25]

Misinterpretations and ambiguities also plague the notion of 'mixed system', the formula that has currently charmed Italy, Russia, Japan, New Zealand and other countries. The notion originates with the German electoral system and its popularity is largely due to a misunderstanding. The German system is mixed in the sense that half of the members of the *Bundestag* obtain a personalized vote (in single member constituencies), but is proportional in the far more important respect that the seats are all allocated proportionally on the basis of the PR list voting.

Most alleged electoral experts are equally misguided in attributing importance to the German additional member system (AMS), that is, to its variable *Bundestag* membership. For instance, Pippa Norris writes that the most striking phenomenon in recent years has been the shift in New Zealand, Italy and Japan, 'away from the extremes of proportional *and* majoritarian systems toward the middle ground of the "additional member system" used in Germany.[26] But Italy and Japan are incorrect examples and AMS is not a middle ground of anything, for it only ensures proportionality. Let it be added that not only the German system *is not mixed in outcome*, since it produces a fully proportional parliament, but that it is equally wrong to assume that Germany displays a three-party format because it mixes PR with plurality. Parties have been reduced in Germany by the Constitutional Court – which has outlawed communists and neo-nazis – not by the electoral system.

Germany and its false witnessing aside, when is a mixed system veritably mixed? And what are the merits of plurality-PR mixes? A frequently held opinion is that mixed systems are 'the most attractive forms of solution to meet otherwise contradictory imperatives'.[27] I agree that we are faced with contrary (though not contradictory) imperatives, namely, (i) the function of mirroring (exact representation) and (ii) the function of functioning (efficient government). But are mixed systems a solution that combines – as the claim goes – the best of both worlds?

Well, let me first provide this definition: A veritable mixed system is such if and only if, *both* the voting method and the allocation of seats are in part majoritarian and in part proportional. Thus a veritable mixed system must combine a proportional with a majoritarian translation of votes into seats. The current Italian, Japanese and Russian electoral systems qualify as mixed under the aforesaid criterion. In Italy (since 1994), 75 per cent of the seats are filled via plurality districts, while the remaining 25 per cent of the seats are filled with proportional criteria. In Japan, the mix is of 300 plurality and 200 proportional seats, whereas in Russia it is even (50/50). In Italy, the result of its mixed system across two elections has been, I have already noted, counterproductive. In Russia, under existing conditions no electoral system can be expected to do much; yet the choice was a poor choice.[28] And in Japan, three years of disappointing coalition maneuvering have helped the LDP to restore its own single-party government.[29]

So far with the veritable mixed systems. Other countries are equally called mixed, albeit misleadingly, for here we fail to distinguish between two different kinds of mixtures. In the first kind – the one that is correctly called *mixed* – we have plurality-proportional mixes both in input and in output and this – we have seen – is the case of Italy, Japan and Russia.[30] In the second one – that can be called *mixed-proportional* – the mixture is incomplete: it is only in input, for the output is fully proportional. Indeed, in Germany as well as in New Zealand a proportional compensation is provided (in parliamentary seats) for any disproportionality arising from the plurality elections. Hence the systems in question unequivocally perform as proportional systems based, in part, on personalized voting. The interesting case in this category is New Zealand,[31] in that here we have a switch from plurality to PR. And while the German 'proportional mix' has been of almost no consequence, New Zealand's switch has already brought about the novel experience of coalition uncertainty.[32]

Overall, the record of both the veritable and the mixed proportional mixes has been erratic. But this record still is, for most countries, a very short one. And since one or two elections cannot tell with any assurance how electoral hybrids might work when routinized, my objection is, in terms of principle, that electoral systems should have *one logic* which conforms to their purpose. Hence all the mixed systems – thereby including the incomplete ones – are objectionable in that they confuse voters and, secondly, require parties to become Janus-faced. PR permits – as Fahrquharson puts it – 'sincere voting', i.e., encourages voters to freely express their first preferences, while majoritarian electoral systems require voters to engage in 'strategic voting', i.e., to express second best, calculated preferences (attuned to the likely winners). To require an ordinary voter to engage simultaneously in sincere (proportional) and in strategic (majoritarian) choices is a sure way of blurring them. By the same token, parties, too, are prompted to engage in schizophrenic behaviour. So, are we looking at the better of two worlds or, instead, at the best way of producing a bastard, a parliament that serves no purpose? For the ultimate question always is: Electoral systems to what end?

The ultimate end of PR is *representative justice*. The ultimate end of majoritarian elections is *governing capability*. Clearly these are contrary goals. To be sure, these goals are amenable to trade-offs: more governability in exchange for less proportionality, or instead, more proportional justice if at the cost of less governability. But these trade-offs should not lead to solutions that are neither fish nor fowl, which is to say to *non-solutions*. One of the two ends – representativeness or governability – must have clear priority and prevail over the other.

Note that I do not hold that one goal is intrinsically superior to the other. I hold that we are confronted with a choice that should not be eluded by 'mixes'. Thus while Arend Lijphart believes that PR is inherently superior to plurality and that a consociational model of governance is inherently superior to the Westminster model, my view is, instead, that when a proportional parliament produces paralyzed coalition governments, then we should seek majoritarian electoral remedies. Unfortunately we hardly know how to do that.

THE INFLUENCE ON PARTIES *PER SE*

Let me turn to the last item on my agenda. Thus far I have dealt with the impact of the electoral system on the voter and its effects on the party system. As I have indicated at the outset, this is the causal path that we are logically required to follow. Yet it is clearly the case that the electoral system also shapes parties *per se*. When the whole is affected, its parts are affected; and, conversely, the parts affect the whole to which they belong.

With a majoritarian system one either wins or loses (in each constituency), whereas in a proportional system, winning and losing are only a matter of greater or smaller shares. And if the very notion of winning is different, at the very least the tactics of party competition must be different. In one case the loser loses all; in the other it just loses something (perhaps just one or two percentage points). So, different electoral systems bring about (cause) different ways of competing: and this affects how parties are, i.e., their competitive nature.

A similar point can be made with regard to the notion of responsibility. When an electoral system maintains or brings about two-partism, by the same token it brings about single-party government and thus a clearly identifiable responsibility: who is responsible, in governing, for what. When, instead, electoral systems cause multi-partism, by the same token they generally bring about coalition governments. If so, the more numerous the coalition partners (e.g., in Italy they have generally been five) and the more frequent the coalition changes, the less the voter can attribute responsibility to any specific party. With coalition governments, responsibility becomes fuzzy. One may thus say that different electoral systems engender 'differently responsible' and/or 'differently irresponsible' parties (in the sense that I have just indicated), in that few parties facilitate and many parties obfuscate, the perception of responsibility in party governance.

However, the single most important direct effect of the electoral system on parties *per se* bears on whether party splitting is penalized and party aggregation rewarded. When a nation-wide two-party system is in place, a plurality system is a powerful maintaining factor of two-partism. And we have also seen that double ballot systems can be rendered strongly aggregative. Conversely, PR systems hardly penalize (unless they are strongly impure) party fragmentation and party splits and thus allow for small-to-minute parties. Thus, whether we have few large parties or a host of small-sized parties is a direct consequence of the electoral system. In short, electoral systems control (in the manner indicated by my laws) party numbers.

It is also assumed that a single-member district system enhances 'personalized' politics, whereas list systems of proportional representation reinforce 'party-based' or party-centered politics. On the same grounds, majoritarian systems are assumed to lead to constituency based (local) politics and thus to decentralized parties, whereas PR is assumed to uphold centralized and stronger parties. Yet these seemingly obvious expectations turn out to be fraught with exceptions as we are now dealing with *indirect* or derivative effects and thus with distal causality. The more a causal trajectory or a causal linkage is lengthened, the more it allows for intervening variables. Yes, of its own accord, a single-member district system does enhance person-based and locality-centered politics. But this tendency can be effectively counteracted by party strength (as in England). And another decisive intervening variable here is who controls the financing of politics, the party as a centralized entity or the candidates themselves. The general point is, then, that the more we move into the area of indirect effects, the more we enter into multi-causality and the more the electoral system turns out to be one of many causal factors. I cannot unravel, here, multi-causal complexities.

Are parties in decline? If they are, electoral systems have little say on that. The weakening of parties cannot be ascribed to voting methods. But the effects of electoral systems remain unchanged – as stated – regardless of whether the nature and centrality of parties changes.

A CODA ON ISRAEL

In my argument, Israel represents an extreme case of proportional representation grafted upon almost all conceivable cleavages: left-right, religious-laical and, furthermore, multi-ethnic, multi-religious, multi-lingual and, so to speak, multi-historical lines of fragmentation. Nor has Israel performed as a melting pot, but rather as a boiling pot. It is not only a worst case of pure proportionality (on a par, in purity, only with the Netherlands), but also a worst case of multi-dimensional competition. Israel thus displays the most fragmented and atomized party system for which the notion of system still makes sense, and over the decades its dismembering has been growing.

The Knesset produced by the 1999 elections contains some fifteen parties – four more than in the previous parliament – all of which can be considered relevant (under my definition of relevance) for one of the arithmetically possible coalitions (five in the present Knesset). Fifteen is a shuddering amount of political units for six million inhabitants. To make things worse, the direct election of the Prime Minister has 'smalled' the larger parties. Formerly, Labour and Likud provided a somewhat bipolar structure that disciplined the vagaries and the intricacies of Israel's politics. But Labour had 44 seats in 1992, which fell to 34 in 1996 and has now ended up (within Ehud Barak's One Israel) with less than 26 seats. Similarly, Likud lost 13 seats in the last election and is now down to 19. Remember that one of the arguments in favour of a directly elected premier was that a two-candidate race would produce a coat-tail effect in favour of the runners' parties. I never believed that; yet I am myself surprised by the extent of the reverse effect that has in fact occurred. Contrary to expectations, the premier-centered race has downsized and weakened the party vote.

The Israelis may have become accustomed to what they have, but a more dysfunctional system is hard to conceive. That Shas, the ultra-orthodox sephardic party, should become the third largest party in the country and indeed a pivotal party, is in my view very alarming for the future of Israel. Quite aside from ideological and religious preferences, the bottom line is that Israel cannot afford, on pure and simple financial grounds, the growth of an insulated and parasitical subsociety that drains ever increasing resources away from the common weal. And if this is the case, then Israel can no longer afford the electoral system with which it performs or, better, misperforms.

In the early 1990s, Israel deluded itself into believing that a bad electoral system could be countered by a premiership system established by a popular vote. That the fragmentation and heterogeneity of the party system would cripple the government of the premier just as much as any other type of government was an easy prediction.[33] Yet, that was not the prevailing prediction. Thus, the failure of the Netanyahu government is not only, in my view, the failure of Netanyahu himself, but also attests that it is both wrong to have a non-changeable premier and to expect effective governing with impossible majorities. So the problem of the electoral system once again forcefully comes to the fore.

The last attempt to curb the representation of small parties and thereby to curb their exaggerated power, was in 1989. At the time, Labour and Likud jointly proposed a German-type mixed system in which the German five per cent threshold of exclusion was replaced by the requirement of winning a minimum of four seats (in fact, a lesser barrier). However, as I have pointed out a earlier, a mixed-proportional electoral system of the German variety still is, in outcome, perfectly proportional. So what was the point, or the expected benefit, of that reform? Yes, the point was to divide the territory into 20 three-member electoral districts. This would have been the truly reductive factor. But I wonder whether a redistribution of this kind would have ever been agreed upon.

The failure of earlier reform attempts explains why I have suggested, in passing, a reform that is technically very simple, namely, to introduce into the existing arrangement two (not one as is usually the case) strong majority premiums for the two first parties, e.g., a 20 per cent premium to the first party and a 15 per cent premium to the second one. It is self-evident that this formula would provide strong aggregative incentives. It is equally evident, however, that the formula requires electoral alliances to be ruled out. The premiums must go to single parties. To make sure that these single parties are not electoral camouflages, the electoral law that I am suggesting should stipulate that the premiums are lost if a premium-benefitted party splits in the course of the legislature (and a variable member system for the Knesset would make this punishment easy to implement). And a further reinforcing element against party fragmentation could also be to reduce the Knesset membership to, say, 100 members. This would further raise an electoral quotient that is already automatically raised by the setting aside of 35 per cent of the seats for the majority premiums.

The question might be: why not simply adopt the five per cent German exclusion clause? Well, the five per cent barrier by itself would not be effective and should be assisted – as in my proposal – by the prohibition of electoral alliances and the splitting penalty. At this point, then, the complexities of either one of the two formulas are roughly the same and the respective pros and cons are that the *Sperrklausel* is a rigid and foreknown barrier, whereas my suggestion leaves room for greater flexibility. In either case, the point remains that Israel's existing barriers are of no use whatsoever. When the exclusion was of one per cent, the parties went up to 15. In 1992, the exclusion was raised to 1.5 per cent and the parties went down from 15 to 10; but now the number of parties is again 15.

Whatever the worth of my suggestions, the plain fact is that after 50 years of pure proportional representation, Israel must face the urgent need for an electoral reform that seeks efficient government and penalizes party atomization.

NOTES

1. M. Duverger, *Les Partis Politiques*, Paris, Colin, 1954, 2nd ed., pp.247, 269 (my translation).
2. These and further critiques are spelled out in G. Sartori, 'The Influence of Electoral Systems: Faulty Laws or Faulty Method?', in B. Grofman and A. Lijphart (eds.), *Electoral Laws and Their Political Consequences*, New York: Agathon Press, 1986, pp.43–45.
3. D. Rae, *The Political Consequences of Electoral Laws*, New Haven: Yale University Press, 1971.
4. I discuss them in G. Sartori, *Parties and Party Systems: A Framework for Analysis*, New York: Cambridge University Press, 1976, pp.307–315; and in 'The Influence of Electoral Systems', pp.45–46, 51, 65–66.
5. R. Taagepera and M. Shugart, *Seats and Votes: The Effects and Determinants of Electoral Systems*, New Haven: Yale University Press, 1989.
6. Rae, *The Political Consequences of Electoral Laws*, p.93.
7. Taagepera and Shugart, *Seats and Votes*, p.145
8. Taagepera and Shugart, *Seats and Votes*, p.145
9. On all these points see Sartori, 'The Influence of Electoral Systems', pp.49–52.
10. See Sartori, 'The Influence of Electoral Systems', pp.55–56; and G. Sartori, *Comparative Constitutional Engineering: An Inquiry into Structure, Incentives and Outcomes*, New York: New York University Press, and London: Macmillan, 1997, 2nd ed., pp.37–38.
11. We generally speak of a 'multiplying effect' of PR. This is, however, a manner of speech, for the multiplication is not 'caused' by PR but results from the 'removal of obstacles' brought about by PR.
12. See Sartori, *Comparative Constitutional Engineering*, pp.33–34, and, for the full argument, *Parties and Party Systems*, pp.119–125, 300–319. It is apparent that my relevance criteria apply to parliamentary systems. The number of parties is of lesser importance in presidential systems.
13. See Sartori, *Comparative Constitutional Engineering*, pp.40–45.
14. This typology is developed in Sartori, *Parties and Party System*, pp.125–211 and 273-293. For easier consultation see G. Sartori, 'A Typology of Party Systems', in P. Mair (ed.), *The West European Party System*, Oxford: Oxford University Press, 1990, pp.316–349, a reader that carries the gist of my party theory.
15. The underlying assumption of the hypothesis is that low polarization corresponds to a unimodal, bell-shaped distribution of opinions, and that when most voters cluster around the central, middle area of the political spectrum party competition is (must rationally be) center-converging. Conversely, high polarization corresponds to a bimodal, two-peaked distribution with a hollow center. This entails that competition is centre-fleeing, and that two-camp entrenchments block the swinging of the pendulum. A recent work bearing on these issues is R. Hazan, *Center Parties: Polarization and Competition in European Parliamentary Democracies*, London: Pinter, 1977.

16. High polarization generally results from ideological distance. However, it can also reflect ethnic and/or religious conflict. Let it be added that polarization can equally be party triggered, in the same sense that in a given system parties may find divisive and conflictual politics rewarding.
17. See Sartori, *Comparative Constitutional Engineering*, pp.44–45.
18. More exactly, the new Italian electoral system is 'mixed' in this proportion: 75 per cent of the seats are allocated by plurality, and 25 per cent on a proportional basis. The majoritarian incompleteness, however, does not affect my argument.
19. This formula is implemented by a proportional compensation (on national lists) for the parties admitted to the run-off that drop out. My expectation is that this arrangement would lead to two-cornered final races, and that it would eliminate blackmail at both electoral stages.
20. The percentages are purely illustrative. The advantage of this 'premium method' is that it strongly encourages party aggregation. Its standard alternative – a majority premium for the winning electoral coalition – simply fabricates a heterogeneous majority that maintains all its pre-coalition conflicts.
21. Arend Lijphart, Rafael Lopez Pintor and Yasunori Sone, 'The Limited Vote and the Single Nontransferable Vote: Lessons from the Japanese and Spanish Examples', in Grofman and Lijphart, *Electoral Laws and Their Political Consequences*, pp.154–155.
22. Note, incidentally, that the Japanese system was devised to favour medium-sized parties, and that its proportionality would have been 'normal' had that intent been achieved.
23. To wit, the alternative vote is a 'preferential' majority system, used in single-member districts, in which voters use numbers to mark their preferences on the ballot paper. If no candidate achieves an absolute majority of the first preferences, votes are reallocated until one candidate attains the required 50 per cent majority. The alternative vote is used in Australia.
24. R. Rose, 'Elections and Electoral Systems', in V. Bogdanor and D. Butler (eds.), *Democracy and Elections*, Cambridge: Cambridge University Press, 1983, pp.32–33 (my emphasis).
25. See, for further consideration, Sartori, *Comparative Constitutional Engineering*, pp.10–12, 61–69.
26. P. Norris, 'Introduction: The Politics of Electoral Reform', *International Political Science Review*, Vol. 16, No. 1 (1995).
27. P. Dunleavy and H. Margetts, 'Understanding the Dynamics of Electoral Reform', *International Political Science Review*, Vol. 16, No. 1, (1995), p.24.
28. In the 1995 Duma election, of the 18 parties running with PR party lists, only four crossed the five per cent threshold of exclusion; thus, nearly 50 per cent of the votes were wasted and this waste produced an enormous overrepresentation of the first four parties. On the other hand, 43 parties competed in the single-member constituencies, and excessively multi-cornered races produced winners with 20 per cent of the constituency vote. It is apparent that some double ballot system would have performed better.
29. Remember that the downfall of the LDP (Liberal Democratic Party) resulted from a split, not from any major defeat. Thus, to the extent that the LDP holds together as the major single party, as its self-interest recommends, it is well positioned to do well in the plurality contests, and to win in proportion (a major one) in the PR arena.
30. *The International IDEA Handbook of Electoral System Design*, International Institute for Democracy and Electoral Assistance, Stockholm, 1997, calls this a 'parallel system' thus correctly distinguishing it from the 'mixed member proportional' (MMP) system, which is New Zealand's name for the German 'personalized proportional system' (*Personalisierte Verhältniswahl*). I object however to the 'parallel system' denomination, for labels are required to be descriptive. Since in this case we exactly have a mixed system, why not say so?
31. The other cases of mixed-proportional systems (Bolivia, Mexico, Venezuela, plus Hungary in a double ballot variety) simply represent a change from one type to another of PR and their witnessing is uninspiring.
32. The 1996 election has produced a two-party coalition government (National Party and New Zealand First) that controls a bare majority (61 seats out of 120) of Parliament. To be sure, very thin majorities also occur in England; but with coalition government 'minimal winning coalitions' perform with great difficulty and represent the worse possible solution.
33. See the evaluation in Sartori, *Comparative Constitutional Engineering*, pp.114–117.

Party Systems and Issue Dimensions: Israel and Thirty-Five Other Old and New Democracies Compared

AREND LIJPHART, PETER J. BOWMAN,
REUVEN Y. HAZAN

Political scientists have had a long-standing interest in the relationship between the number of political parties in a party system and the number of issue dimensions in inter-party competition. Early comparativists like Herman Finer and Carl J. Friedrich already emphasized that the partisan conflict in two-party systems was mainly along the traditional left-right (socio-economic) dimension whereas the parties in multi-party systems were usually divided by additional dimensions of issue conflict, especially the religious dimension. They contrasted the two-party systems and one-dimensional party systems of Great Britain and the United States with the multi-party and multi-dimensional party systems of France and Germany.[1]

This relationship was measured more precisely in a comparative study of 21 democracies in the period from the late 1940s to 1980. It found a strong statistical correlation – $r = 0.75$ – between the 'effective' number of political parties (a term that will be defined below) and the number of issue dimensions dividing them.[2] Rein Taagepera and Bernard Grofman took the analysis a significant step further by pointing that the relationship between the two variables can be closely approximated by the simple equation:

$$N = I + 1$$

in which N is the effective number of parties and I the number of issue dimensions.[3] According to this equation, the number of issue dimensions in a two-party system can be expected to be one, in a three-party system,

Arend Lijphart is Research Professor of Political Science at the University of California, San Diego. Peter J. Bowman is Lecturer in Political Science in the Department of Social Sciences at Mira Costa College. Reuven Y. Hazan is Lecturer in Political Science at the Hebrew University of Jerusalem.

two and so on; each party that is added produces an additional issue dimension and vice versa.

While these findings are certainly impressive, they are based on limited empirical evidence: a heavily Euro-centric and Western-centric set of countries. Of the 21 democracies that were analyzed, 15 were West European (Britain, France, Germany, Italy, the five Nordic states, the three Benelux countries, Switzerland, Austria and Ireland); the other six were the United States, Canada, Australia, New Zealand, Japan and Israel. The only significant elements of diversity among these countries were introduced by Japan – the only non-Western country in the set – and by Israel – the only country that was not already a well-established state before the beginning of the period under consideration.

The purpose of this essay is to re-examine the relationship between party systems and issue dimensions in a comparative analysis that includes more – and especially more diverse – countries, that covers a longer period of time (from the late 1940s, or from the date of independence or democratization, until the middle of 1996) and that measures the effective number of parties more accurately. Our criteria for inclusion are continuous democracy from 1977 or earlier until mid-1996 and a population of at least 250,000. These criteria yield a set of 36 countries: the 21 countries already included in the earlier study, plus the three new Southern European democracies (Spain, Portugal and Greece), three Latin American countries (Costa Rica, Venezuela and Colombia), four Caribbean island states (Jamaica, Barbados, the Bahamas and Trinidad),[4] India, Papua New Guinea, Mauritius, Botswana and Malta. The addition of these fifteen countries allows us to pay special attention to any differences that may appear between old and new states and between old and new democracies. Israel is in an unusual position in these respects: it is by now clearly one of the older democracies, but still a relatively new state – and hence deserves special attention. We shall also introduce two refinements in the measurement of the effective number of parties in party systems.[5]

PARTY SYSTEMS AND NUMBERS OF PARTIES

It has long been accepted in political science that, in characterizing party systems, both the numbers of parties and their relative strengths should be taken into consideration. When Finer and Friedrich spoke of two-party systems, for instance, they did not mean that such systems literally consisted of only two parties; they simply counted the major parties and ignored the minor ones. Douglas W. Rae pioneered a precise index based on both numbers and relative sizes of parties: the index of party system fragmentation.[6] Markku Laakso and Rein Taagepera transformed Rae's index into the 'effective number of parties', which has become the standard index in comparative analyses. This number (N) is calculated as follows:

$$N = 1/\Sigma s_i^2$$

in which s_i is the proportion of seats in a legislature that are held by the i-th party.[7]

The great advantage of the Laakso-Taagepera index is that it yields values that can be interpreted in the familiar number-of-parties context. For instance, in a two-party system with two equally strong parties, the effective number of parties is exactly 2.0. If one party is considerably stronger than the other, for instance, if their respective seat shares are 70 and 30 per cent, the effective number of parties is 1.7 – in accordance with our intuitive judgment that the party system is moving away from a pure two-party configuration in the direction of a one-party system. Similarly, with three exactly equal parties, the effective-number formula yields a value of 3.0. If one of these parties is weaker than the other two, the effective number of parties will be somewhere between 2.0 and 3.0, depending on the relative strength of the third party. For example, when three parties hold 42, 42 and 16 per cent of the legislative seats, the party system looks like a two-and-a-half party system and the effective number of parties is 2.6.

The problem of how to count parties of different sizes is solved satisfactorily by using the effective-numbers measure. However, this measure does not solve the question of what a political party is. The usual assumption in political science is that organizations that call themselves 'political parties' are, in fact, political parties. This assumption works well for most parties and most countries, but is problematic in two situations: parties that are so tightly twinned that they look more like one party than two parties and, conversely, parties that are so factionalized or uncohesive that they look more like two or more parties than one party. These problems cannot simply be ignored. We are interested in the numbers of parties in party systems because they indicate the degree to which party systems are fragmented. It is worth remembering in this connection that Rae calls his index, on which the Laakso-Taagepera index is based, the index of party system *fragmentation*. Clearly, a three-party system in which all three parties are cohesive and disciplined is less fragmented than a three-party system (with the same party sizes) in which one of the three is highly factionalized. Conversely, a three-party system in which all three parties are completely independent entities is more fragmented than when two of the parties are closely and perpetually allied with each other.

The twinned-parties problem can be solved relatively easily. The relevant cases are the following five closely allied parties: the Christian Democratic Union (CDU) and Christian Social Union (CSU) in Germany;

the Liberal and National parties in Australia; and the three pairs of parties that resulted from splits along the linguistic dividing line in Belgium: two Christian Democratic parties since 1968, two Liberal parties since 1971 and two Socialist parties since 1978. In particular, the two German and the two Australian parties are often treated as single parties by political scientists. For instance, Manfred G. Schmidt writes that the three 'major established parties' in Germany are 'the CDU–CSU, the SPD [Social Democrats] and the Liberals'.[8] A key characteristic of such tightly allied parties is that in cabinet formations they either enter the cabinet together or choose to be in the opposition together.

It only makes sense to consider counting two tightly allied parties as less than the normal two parties if their close collaboration is of long standing. Both duration and degree of closeness distinguish the above five pairs of parties from other examples of electoral alliances that are mere 'marriages of convenience'. Electoral systems with single-member district elections give small and medium-sized parties a strong incentive to form such alliances, but these alliances tend to be ad hoc, temporary and shifting; examples are France, India, and Mauritius. Similar temporary and shifting alliances can also be found in countries that use proportional representation, such as Israel, the Netherlands, and Portugal. In list systems of proportional representation, the lists on the ballot are often referred to as 'party lists', and we generally assume that these lists can indeed be counted as parties.

Our solution to the problem of tightly twinned parties is based on the notion that such parties are, in practice, somewhere in between one party and two parties and can plausibly be counted as one-and-a-half parties. The effective number of parties in systems with such tightly allied parties can be calculated by first calculating two effective numbers, based on the two-party assumption and on the one-party assumption and then averaging these two numbers. This is a compromise and may not be the most perfect and elegant solution, but it reflects the reality of these partisan actors better than counting them as either two parties or one party.

We propose a similar solution for highly factionalized parties: the Liberal and Conservative parties in Colombia; the Indian Congress party; the Italian Christian Democrats; the Liberal Democratic party in Japan; and the Democratic party in the United States. These are not the only parties in modern democracies that lack perfect cohesion – in fact, it is generally wrong to view parties as 'unitary actors'[9] – but they are the most extreme cases in which analysts have tended to conclude that the party factions are very similar to separate parties.

The big challenge in finding a compromise solution for counting factionalized parties is that the two numbers to be compromised are not immediately obvious: at one end, there is the one-party alternative; but what is the number of parties at the other end? In Italy and Japan, where the intra-party factions have been the most distinct and identifiable, the number of factions has been quite large: if these factions are counted as parties, measured in terms of the effective number of parties, both the Italian Christian Democrats and the Japanese Liberal Democrats would have to be counted as five to six parties. This is clearly excessive since it would make the overall party system of these two countries the most extreme multi-party systems in the world! Our proposal for the alternative at the multi-party end is much more modest: Treat each factionalized party as two parties of equal size. The compromise is then to average the effective number of parties based on the one-party assumption and the effective number based on the two-equal-parties assumption.

The result is that factionalized parties are counted as one-and-a-half parties – exactly the same solution that we propose for closely allied parties. This solution for factionalized parties is both a rougher approximation and more unconventional and so, likely to be more controversial. It is worth emphasizing again, therefore, that the number of parties should reflect the degree of fragmentation of the party system. This means that severe intra-party fragmentation must be taken into account. It is also important to emphasize that our adjustment for factionalized parties is a very modest one and, if it errs, that it errs on the side of underestimation instead of overestimation.

Table 1 shows the effective numbers of parties in 36 democracies – based on the partisan composition of the lower, and generally more important, house of bicameral legislatures or the only chamber of unicameral legislatures – averaged over all elections between 1945 and the middle of 1996. They are listed in decreasing order and cover a wide range: from 5.98 parties in Papua New Guinea to a low of 1.35 parties in Botswana. These numbers of parliamentary parties are based on the one-and-a-half parties assumptions for both closely allied and factionalized parties. In deference to the more conventional approach, which accepts the parties' own definition of 'parties', the table also shows the effective numbers of parties based on this alternative, more conventional, definition – closely allied parties are counted as two and factionalized parties as one – for the relevant countries. Moreover, at the end of this article, we shall examine whether our approach or the conventional approach yields the stronger correlation with the numbers of issue dimensions in the 36 democracies.

SEVEN ISSUE DIMENSIONS OF PARTISAN CONFLICT

In their developmental theory of cleavage structures and party systems, Seymour Martin Lipset and Stein Rokkan argue that two successive revolutions – the national and industrial revolutions – each generated

TABLE 1
AVERAGE EFFECTIVE NUMBERS OF PARLIAMENTARY PARTIES (ENPP)
RESULTING FROM ELECTIONS IN 36 DEMOCRACIES, ALTERNATIVE AVERAGES
FOR EIGHT DEMOCRACIES, AND THE NUMBER OF ELECTIONS ON WHICH
THESE AVERAGES ARE BASED, 1945–1996

	ENPP	Alternative ENPP	Number of elections
Papua New Guinea	5.98	–	4
Switzerland	5.24	–	13
Finland	5.03	–	15
Italy	4.91	4.16	14
Netherlands	4.65	–	15
Israel	4.55	–	14
Denmark	4.51	–	21
Belgium	4.32	5.05	17
India	4.11	3.34	6
Iceland	3.72	–	16
Japan	3.71	3.08	19
France	3.43	–	10
Venezuela	3.38	–	8
Luxembourg	3.36	–	11
Norway	3.35	–	13
Portugal	3.33	–	8
Sweden	3.33	–	16
Colombia	3.32	2.22	14
Germany	2.93	3.23	13
Ireland	2.84	–	15
Spain	2.76	–	7
Mauritius	2.71	–	6
Austria	2.48	–	16
Costa Rica	2.41	–	11
United States	2.40	1.93	25
Canada	2.37	–	16
Australia	2.22	2.50	21
Greece	2.20	–	8
United Kingdom	2.11	–	14
Malta	1.99	–	6
New Zealand	1.96	–	17
Trinidad	1.82	–	7
Barbados	1.76	–	7
Bahamas	1.68	–	5
Jamaica	1.62	–	7
Botswana	1.35	–	7

Source: Based on data in Thomas T. Mackie and Richard Rose, *The International Almanac of Electoral History*, 3rd ed., London: Macmillan, 1991; Thomas T. Mackie and Richard Rose, *A Decade of Election Results: Updating the International Almanac*, Glasgow: Centre for the Study of Public Policy, University of Strathclyde, 1997; Dieter Nohlen, ed., *Handbuch der Wahldaten Lateinamerikas und der Karabik*, Opladen: Leske und Budrich, 1993; V. B. Singh, *Elections in India, Volume 2: Data Handbook on Lok Sabha Elections, 1986–1991*, New Delhi: Sage Publications India, 1994; Arend Lijphart, *Electoral Systems and Party Systems: A Study of Twenty–Seven Democracies, 1945–1990*, Oxford: Oxford University Press, 1994; and data provided by Pradeep K. Chhibber, Michael Coppedge, Brian F. Crisp, Gary Hoskin, Mark P. Jones, J. Ray Kennedy, Hansraj Mathur, Shaheen Mozaffar, Ben Reilly, and Andrew S. Reynolds.

two dimensions of political issues, yielding a total of four such dimensions: religious, cultural-ethnic, socio-economic and urban-rural.[10] In addition to these four basic dimensions, other scholars have identified three further important dimensions of partisan conflict in modern democracies: foreign policy, regime support and materialist versus postmaterialist dimensions.[11]

How can the issue dimensions of party systems be determined? Official party programmes should be read with some skepticism, but they do offer clues to where parties stand on public policies, especially if they are supplemented by other formal party pronouncements, debates in party conferences and speeches by party leaders in parliament and elsewhere. Moreover, we can observe the actual policies pursued by a party when it is in power, or the policies promoted by a party when it shares governmental power with one or more partners in a coalition. Party programmes must be distinguished from the characteristics of the voters that parties represent. For instance, the fact that a party receives exceptionally strong support from Catholic voters does not automatically make it a Catholic party, nor necessarily indicates that religion is an important issue dimension. On the other hand, there is usually a mutual relationship between a party's programme and the objective and subjective interests and needs of the party's supporters.

A second guideline for the identification of the issue dimensions of partisan conflict is that the focus should be on the differences between, rather than within, parties. This means that some important sets of issues in a country may not constitute issue dimensions of its party system: they may divide parties internally instead of from each other. Third, our analysis will be restricted to the issues dividing what Giovanni Sartori calls the 'relevant' parties: (1) those large and/or centrist enough to have coalition potential; and (2) those that are large but extreme and hence do not have coalition potential, but that are sufficiently large to have 'blackmail potential'.[12] Finally, our focus will be on durable issue dimensions; partisan differences that may emerge in one election but fade away soon afterwards will be ignored.

Table 2 indicates which of the seven issue dimensions have been present in each of our 36 democracies. A distinction is made between dimensions of high salience (H), those of only medium intensity (M) and those that varied between high and low intensity over time (also rated M). The judgments on which the table is based are necessarily subjective, but most of them are straightforward and uncontroversial. The few difficult cases will be pointed out in the discussion of each of the issue dimensions.

1. *The socio-economic dimension.* The socio-economic issue dimension is listed first in Table 2 because it is the most important of the issue dimensions and because it was present in all of the democratic party

TABLE 2

ISSUE DIMENSIONS OF 36 DEMOCRATIC PARTY SYSTEMS, 1945–1996

	Socio–economic	Religious	Cultural–ethnic	Urban–rural	Regime support	Foreign policy	Post–materialist	Number of dimensions
Finland	H	M	H	M	M	–	–	3.5
Belgium	H	H	H	–	–	–	–	3.0
Germany	H	H	M	–	–	–	M	3.0
India	H	H	M	–	M	–	–	3.0
Israel	H	H	–	–	–	H	–	3.0
Italy	H	H	–	–	M	M	–	3.0
Netherlands	H	H	–	–	–	–	H	3.0
Norway	H	H	–	M	–	–	M	3.0
Papua N.G.	H	M	H	–	–	M	–	3.0
Switzerland	H	H	M	M	–	–	–	3.0
France	H	M	–	–	M	M	–	2.5
Japan	H	M	–	–	M	M	–	2.5
Portugal	H	M	–	–	M	M	–	2.5
Colombia	H	M	–	M	M	–	–	2.5
Denmark	H	M	–	M	–	M	–	2.5
Spain	H	M	H	–	–	–	–	2.5
Sweden	H	M	–	M	–	–	M	2.5
Costa Rica	H	H	–	–	–	–	–	2.0
Luxembourg	H	H	–	–	–	–	–	2.0
Venezuela	H	H	–	–	–	–	–	2.0
Iceland	H	–	–	M	–	M	–	2.0
Malta	H	M	–	–	–	M	–	2.0
Mauritius	H	–	H	–	–	–	–	2.0
Ireland	H	–	–	–	–	M	–	1.5
Jamaica	H	–	–	–	–	M	–	1.5
UK	H	–	–	–	–	M	–	1.5
Canada	M	–	H	–	–	–	–	1.5
Trinidad	M	–	H	–	–	–	–	1.5
Australia	H	–	–	M	–	–	–	1.5
Austria	H	M	–	–	–	–	–	1.5
Botswana	H	–	M	–	–	–	–	1.5
Greece	H	–	–	–	M	–	–	1.5
Barbados	H	–	–	–	–	–	–	1.0
New Zealand	H	–	–	–	–	–	–	1.0
United States	M	–	M	–	–	–	–	1.0
Bahamas	M	–	–	–	–	–	–	0.5
Total	34.0	16.5	9.5	4.0	4.0	6.5	2.5	77.0

Note: H indicates an issue dimension of high salience, and M a medium-salience dimension or those that varied between high and low intensity over time.

systems in the 1945–96 period. Many studies have shown that there are significant differences between the socio-economic policies advocated and pursued by leftist-oriented and rightist-oriented parties and governments. Leftist governments have systematically produced a higher rate of growth of the public sector of the economy, larger central government budgets, more income equalization, greater efforts to reduce unemployment and more emphasis on education, public health and social welfare spending than rightist governments. The evidence can be summarized in the following statement by Edward R. Tufte: 'The single most important determinant of variations in macroeconomic performance from one industrialized democracy to another is the location on the left-right spectrum of the governing political party. Party platforms and political ideology set priorities and help decide policy'.[13]

Left-right differences on socio-economic issues have generally declined since the 1960s, culminating in the 'Third Way' phenomenon in countries like Britain and Germany in the 1990s: British Labour and the German Social Democrats moderated their platforms and redefined their partisan identities to adopt positions favouring lower taxes, reduced social spending and the acknowledgment of the advantages of the free play of market forces. Their moves toward the centre were rewarded with big election victories in 1997 and 1998 respectively. However, over the whole period under consideration for each of the 36 countries, including Israel, the socio-economic issue dimension cannot be said to have disappeared in any of them, or to have even moderated from 'high' to only 'medium' salience in most countries.

Table 2 assigns 'medium' ratings only to the United States, Canada, the Bahamas and Trinidad. The United States is exceptional, as Lipset has repeatedly emphasized, in that it has never developed a Socialist or Social Democratic party.[14] Canada does have such a party but it is relatively small and the two major Canadian parties have both been determinedly centrist. In the two-party systems of the Bahamas and Trinidad, the dominant parties have also both stuck very close to the political centre. One trait that the four countries have in common is that they all have plurality electoral systems, which are often credited with creating centre-seeking parties. However, this explanation is not persuasive because eight other democracies also have plurality elections but 'high' ratings on the socio-economic dimension (Barbados, Botswana, India, Jamaica, Mauritius, Papua New Guinea, the United Kingdom and, until 1996, New Zealand). Another trait that unites this small group of four countries is that they all happen to be located in the Western hemisphere. Two are old and two are new democracies; the difference between old and new democracies is clearly not significant here. The other 32 democracies that all merit a 'high' rating on the socio-economic dimension also include both old and new democracies.

The Israeli party system belongs to this large majority of party systems and is not an exceptional case.

2. *The religious dimension*. Differences between religious and secular parties constitute the second most important issue dimension. Such differences can be found in more than half of the 36 democracies. In twelve countries that are largely Catholic and/or Protestant, there are, or have long been, many parties that explicitly call themselves 'Christian': Belgium, Costa Rica, Denmark, Finland, Germany, Italy, Luxembourg, the Netherlands, Norway, Sweden, Switzerland and Venezuela. Where, in these twelve party systems, the religious–secular difference has been important throughout the period under consideration, a 'high' rating is assigned in Table 2 and a 'medium' score to the others. In six mainly Catholic countries, religious divisions have on average been less prominent and explicit but still merit at least a 'medium' rating: Austria, Colombia, France, Malta, Portugal and Spain. In three mainly non-Christian countries, a religious issue dimension has also been present: Israel, India and Japan. This dimension has been and continues to be, extremely important in Israel, where the National Religious Party and, even more clearly, the ultra-Orthodox parties have long been highly effective advocates of orthodox religious policies. In India, the Bharatiya Janata party is usually described as a 'Hindu nationalist' party. In Japan, the Komeito party became a significant political presence in the 1970s; it is the political representative of the Buddhist Soka Gakkai sect.

Like the socio-economic issue dimension, the religious dimension has generally declined in importance in the post-World War II period. In the European countries with mixed Catholic and Protestant populations and histories of Catholic–Protestant antagonism, inter-religious tensions have largely disappeared and the two groups have even tended to unite politically. The Christian Democratic Union of postwar Germany was founded as a joint Catholic–Protestant party. In the Netherlands, the Catholic party and the two main Protestant parties presented a joint list in the 1977 parliamentary elections and merged into a single party organization soon thereafter. Moreover, both the religious parties and their anticlerical opponents have moderated their claims and counterclaims to a large extent. On the other hand, religious and secular parties are still divided on a wide range of moral issues, such as questions of marriage and divorce, gay rights, birth control, abortion, sex education, pornography, and so on. These issues have become especially prominent since the late 1960s. Moreover, it was not until the second half of the period that the relatively small religious parties of Japan, Denmark, Finland and Sweden became electorally important and not until the early 1990s that they clearly established their coalition potential by actually entering coalition cabinets.

Two much more significant exceptions to the decline in the salience of the religious issue dimension, noted above, are India and Israel. The Bharatiya Janata party has greatly increased its strength in India; its leader first became Prime Minister in an extremely short-lived coalition cabinet in 1996 and then in a more durable cabinet formed after the 1998 elections (but brought down in 1999). In Israel, too, the religious issue dimension has become increasingly salient and contentious and is probably stronger in the 1990s than it has ever been before. The distinction between old and new democracies does not appear to play much of a role with regard to the presence of a religious dimension. Of the fourteen countries without this dimension, half are old and half are new democracies.

3. *The cultural-ethnic dimension.* The cultural-ethnic issue dimension can be expected to be of special importance in plural societies – that is, societies that are sharply divided along ethnic, linguistic, racial, cultural, or religious lines into virtually separate subsocieties with their own political parties, interest groups and media of communication. Where different groups speak different languages, the formation of such distinct subsocieties is highly probable. Of our 36 democracies, nine can be regarded as plural societies: Belgium, Canada, India, Israel, Mauritius, Papua New Guinea, Spain, Switzerland and Trinidad. All but one of the plural societies are linguistically divided countries. India, with its more than a dozen officially recognized languages is an extreme case and Papua New Guinea is even more fragmented along linguistic lines. About two-thirds of the population of Mauritius is of Indian and one-third of African descent; the Indian community is a microcosm of the linguistic and religious divisions of India. Israel is a plural society not just because of the division between Jewish and Arab citizens, but even more as a result of the sharp split between religious and secular Jews. The only exceptional case is Trinidad, where the common language is far from sufficient to bridge the deep and all-pervasive cleavage between Creoles and East Indians.

The cultural-ethnic dimension is, indeed, of at least some importance in eight of the nine plural societies. In most of these, cultural-ethnic issues have high salience. The two rather surprising exceptions are multi-lingual Switzerland and even more multi-lingual India, which in addition is deeply divided by caste differences. In these two countries, religious differences between Protestants and Catholics in Switzerland and between Hindus, Moslems and Sikhs in India are the much more salient differentiators between the parties at the national level.

Israel is the most significant exception: a plural society in which the party system, in our judgment, should not be assigned a cultural-ethnic issue dimension in spite of the presence of Arab and Russian immigrant parties and the split between Ashkenazi and Sephardi. The Jewish–Arab division is clearly an ethnic division, but the Arab parties have generally not been regarded as acceptable coalition partners by the other parties. According to Sartori's criteria, mentioned above, the Arab parties should not be taken into consideration in determining the issue dimensions of partisan conflict: they have not had coalition potential and they have been too small for most of the period to have blackmail potential. Only after the development of the Israeli party system into a two-bloc competitive configuration, did the Arab parties begin to acquire blackmail potential:[15] this became evident by 1984, when they helped the other parties on the left form a 'blocking majority' of 60 MKs (Members of Knesset), which forced the formation of a national unity government. By the 1990s, it can be argued that they practically acquired coalition potential to the extent that they provided vital external support for the 1993–96 Rabin and Peres minority governments, which prevented these governments from being voted out of office. Moreover, it has only recently become acceptable, albeit controversial, to make major decisions with the crucial support of the Arab parties, such as the Oslo II agreement in 1995, which passed on a 61–59 vote and hence lacked a 'Jewish majority' in the Knesset. The Arab parties still did not become actual coalition partners, however. In any case, both the period of blackmail potential since the 1980s and the brief period of semi-coalition status in the 1990s are much too short to qualify Israel for a cultural-ethnic issue dimension for the entire 1949–96 period (see the last section for a discussion of Israel in the 1990s).

It is also only in the 1990s that the Israeli party system can be said to have acquired a cultural-ethnic dimension on account of the appearance of explicitly Russian immigrant parties. Again, their presence and obvious importance in the party system have come too late to affect our rating for the entire 1949–96 period. The Ashkenazi–Sephardi division is of much longer standing, but in the early years it was more a factor that clearly affected voting behaviour than an explicit programmatic difference between the parties. It also gradually faded until the appearance of Shas in 1984. We have opted not to credit Israel with a cultural-ethnic dimension on the basis of the Ashkenazi–Sephardi split, but we agree that a reasonable argument can be made in favour of assigning at least a medium-salience dimension. We shall return to this question and to the general subject of the drastic changes in the Israeli party system in the 1990s at the end of this article.

Canada is given a 'high' rating, based notably on Ottawa's strained relations with the province of Quebec. Citing its own unique political, ethnic and linguistic significance, Quebec has engaged in a protracted struggle to secede from the Canadian federation, almost achieving success with a 1995 referendum that, only by the slimmest of margins, kept the mainly French-speaking province a part of Canada. This conflict is not just a central-regional conflict, but a partisan split between the Quebec Party (Parti Québecois) and the anti-secessionist Liberal Party. The 1998 provincial elections yielded a decisive victory for the ruling Quebec Party, which won 75 seats to the Liberals' 48 seats. However, the Liberals actually won a slightly higher share of the vote than the Quebec Party – 44 per cent compared with 43 per cent – and the election outcome, therefore, gave mixed signals with regard to the likely success of another attempt to achieve secession by means of a provincial referendum. The question at the heart of this matter remains whether Quebec's leaders truly want independence or, in a more Machiavellian interpretation, merely want to place themselves in a strategic position of greater political leverage with Ottawa in the future.

In three countries that can be classified as semi-plural, the cultural-ethnic dimension is of some importance, too: Finland, Germany and the United States.[16] In Finland, the Swedish-speaking minority and the Swedish People's party are both very small, but the party has been a highly effective political actor and a frequent partner in coalition governments. Because the Christian Social Union of Bavaria is counted as a 'half' party and also because of the emergence of the Party of Democratic Socialism as a specifically East German party since unification in 1990, Germany is given a 'medium' score.

No American party has an exclusively ethnic base, but the Democrats have been much more representative of and sensitive to the interests of ethnic and racial minorities than the Republicans and, when affirmative-action and other special minority programmes have become controversial, Democrats have tended to support and Republicans to oppose them. Democratic sensitivity to Hispanic-American issues is especially notable in California, where many state Democrats opposed California's Proposition 187, the controversial 1994 ballot initiative that proposed the banning of public services such as health care and education to illegal immigrants. When the Republicans, led by then-governor Pete Wilson, strongly endorsed this initiative, many Latino voters responded in 1998 by helping elect a Democratic governor, Gray Davis, who has since reached out to Mexican-Americans with more inclusive policies and gestures, such as warmer political and economic relations between California and Mexico.[17]

In one non-plural and ethnically largely homogeneous country, Botswana, tribal differences have had a sufficient impact on the party system to warrant a 'medium' score on the cultural-ethnic dimension. Finally, when we classify the twelve countries with a cultural-ethnic issue dimension according to whether they are old or new democracies, we find that they are again evenly split between the two categories.

4. *The urban-rural dimension.* Differences between rural and urban areas and interests occur in all democracies, but they constitute the source of issue dimensions in the party systems of only eight countries and only with medium salience. Israel's position on this dimension is not exceptional: together with 27 other democracies, it lacks the urban-rural issue dimension. However, in this respect there is a major difference between old and new democracies: of the eight countries with this issue dimension, seven are old democracies and only one, Colombia, is a new democracy.

Where agrarian parties are found, mainly in the Nordic countries, they have tended to become less exclusively rural and to appeal to urban electorates, too, prompted by the decline of the rural population. A clear sign of this shift is that the Swedish, Norwegian and Finnish agrarian parties all changed their names to 'Centre Party' between 1957 and 1965. The Danish Liberals and the Icelandic Progressives also originated as agrarian parties, but similarly try to portray themselves as centre parties. The Swiss People's Party and the Colombian Conservatives can also be regarded as parties that are to some extent representative of rural interests. The Australian National party used to be called the 'Country Party' and has been the traditional defender of rural and farming concerns. In deference to its classification as a 'half' party, however, Australia is only assigned a 'medium' score on the urban-rural dimension.

5. *The dimension of regime support.* This dimension may occur in democracies as a result of the presence of important parties that oppose the democratic regime; these are typically Sartori's 'blackmail' parties. In our 36 democracies, the dimension of regime support has been present mainly in European and Asian countries with sizable Communist parties: France, Italy, Finland, Portugal, Greece, India and Japan. However, the trend toward 'Eurocommunism' has entailed basic changes in Communist attitudes toward both democracy and foreign policy and the Indian and Japanese Communist parties have similarly become more moderate. For this reason, none of the party systems is given more than a 'medium' rating on this dimension. The only other country with a sizable Communist party is Iceland, but the Icelandic Communists may be said to have been Eurocommunists since the late 1930s; they joined with a Socialist faction to form a new party that was explicitly pro-parliamentary and pro-democratic and that resigned from the Comintern.

Israel could arguably be assigned a score on the regime support dimension for two reasons. One is that the ultra-Orthodox parties basically favour a straightforward theocracy instead of democracy; in practice, however, they tacitly accept the democratic regime – and the benefits they derive from it. Second, the Jewish–Arab division represents a regime support dimension as well as the cultural-ethnic dimension discussed above: the Arab parties are regarded as anti-system by the other parties and are hence not regarded as suitable participants in governing coalitions; conversely, the conception of Israel as a Jewish state is hard to accept for many in the Arab parties. However, as explained earlier, the Arab parties became relevant parties according to Sartori's criteria only in the 1980s and therefore cannot be said to produce either an ethnic dimension or a regime support dimension in the entire period from 1949 to 1996. Hence we do not assign a regime support dimension to Israel in Table 2.

Colombia is assigned a 'medium' score for a quite different reason than in the European and Asian cases: the prominent role of the AD-M19 party, which originated as a revolutionary movement, but later participated in elections and even entered the cabinet in the early 1990s. Four of the eight countries with a regime support dimension are old and four are new democracies – another even split.

6. *The foreign policy dimension.* A great variety of foreign policy issues have divided the parties in twelve of our 36 democracies: the traditional, but declining, pro-Soviet stance of the European Communist parties; opposition to NATO membership in France and Iceland; opposition to membership in the European Union and its predecessors in Britain, Denmark, France, Ireland and Malta; relations with the United States in Japan and Jamaica; relations with Australia in Papua New Guinea; relations with Libya in Malta; and different attitudes of the Irish parties toward the Northern Ireland problem. None of these was either prominent or durable enough, however, to merit more than a 'medium' rating.

The only country with a 'high' score in Table 2 is Israel. Here the issue is a nationalist-territorial one and the debate is 'between those who follow the maximalist territorial tradition of the Revisionists and those who adhere to the more moderate territorial demands of the Socialist–Zionist school'.[18] This issue dimension has been present in Israel throughout the country's existence, but became especially prominent after the occupation of Arab territories in 1967. Its salience has increased in recent decades and, by the 1990s, the foreign policy issue dimension had reached a peak of intensity. Major international agreements, like the 1993 and 1995 Oslo Accords, have been bitterly contested among Israel's political parties. The 1998 Wye River accord was responsible for bringing down the Israeli cabinet in early 1999, and even forced new elections. Israel is, therefore, exceptional in two respects: it is the only country with a 'high' score on this dimension, and the dimension has greatly increased in intensity.[19]

Of the twelve countries in which the foreign policy dimension is of some importance, eight are old and four are new democracies. This is

not a striking difference, however, considering that our set includes
slightly more old than new democracies: 21 versus 15.

7. *The materialist versus postmaterialist dimension.* This dimension
revolves around the two issues of participatory democracy and
environmentalism, which both fit the cluster of values of what Ronald
Inglehart calls 'post-materialism'. Inglehart found that, especially among
young middle-class people in Western democracies, a high priority is
accorded to goals like 'seeing that the people have more say in how things
get decided at work and in their communities' and 'giving the people
more say in important government decisions'. Moreover, in the richer
nations the cluster of postmaterialist values also included the objective of
'trying to make our cities and countryside more beautiful'.[20] As Table 2
shows, postmaterialism has become the source of a new dimension in
only a few party systems. The explanation is that it has emerged only in
the more developed countries and only recently and that, as result, the
postmaterialist parties have remained small and generally without clear
coalition potential. However, the Norwegian and Swedish Centre parties
have made a smooth transition from old-fashioned rural to modern
environmentalist values and two new Dutch parties, Democrats '66 and
Radicals, espoused participationist proposals as early as the late 1960s
and entered a coalition cabinet in 1973. Germany is also given a
'medium' rating on this dimension because of the prominence of the
Green party; it has participated in several governments at the state level
and it was widely considered to have coalition potential at the national
level as well – even before it actually entered a national cabinet, as the
junior partner of the Social Democrats, in 1998.

   The only four countries with a significant postmaterialist dimension
are all old democracies, which are also the wealthier democracies.
Postmaterialism can be seen as a luxury that only prosperous countries
can afford.

ISSUE DIMENSIONS AND PARTY SYSTEMS

The last column of Table 2 shows the number of issue dimensions in
each of the 36 democracies. This number could, in principle, range from
0 to 7 dimensions, but the actual range is only from 0.5 to 3.5. The
countries with the same total scores are grouped together in the table
and these groupings are listed in decreasing order of their number of
issue dimensions. Within each category, countries that have the same
pattern of issue dimensions are listed first. In the group with 2.5 issue
dimensions, France, Japan and Portugal have the same 'high' socio-
economic dimension plus the same 'medium' religious, regime support
and foreign policy dimensions. Costa Rica, Luxembourg and Venezuela

form a similar subgroup with 'high' socio-economic and religious dimensions in the 2.0 category. And five countries with a British political heritage form two subgroups in the 1.5 category: the first, consisting of Ireland, Jamaica and the United Kingdom, with 'high' socio-economic and 'medium' foreign policy dimensions and the second, composed of Canada and Trinidad, with 'medium' socio-economic and 'high' cultural-ethnic dimensions.

We now return to the question posed at the beginning of this article: How are the numbers of issue dimensions related to the effective numbers of political parties? In terms of pure logic, no strong link is necessary: the two parties in a two-party system could differ on all of the seven issue dimensions; conversely, even an extreme multi-party system might have no issue dimensions at all if, for instance, all of the programmatic differences were intra-party instead of inter-party divisions. However, there are two reasons to expect a strong and mutual empirical link between the two variables. First, when there are several dimensions of political conflict in a society, one would expect that a relatively large number of parties are needed to express all of these dimensions, unless they happen to coincide with each other. Second, issue dimensions have been defined in terms of differences between instead of within parties; this means that party systems with few parties cannot easily accommodate as many issue dimensions as multi-party systems. The first argument treats the number of issue dimensions as the independent (explanatory) variable; in the second, the number of parties is the independent variable.

The correlation coefficient that was found in the earlier study of 21 mainly West European democracies in the period between the late 1940s and 1980 was 0.75.[21] For our new set of 36 much more diverse countries, the correlation is even stronger: 0.84. This means that the earlier finding cannot be attributed to the fact that it was based on a rather homogeneous set of Western, highly industrialized democracies. Our new finding strongly confirms the generally close link between party systems and issue dimensions.

Our test differs from the earlier one in three respects: (1) a larger number, and greater diversity, of countries; (2) a longer time span; and (3) refinements in the counting of the effective number of parties in eight countries that have either closely allied or factionalized parties. Does the third difference explain a portion of the stronger correlation that we found? This possibility can be tested by regressing the *unadjusted* effective number of parties – in which closely allied parties are counted as two separate parties and a factionalized party as just one party – on the number of issue dimensions. As explained above, we detected an urban-rural dimension in Australia on account of its National party and a cultural-ethnic dimension in Germany because of the presence of the Christian Social Union; however, because these two parties were counted as only 'half' parties, we gave the two countries only 'medium' ratings on the respective dimensions. In the new regression, they are treated as full-fledged separate parties and the two countries' ratings should therefore be raised from 'medium' to 'high' on the affected dimension – which gives Australia a total score of 2.0 and Germany a total score of 3.5. The correlation coefficient is 0.79 – still very strong but slightly lower than the 0.84 coefficient based on the adjusted effective numbers of parties. Therefore, our one-and-a-half parties assumption appears to have worked quite well.

However, although our correlation for the 36 democracies is stronger than the earlier one for 21 democracies, our regression equation deviates more from Taagepera and Grofman's simple relationship of N = I + 1. Their empirical result for 21 countries (with issue dimensions as the independent and parties as the dependent variable) was:[22]

$$N = 0.834I + 1.264.$$

The corresponding expression based on our data for 36 countries is:

$$N = 1.304I + 0.373.$$

One explanation for the greater deviation from N = I + 1 is that in the longer period (from the late 1940s to 1996) the effective numbers of parties have tended to increase somewhat and that the number and intensity of the issue dimensions has generally declined. Another explanation is the inclusion in the 36-country set of Botswana, Jamaica and Trinidad, with effective numbers of parties well below 2.0 but with 1.5 issue dimensions each. Yet another is the influence of two outliers: the 21-country comparison included the French Fourth Republic with a very high total number of issue dimensions[23] – 4.5, compared with a maximum of 3.5 dimensions in the 36-country study – and 4.9 parties and the latter study includes Papua New Guinea with an extremely high number of parties, 5.98, but only 3.0 issue dimensions.

Figure 1 presents the positions of each of the 36 countries graphically. Somewhat arbitrarily, it treats the effective number of parties as the independent variable and the number of issue dimensions as the dependent variable. It also shows the regression line, drawn as a solid line, as well as Taagepera and Grofman's predicted regression line as a dotted line. The figure shows that the Taagepera-Grofman regression line is still a reasonable approximation of the regression line that is based on our empirical data.

Figure 1 shows that the new democracies do not form a pattern that is at all different from the old democracies. Old and new democracies alike cluster very closely around the regression line. The main outliers, but still only modest outliers, are the Bahamas, the United States, Papua New Guinea, Norway, Germany and Spain – three old and three new democracies.

Israel was shown to be quite exceptional with regard to two of the

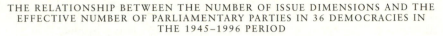

FIGURE 1

THE RELATIONSHIP BETWEEN THE NUMBER OF ISSUE DIMENSIONS AND THE
EFFECTIVE NUMBER OF PARLIAMENTARY PARTIES IN 36 DEMOCRACIES IN
THE 1945–1996 PERIOD

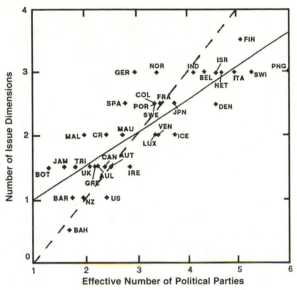

Note: The 36 Democracies are identified by the first three characters of their English names,
except that AUL means Australia, AUT Austria, CR Costa Rica, JPN Japan, NZ New
Zealand, PNG Papua New Guinea, UK United Kingdom, and US United States.

dimensions: not just high salience but also growing salience and
intensity on the religious and foreign policy dimensions. However,
Israel's combination of 4.55 effective parties and 3.0 issue dimensions
does not appear to be exceptional at all: Israel's position is very close to
the regression line in Figure 1. We must, however, mention two
qualifications. One is that, as discussed earlier, it can be argued that
Israel deserves at least a 'medium' rating on the cultural-ethnic
dimension because of the Ashkenazi–Sephardi division. This would
increase the total number of issue dimensions to 3.5 and it would move
Israel to a higher position in Table 1 – and away from the regression line.
Second, our operational rule to count lists as parties (in countries with
list systems of proportional representation) tends to depress the effective
number of parties in countries where parties frequently present joint lists
– of which Israel is the most extreme case. If we were to disaggregate
such joint lists in the Israeli case, the effective number of parties would
undoubtedly go up by at least half a party. If both of these 'corrections'
were made, of course, Israel would be back in a position close to the
regression line.

THE CASE OF ISRAEL IN THE 1990s

Another exceptional aspect of the Israeli party system and its issue
dimensions in recent years, apart from the growing intensity of the
religious and foreign policy dimensions, is that the cultural-ethnic and
regime support dimensions have clearly become relevant and highly
salient in the 1990s. As discussed earlier, this results partly from the
changed status of the Arab parties, partly from the appearance of the
new Russian immigrant parties and partly from the solidification of the
Ashkenazi–Sephardi division as a dimension separating political
parties.[24] The total number of issue dimensions in the Israeli party
system in the 1990s has therefore increased to 5.0 – that is, five of the
seven possible issue dimensions. This is a remarkably high number
compared with the numbers of issue dimensions found in the other 35
democratic party systems in the 1945–96 period, the highest of which is
3.5 and is found in only one country (Finland); moreover, if we were to
measure the numbers of issue dimensions in these 35 countries in the
1990s, most of them would have the same or slightly fewer, instead of
more, issue dimensions than before 1990. The number of issue
dimensions in Israel in the 1990s (5.0) is also even higher than the
highest number counted in the earlier study: the 4.5 issue dimensions
found in the fragmented party system of the French Fourth Republic.

At the same time, the effective number of parties in Israel has also
been high in the 1990s; in particular, the 1999 election produced a
dramatic rise to 8.68 effective parties in the Knesset. The previous high
in the elections since 1949 occurred a long time ago – 5.96 parties in the
1955 election – but the second highest previous number was produced
by the 1996 election: 5.61 parties. The average effective number of
parties in the three elections in the 1990s is 6.23. The slightly more than
six effective parties and the five issue dimensions in Israel in the 1990s
are remarkably close to the Taagepera-Grofman equation, which
predicts that the number of parties will exceed the number of issue
dimensions by one. This very close correspondence might be a
fortuitous result, but the Israeli party system in the 1990s does provide
a bit of additional evidence of the tendency of the effective number of
parties and the issue dimensions of partisan conflict to be strongly and
directly related to each other.

Both generally and in the case of Israel, we have been emphasizing
mutual causation: a growing number of parties facilitates the emergence
of new issue dimensions and vice versa. A final question that is worth
asking is whether there are other independent variables that affect the
number of issue dimensions and/or the number of parties. We suggest
that three such important influences have been at work in Israel. First,
the number of issue dimensions is also closely related to the number and

depth of cleavages in a society. For instance, in a religiously divided society, it is possible and even likely, that the party system will have a religious issue dimension, whereas such a dimension is impossible in religiously homogeneous societies. Accordingly, Israel's growing number of issue dimensions is not unexpected in view of the increasing fragmentation in Israeli society. Second, the growing polarization in Israeli politics, combined with the fact that the forces of the 'left' and those of the 'right' have become so evenly divided – exemplified by Netanyahu's razor-thin victory over Peres in 1996[25] – have made the Arab parties important enough political actors to be counted in the 1980s and 1990s (according to Sartori's criteria).

Third, the usual institutional explanation of the number of parties is the electoral system. Israel's extreme system of proportional representation is clearly an important factor behind its multi-party system, but cannot, by itself, explain the increased fragmentation of the party system in the 1990s. After all, virtually the same electoral system produced only 3.12 effective parties in 1981 but 8.68 parties in 1999; the only significant change in the electoral system was that the electoral threshold was raised from one per cent to 1.5 per cent – but this should have had the effect of slightly reducing instead of increasing the effective number of parties. The crucial institutional change was the directly elected Prime Minister in the 1996 and 1999 elections;[26] it led many voters to give their Prime Ministerial vote to one of the major party candidates but their parliamentary vote to one of the small parties – a pattern that clearly hurt the two large parties, helped the smaller parties and dramatically increased the effective number of parties in the Israeli party system. Prior to the 1999 elections, there was growing sentiment in favour of abolishing the direct election of the Prime Minister and returning to the pre-1996 system of selecting Prime Ministers and forming cabinets. However, the greatly increased strength of the smaller parties in the Knesset, who owe their gains at least partly to the new system, makes a return to the old system considerably less likely.

To end on a comparative note, it is worth emphasizing that Israel's experience of growing multi-partism as a result of the introduction of the direct election of the chief executive runs counter to the pattern in most Latin American presidential democracies, which also combine the popular election of the chief executive (president) with proportional representation in legislative elections. The experts' consensus is that, because the presidency is the biggest political prize to be won and because only the largest parties have a chance to win it, these large parties have a great advantage over small parties, which tends to carry over into legislative elections, even when the latter are by proportional representation.[27] This tendency toward moderate multi-partism is especially strong when the presidential election is decided by plurality instead of a two-stage majority-runoff procedure (where small parties may want to try their luck in the first round) and when the legislative elections are held at the same time or shortly after the presidential elections.[28]

In 1996 and 1999, Israel actually fulfilled both of the above conditions: although the formal Prime Ministerial election procedure was majority-runoff, only two candidates competed and the election was completed in one round; hence the system resembled plurality and the two elections, Prime Ministerial and parliamentary, were held on the same day. Nevertheless, the outcome was a growth instead of a decline in multi-partism. The most plausible explanation for the deviant outcome in Israel, we submit, is that, in contrast with the Latin American countries, Israeli society is much more fragmented – in terms of both the number of groups and the depth of the cleavages dividing the groups – and that Israelis have much stronger loyalties to their sub-cultural communities and to the political parties representing these communities.

NOTES

We would like to thank Abraham Diskin and Emanuel Gutmann for their very helpful comments on the first draft of this article.

1. Herman Finer, *The Theory and Practice of Modern Government*, rev. ed., New York, Henry Holt, 1949; Carl J. Friedrich, *Constitutional Government and Democracy*, rev. ed., Boston: Ginn, 1950.
2. Arend Lijphart, *Democracies: Patterns of Majoritarian and Consensus Government in Twenty-One Countries*, New Haven: Yale University Press, 1984, pp.127–49.
3. Rein Taagepera and Bernard Grofman, 'Rethinking Duverger's Law: Predicting the Effective Number of Parties in Plurality and PR Systems – Parties Minus Issues Equals One', *European Journal of Political Research*, Vol. 13, No. 4 (1985), pp.341–352.
4. Trinidad's official name is 'Trinidad and Tobago', but for brevity's sake we shall take the liberty of referring to it simply as 'Trinidad'.
5. Our analysis is based on data presented in Chapter 5 and Appendix B of Arend Lijphart, *Patterns of Democracy: Government Forms and Performance in Thirty-Six Countries*, New Haven: Yale University Press, 1999.
6. Douglas W. Rae, *The Political Consequences of Electoral Laws*, New Haven: Yale University Press, 1967, pp.53–58, 62.
7. Markku Laakso and Rein Taagepera, 'Effective" Number of Parties: A Measure With Application to West Europe', *Comparative Political Studies*, Vol. 12, No. 1 (1979), pp.3–27. We shall focus on the effective number of *parliamentary* parties, based on the proportions of seats in the legislature; the Laakso-Taagepera index can also be calculated on the basis of the proportions of the parties' votes and it then becomes the effective number of *elective* parties.
8. Manfred G. Schmidt, 'Germany: The Grand Coalition State', in Joseph M. Colomer (ed.), *Political Institutions in Europe*, London: Routledge, 1996, p.95.
9. Michael Laver and Norman Schofield, *Multi-party Government: The Politics of Coalition in Europe*, Oxford: Oxford University Press, 1990, pp.14-28.
10. Seymour Martin Lipset and Stein Rokkan, 'Cleavage Structures, Party Systems and Voter Alignments: An Introduction', in Seymour M. Lipset and Stein Rokkan (eds.), *Party Systems and Voter Alignments: Cross-National Perspectives*, New York: Free Press, 1967, pp.1–64.
11. See Arend Lijphart, 'Political Parties: Ideologies and Programmes', in David Butler, Howard R. Penniman and Austin Ranney (eds.), *Democracy at the Polls: A Comparative*

Study of Competitive National Elections, Washington, D.C.: American Enterprise Institute, 1981, pp.28–29.

12. Giovanni Sartori, *Parties and Party Systems: A Framework for Analysis*, Cambridge: Cambridge University Press, 1976, pp.121–124.

13. Edward R. Tufte, *Political Control of the Economy*, Princeton: Princeton University Press, 1978, p.104.

14. Seymour Martin Lipset, *American Exceptionalism: A Double-Edged Sword*, New York: Norton, 1996, pp.77–109.

15. Reuven Y. Hazan, 'Party System Change in Israel, 1948–1998: A Conceptual and Theoretical Border-Stretching of Europe?', in Paul Pennings and Jan-Erik Lane (eds.), *Comparing Party System Change*, London: Routledge, 1998, pp.151–166.

16. In addition to these three, we classify six other countries as semi-plural: Austria, Colombia, France, Italy, Luxembourg and the Netherlands.

17. The Republicans have made inroads toward Hispanic voters in Texas, where Governor George W. Bush has adopted a more inclusive approach to Latinos in the state. This development has important implications beyond Texas politics because by early 1999, Bush had become the front-runner for the Republican presidential nomination in the year 2000.

18. Ofira Seliktar, 'Israel: Fragile Coalitions in a New Nation', in Eric C. Browne and John Dreijmanis (eds.), *Government Coalitions in Western Democracies*, New York: Longman, 1982, p.295.

19. The foreign policy dimension is arguably the most critical one in Israel, given the country's geography and tense relations with its Arab neighbours; few countries – including countries that are not in our set of 36 nations – have a foreign policy dimension that is as critical as it is in Israeli politics. Moreover, Israel's foreign policy dimension is reinforced by the fact that it largely coincides with the religious issue dimension. The fall of the Netanyahu government in early 1999 can be explained in terms of the Israeli-Palestinian conflict and the stance toward it of the orthodox National Religious Party (NRP) that was in the cabinet. This party, along with other rebels in the coalition, pressured Prime Minister Netanyahu to move slowly, if at all, on the implementation of the Oslo accords and the signing of the Wye River agreement and they threatened to bolt the fragile cabinet if their wishes would not be respected.

20. Ronald Inglehart, *The Silent Revolution: Changing Values and Political Styles Among Western Publics*, Princeton: Princeton University Press, 1977, pp.40–50.

21. Lijphart, *Democracies*, p.148.

22. Taagepera and Grofman, 'Rethinking Duverger's Law', p.350.

23. Lijphart, *Democracies*, p.130.

24. This dimension already intensified in the 1970s and 1980s, exhibited by the high ratio of Sephardi voters for the Likud as opposed to those of Labour, but it then slightly decreased its relevance, only to return with a vengeance in the 1999 elections.

25. The results of the Knesset elections in 1999 still exhibit this even split. The coalition partners in the outgoing Netanyahu government and their associated parties, won 60 of the 120 seats, while those parties opposed to the Netanyahu government won an identical number of seats. See Reuven Y. Hazan and Abraham Diskin, 'The 1999 Direct Election of the Prime Minister and the Knesset in Israel', *Electoral Studies*, forthcoming.

26. Reuven Y. Hazan, 'Presidential Parliamentarism: Direct Popular Election of the Prime Minister, Israel's New Electoral and Political System', *Electoral Studies*, Vol. 15, No. 1 (1996), pp.21–37.

27. Of the three Latin American democracies included in our study – all characterized by presidentialism, proportional representation and multi-partism – Colombia's and Venezuela's multi-partism is very moderate with only 3.32 and 3.38 parties respectively and Costa Rica's party system with only 2.41 effective parties is actually more like a two-and-a-half party system than a true multi-party system (see Table 1).

28. Matthew Soberg Shugart and John M. Carey, *Presidents and Assemblies: Constitutional Design and Electoral Dynamics*, Cambridge, Cambridge University Press, 1992, pp.206–58; Mark P. Jones, *Electoral Laws and the Survival of Presidential Democracies*, Notre Dame: University of Notre Dame Press, 1995, pp.88–118.

Changing Conditions of Party Competition: A New Model Party?

GORDON SMITH

What happens when social cleavages lose their force? This question has been around for some time, but with each round of national elections it becomes increasingly apparent that the historical lines of social division in Europe – principally those of religion and social class – are steadily losing relevance even as passive indicators of voting behaviour. The consequences could be profound: as electorates become less structured, higher levels of volatility will become evident, ultimately building up potential for radical change.

The effects would not merely be felt on the fortunes of individual parties, but would change the character of party competition. Party competition in Europe is still firmly embedded in the left-right axis: in how parties present themselves; in the basis of coalition formation; in party-placement according to the judgements of voters. If party competition were to be altered fundamentally, would the labels of 'left' and 'right', if not discarded entirely, be emptied of substantial meaning? Given such a scenario, it is reasonable to conclude that individual parties have to re-think their competitive stance, their ideology and their structure. In other words, what are the chances of a new type of party coming into being which could serve as a model for others to follow?

ELECTORAL DEALIGNMENT AND ISSUE-POLITICS

Such a line of argument can, of course, be easily over-stated. It may imply that political life is becoming more unstable, or anyway increasingly unpredictable, when after all, Western Europe, at least, remains highly stable. The erosion of social cleavages is a gradual process and the major parties continue to rely on their appeal to one or another section of society for a large share of support. If it were the case that a widespread electoral dealignment had been occurring, then there

Gordon Smith is Emeritus Professor of Government at the London School of Economics and Political Science.

would be strong evidence that old-established parties, in particular, were affected. Yet Peter Mair's analysis showed only a rather muted picture of electoral change.[1] Taking a ten-year span of the electoral cycle for West European countries and comparing the aggregate performance of parties competing at its commencement with their performance at the end of the cycle, it was apparent that the extent of any de- or realignment had been modest. These 'old' parties (in his terminology) had – in percentage terms – lost ground, although by far less than was currently believed. There was another factor to be taken into account: over the whole period, the size of electorates had increased substantially and the 'old' parties were successful in securing a large slice of the expanded electorates. On balance, it can reasonably be argued, these 'old' parties had maintained their position: losing somewhat in their share of the vote, but as compensation seeing a significant increase in the actual size of their support. There are no strong grounds for believing that their position has since sharply deteriorated.

Yet two caveats have to be made. One is that, even though their percentage losses in any one period may not have been serious, the cumulative effect over a longer period would be large. The other reservation is that the negative balance will be even more pronounced if, as seems likely, the size of electorates in the future grows more modestly than in the past. At the very least, it can be concluded that those parties which were rooted in the cleavages of European society will become more vulnerable to the effects of electoral change and less able to withstand the competitive pressures, unless they adapt themselves to the new conditions.

One of these pressures emanates from the impact of issue-politics on the political system generally and the parties in particular. With the influence of higher levels of education and access to wide sources of information, there is a much wider awareness of public issues. By its nature, issue-politics relates to the strongly-held beliefs of minorities determined to bring their demands to the attention of the wider public and the parties. Even otherwise loyal party supporters are quite prepared to take up issues that are not on the agenda of the party leadership and may run contrary to party policy. Such developments may well be healthy for a democracy, but present considerable problems for the parties.

Rather than leading to a greater involvement, electoral dealignment can point in another direction, towards a disengagement from politics, apathy and indifference, shown in one way by a declining turnout at elections. The danger to established parties of this non-involvement is that an apparently apathetic section of the population may suddenly become activated by a grievance or a sharp crisis and mobilized by a single-issue, protest party or even an anti-system one.

PARTIES AND ISSUE-HANDLING

Whichever aspect of a dealigned electorate is taken, the problems of established parties in maintaining their positions are likely to intensify and that is most readily seen with regard to issue-politics. Almost anything can become an 'issue' and parties ignore them at their peril. Just as with treating the extent of dealignment with caution, however, so it is also important not to exaggerate the consequences of dealignment in relation to issue-politics.

The resolution of an issue is an outcome that should leave all those most closely concerned satisfied – in other words that the problem has been solved. In fact, of course, such a neat result is not usually forthcoming and parties – normally the governing ones – have to extricate themselves in one way or another if the 'costs' of meeting demands are too high. Unacceptable costs would include: threats to party unity and implementation of the party's programme; antagonizing significant sections of the electorate; harming relations with important interests.

A party's strength lies just as much in its ability to 'handle' problems satisfactorily as in seeking to satisfy the demands made on it.[2] Parties have to act as efficient 'gatekeepers' so as not to be overwhelmed. All kinds of tactics are covered by the label of 'issue-handling': simple delay; buying-off proponents; counter-attack; marginalizing groups or party factions; issue-conflation; issue-substitution; and displacement. It is also the case that many problems do not have a widely acceptable solution; issue-handling is a vital part of the political process.

Not all issues are amenable to such tactics, especially not those that have been termed 'maverick issues'.[3] Particularly relevant are those issues that are value- rather than resource-related, since strongly held values tend to be non-bargainable and not susceptible to tactical manoeuvres employed by parties. Such issues have disruptive potential, especially if they do not conform to a unilateral ordering – in other words, do not fit within the left-right structuring of party systems. The destabilizing effects will be felt by individual parties, but a maverick issue can also bring about a decisive change in a party system, most obviously through the arrival of new parties, or through a split in an existing one, but also in causing the break-up of a previously stable coalition alignment.

Too heavy an emphasis on trends of electoral dealignment and the consequent growth of issue-politics runs the risk of down playing the role of parties: they do not just react passively to societal and electoral change. That much is evident from the variety of tactics used in reacting to uncomfortable issues. Parties are themselves strategic and pro-active players. They have a vested interest in their own survival as organizations, irrespective of changes in the original conditions that first led to their foundation. The ability of parties to mould electoral opinion, set the terms of political debate and shape the institutional context in which they operate further underlines their independent role.

PERSISTENCE OF LEFT AND RIGHT

A balance has to be struck between the increasing fluidity of electoral behaviour on the one side and the resources available to parties on the other. Yet the balance is not static and parties have continually to re-adjust their positions and strategies in order to counter the threat of electoral erosion. One position that is most difficult for a party to shift decisively is its primary location on the left-right spectrum. Nor, of course, is it necessarily in its interests to do so. The left-right placement is one of the enduring features of European politics. Parties rely heavily on their traditions to bind the loyalties of members, but more widely to give the electorate at large a sense of what a party 'stands for' and that may otherwise not be readily apparent from its programmematic intentions.

Increasing electoral volatility appeared to show that voters were not only less tied to individual parties, but also that voting behaviour was no longer so influenced by left/right considerations. Yet the analysis made by Bartolini and Mair showed that overall volatility had not been greater than in the inter-war years.[4] Moreover, most movement took place between parties that were fairly closely linked, within a 'bloc' rather than between blocs. In other words, voters move between parties of the left or right and are far less inclined to transfer from a party of the left to one on the right. As a consequence, the effect of electoral volatility is contained.

From a different perspective, however, the situation may be less static than it first appears. If voters are reluctant to make a decisive move, then parties have an incentive to take advantage of declining loyalties to individual parties, pitching their appeal somewhat wider and thus better adjusting themselves to the demands of issue-politics. In itself, this process is hardly new: parties moderate their stance in order to broaden their appeal, compete for the centre-ground and major parties engage in centripetal competition to maximize support. Such competition, however, still conforms to the contest between left and right, even though both are watered down. Essentially, this process of steady dilution continues to characterize European politics. Nevertheless, at some stage a critical juncture could be reached when the old parameters cease to apply.

CONDITIONS FOR A NEW MODEL

Electoral detachment from individual parties is a feature of the present era and the weakening of party ideologies makes it easier for voters to

switch between parties of left and right. Thus, there is an incentive for
a party not merely to follow electoral drift, but to devise a preemptive
strategy. Why just wait for voters to move? If successfully implemented,
the electoral rewards of such a strategy could be large. There are plenty
of pitfalls on the way; failure would lead to a loss of credibility with no
easy way back to its former position. Parties cannot just quietly abandon
their long-held left or right positions and in other ways carry on as
before. Much more is required. Moving 'beyond left and right' has all
kinds of consequences for the nature of a party: its basis of appeal;
competitive stance; internal organization; and its leadership.

Considering the problems likely to be encountered, it might seem
that a brand-new party would be better able to attract wide support
without first having to re-invent itself. The drawbacks, however, are
obvious: with little or no organizational infrastructure and no secure
electoral base, the new party would probably be over-dependent on its
leader to secure a wide following. Such charismatic leaders need to
incorporate a strong 'message', usually of an anti-system nature if they
are to be successful. But such a rallying-call has the effect of alienating
many, as much as it attracts others. Rather than stamping a new party
out of the ground, a new model has a better chance of emerging from
among established parties.

In order to appreciate what could be involved, some broad
conditions can be specified – based in part on the experience of the
British Labour Party – to show how they have been applied in the British
case. and how a new model might be relevant for other parties. The
conditions can be summarized under three headings:

Ideology. The term here is used in a loose sense and refers to a party's
view of society, its Weltanschauung. It will be implicit in the party
programme, but just as much in the history, traditions and symbols of
the party. They give it coherence and a sense of purpose.
Nevertheless, they have to be forfeited in order to justify the new
model. The problem is, then, what to put in their place. It has to be
a rationale for the party that does not estrange the party's hitherto
loyal supporters, whilst simultaneously giving other sections of the
electorate few grounds for concern.

Party leadership. Without purposeful leadership it is doubtful whether
the impetus to create a new-type party could be maintained. The
party leader needs to have undisputed authority, effectively be in
control of the party's organization and have considerable freedom to
interpret policy. It has to be assumed that the leader will already have
a high standing in the party, but there will also have to be some
charismatic quality, a sense of personal mission, perhaps, if the
party's brand-new ideology is to be acceptable to party supporters
and a wider electorate.

Concentration of authority. It is inevitable that a new party ideology will be far more diffuse and its interpretation in terms of policy initiatives uncertain. Inevitably, too, many activists and factions will be hostile to change. Centralization of authority may be essential until the party is fully secured in its new position. The danger is that inner-party democracy will be permanently weakened. Concentration of authority is also required for the efficient presentation and management of government policies for dissemination in the public domain.

IDEOLOGY AND NEW LABOUR

Labour's massive victory in 1997 owed less to fundamental rethinking of the party's ideological position than electoral rejection of the Conservatives: after 18 years in office the ruling party was jaded and deeply divided.[5] Nevertheless, the badge of 'New Labour' was a positive attraction – some two million voters switched directly from the Conservatives – and specific policy commitments together with the major reforms within the party were sufficient to show that New Labour had banished its old-style, class-based image.

In fact, the wide-ranging debate on the 'third way' has been a feature of subsequent years; the debate mirrors similar concerns of other social democratic parties. The Labour Party itself has no worked-out theory of society and it would anyway be at odds with its pragmatic nature. This reservation by no means diminishes the significance of the third way discourse. Its vague meaning is a valuable support for the leadership: it is an unofficial credo at the same time as a useful rationalization of power, but also a flexible tool of policy-making.

The experience of Thatcherism in Britain acted as a catalyst for Labour attitudes. Although rejecting many of its policies, the party could not countenance the entire rejection of the market philosophy; too much had changed meanwhile in the economy and society. Instead, the third way seeks to combine elements of it to bring about a renewal of social democracy. A leading exponent, Anthony Giddens, has argued that on a socio-economic level, the third way 'is a response to two deficient philosophies, the old Keynesian welfare consensus (Old Left) and the New Right/neo-liberalism. The Third Way is an attempt to go beyond them'.[6] Going 'beyond' is thus not the same as taking a 'centre' position, between left and right, but expresses a kind of 'transcending dualism'. How this thinking may work out in practice can only properly be judged after several years when a number of its policies have been implemented.[7]

LEADERSHIP AND NEW LABOUR

As yet, the third way hardly provides a firm basis for policy-making, but this deficiency is not at all a disadvantage. It allows an open-minded approach which has always suited Labour; moreover the third way gives wide freedom of interpretation to the leadership. The fact that it is only one model of how social democracy could develop is not a handicap. The very imprecision of the third way – it has no hard core – is an important merit. As Prime Minister, Tony Blair, in his writing, has closely identified himself with the third way, so that his interpretations carry the ring of authority in the party.[8] Blair has come to personify New Labour. This development is in line with Herbert Kitschelt's argument that, 'Social democrats are most able to respond to a highly competitive situation and a strong challenge of market liberalism if they have an autonomous leadership'.[9]

Blair's stature grew impressively in the course of the 1997 election campaign and was further strengthened by the massive scale of Labour's victory. Thanks to his huge parliamentary majority, the Prime Minister enjoyed an almost unquestionable authority over the parliamentary party and his ministerial colleagues. Although critics could see dangers in the threat to parliamentary democracy, the increasingly presidential style of government won broad popular support, as shown by Blair's historically high poll ratings.

CONCENTRATION OF AUTHORITY

In the past, activists and left-wing factions were a powerful check on the leadership of the Labour Party. The trade unions, too, represented a force within the party that had to be placated. This situation changed in the 1980s: undesirable activists were excluded, in particular through the banning of Militant Tendency – 'a party within a party' – and membership was declared incompatible with that of the Labour Party. Throughout the 1980s, as well, the influence of the trade unions weakened, as they were forced to be on the defensive by the policies and legislation of the Conservative government, along with the decline of industries that had been the backbone of union power.

An equally important development has been the erosion of the authority of the party's annual conference, nominally still the sovereign body of the party. Delegates from the constituencies used the conference as a forum, frequently to oppose the leadership's policies and the conference had control of the party programme. That changed in 1997. Instead, party policy is formulated by a rolling programme of consultation within a 'national policy forum' over which the government will certainly have decisive influence. The reform was justified on the need to prevent obstructionism on the part of activists and avoid the risk of confrontation between the government and party.[10]

What of the parliamentary party? Moshe Maor has argued that the two major British parties have increased centralization of decision-making, giving them increased strategic flexibility, but also 'enhancing the autonomy of their parliamentary party'.[11] And yet this assessment is quite at odds with the present reality of Labour's parliamentary party. Far from its large majority giving maximum scope for dissent and with no real danger to the government, the parliamentary party has thus far proved to be a largely quiescent body, content to follow the government's lead.[12] One could even speak of a downgrading of parliamentary authority: the government's preference for direct communication with the public and cultivation of the media as a more efficient way of getting its policies across is a rational course to take. The Prime Minister's personal preference for a wider stage, European as well as national, is also a factor. Why bother with the distractions of parliamentary debate if the wider public can better be addressed in other ways?

IMPLICATIONS OF NEW LABOUR

The three elements of New Labour all hang together: a loose ideology capable of wide interpretation; a leader able to exploit its wide ambit; and control over the party to minimize the risk of challenge to the leader. It is a powerful combination. Relatively free of pressures from within the party, the leader is able to concentrate on the wider electorate and speak on behalf of 'the people' or 'the nation' as inclusive concepts.

Integral to New Labour – and perhaps a further condition for the model – is the attention that has to be given to public sentiment and the means to influence it. This priority is shown by the way issues are handled, the tapping-in to so-called 'focus groups' to determine government tactics, the readiness to back away from decisive action when it runs counter to public opinion or the opposition of important consumer or producer interests. Presentation and coordination of government policies is a central task of government. The now re-titled Government Information and Communication Service ('Communication' added), is a key part of government machinery, flanked by the host of 'political advisers' to ministers and by the tireless 'spin-doctors' dedicated to putting the best gloss on government actions.[13] It is tempting to take a cynical view of this style, but the nature of the new model may require such orchestrated support if the party itself is denuded of many of its former functions and if the uncertainties of issue-politics are to be contained.

Faced with the attractions of Labour's new model, opposition parties find difficulties in how they can best react. Troublesome regional parties have been 'bought off', at least for a while, by measures of devolution at a national level.[14] The Liberal Democrats hover uneasily between co-operation and muted opposition, leaving the Conservatives hoping that something will turn up to restore their fortunes. That 'something' was allowed for by Otto Kirchheimer, namely in a resurgence of 'opposition in principle'.[15] Yet apart from an appeal to national sovereignty against the inroads of further European integration a principled opposition to New Labour is difficult to foresee.

Nevertheless the continuing dominance of New Labour should not be taken for granted. One measure of a dominant party, for instance, posits the winning of three successive elections as the criterion. An alternative guide is for a party's ideas to be dominant for an era. On both tests, the Thatcher years made the Conservative Party dominant. Just mid-way through Labour's first parliamentary term, caution in extrapolation is essential.

There is a further reason for caution: the New Labour model is heavily dependent on its leader. Can such a style of personal leadership be securely institutionalized? Without Blair, the third way could lose coherence and conviction. Moreover, any successor would have to cope with a resurgent party prone to factional in-fighting, just as the Conservative Party has experienced in the post-Thatcher years.

THE MODEL IN COMPARATIVE PERSPECTIVE

Quite apart from problems New Labour may face in the future, there is a niggling question: is its model really new? Writing in the 1960s, Kirchheimer had forecast the emergence of a new type of party, the catch-all party.[16] Not only would the catch-all party ditch its 'ideological baggage' in response to fundamental changes in society, but it had other important characteristics relating to its organization and societal links. These features included: the increasing power of the party's top leadership; a diminished role for individual members; an appeal fashioned for the whole electorate; and dealing with all kinds of interest groups, not just a favoured few.

In all these respects, there is little to distinguish New Labour from its catch-all forerunner. Kirchheimer had continental European parties specifically in mind in formulating his argument, both Christian as well as social democratic ones, especially the CDU and SPD in Germany in becoming 'people's parties'.[17] Yet the changes in such parties were more ideological than organizational and their electoral appeal was by no means 'catch-all', since they continued rely mainly on support from particular social groups and interests. In important ways New Labour conforms to Kirchheimer's original specifications more closely than other parties that had made partial changes much earlier. Indeed, with the techniques of communication, policy presentation and coordination, the party has now developed, New Labour has gone beyond the simple catch-all model . The party, too, had no cumbersome baggage to get rid of in the first place; instead it has the flexible suitcase of the third way.

Can the New Labour example be replicated elsewhere? Certainly, there are no special difficulties in adopting a variation of the third way and some social democratic parties have taken this course. More problematic is securing the centralization of authority in a party, since organizational structures vary from one country to another. Thus, in a federal state or a strongly regional one, it may prove difficult to subject local units without risking party unity and without centralization the party leader would lack the wide freedom to do so. In most cases, one or more aspect of the model could be employed, but its separate parts are really all interdependent.

At the level of the party system there are other difficulties, since the great majority are multi-party systems and coalition politics is the norm. Unless coalition partners are quite minor and usually compliant, the major one will not have sufficient authority even though it is the dominant player and its leader likewise will probably lack the overriding stature implied by the model. In a multi-party system, too, there is the likelihood that a party will have others nearby in close competition. How can a social-democratic party, for instance, find sufficient competitive space – a problem that New Labour does not have? Kitschelt finds that such space lies on the communitarian-libertarian dimension, but points out that green/new politics parties are often already in occupation.[18] New Labour, in contrast, is able to absorb this dimension to its competitive advantage.

A conclusion has to be that New Labour is not an example that others can follow. Similarly faced with disengaged electorates, parties in other countries are likely to tackle their problems in a totally different way. For the Labour Party, the 1997 election proved a golden opportunity: it had a useful ideology in place; the party leadership was in firm control; and the structure of the party system gave it competitive space. Since then, with the resources of government available, it has made good use of its now dominant position. That combination is unlikely to be replicated elsewhere.

NOTES

1. Peter Mair, 'Myths of Electoral Change and the Survival of Traditional Parties', *European Journal of Political Research*, Vol. 24, No. 2 (1993), pp.121–133.
2. This view is taken by Jan-Erik Lane and Svante Ersson who conclude: 'The West European party systems have reached a stage of development characterized by a floating electorate. One may argue that the Rokkan carpet of cleavages has been pulled away from under the parties', in Paul Pennings and Jan-Erik Lane (eds.), *Comparing Party System Change*, London: Routledge, 1998, p.36.
3. Moshe Maor and Gordon Smith, 'On the Structuring of Party Competition: The Impact of Maverick Issues', in T. Bryder (ed.), *Party Systems, Party Behavior and Democracy*, Copenhagen: University of Copenhagen, 1993, pp.40–51.
4. Stefano Bartolini and Peter Mair, *Identity, Competition and Electoral Availability: European* Electorates, 1885–1985, Aldershot: Gower, 1990.
5. In 1997, Labour won 43.3 per cent of the vote as against 34.4 per cent in 1992. The swing was then further greatly magnified by the disproportionate effect of the relative plurality voting system.
6. Anthony Giddens at a conference held at the London School of Economics, May 1998: *Is There a Third Way? And Has Labour Found It?*
7. Anthony Giddens, *The Third Way: The Renewal of Social Democracy*, Cambridge, The Polity Press, 1998. Giddens lists the components of the third way 'programme' (p.70): the radical centre the new democratic state (the state without enemies) active civil society the democratic family the new mixed economy equality as inclusion positive welfare the social investment state the cosmopolitan nation cosmopolitan democracy.
8. Tony Blair, *The Third Way: New Politics for the New Century*, London: Fabian Society, 1998.
9. Herbert Kitschelt, *The Transformation of European Social Democracy*, Cambridge: Cambridge University Press, 1994, p.253.
10. Andrew Richards has pointed out that although the Labour Party has boosted its individual membership, the irony is that, 'the power and influence of the party member in general and the party activists in particular, have continued to decline'. 'The Life and Soul of the Party: Causes and Consequences of Organizational Change in the British Labour Party', Instituto Juan March, Estudio Working Paper, June 1997.
11. Moshe Maor, *Political Parties and Party Systems: Comparative Approaches and the British Experience*, London: Routledge, 1997, p.132.
12. As a result of the 1997 election, Labour had a massive (176) majority over all other parties in the Commons, but rather than greater freedom for the parliamentary party, the reverse was the case, perhaps because a large proportion of the new entrants were elected thanks to Blair's popularity.
13. Nicholas Jones, *Titans of Spin: The Media and the New Labour Government*, London: Gollancz, 1999.
14. Measures of devolution for Scotland, Wales and London involved the risk of allowing local parties too much freedom. A priority was given to ensure that the leadership's favoured politicians secured the post of first minister (mayor, in case of London) and squeezing out 'awkward' but popular local figures.
15. Otto Kirchheimer, 'The Waning of Opposition in Parliamentary Regimes', in M. Dogan and R. Rose (eds.), *European Politics: A Reader*, New York: Little, Brown, 1971.
16. Otto Kirchheimer, 'The Transformation of Western European Party Systems', in J. LaPalombara and M. Weiner (eds.), *Political Parties and Political Development*, Princeton: Princeton University Press, 1966, pp.177–200.
17. Kitschelt, *The Transformation of European Social Democracy*, p.301.
18. Thus, a quite different response to the weakening of links between parties and electorates is for parties to attach themselves more closely to the state and forming a cartel with other parties. See, Richard Katz and Peter Mair, 'Changing Models of Party Organization: The Emergence of the Cartel Party', *Party Politics*, Vol. I, No. 1 (1995).

PART II
RELIGION AND STATE

Religion and State in Europe and Israel

BENYAMIN NEUBERGER

Europe is a fascinating mosaic of dozens of nation state with a wide range of arrangements between church and state, sometimes varying within the state itself. Great Britain has two Established Churches, one in England and one in Scotland with different arrangements in Wales and Ulster. In France, the separation of church and state does not hold for the departments Haut-Rhin, Bas-Rhin and Moselle (the former Alsace-Lorraine) and in Switzerland, there is separation in the cantons of Geneva and Neuchatel, but not in the rest of the country.

The six basic models of church and state relations include two dictatorial and four democratic models. The former are theocracy and secular absolutism; the latter are the Established Church, the Endorsed Church, the Separation of Church and State and the Recognized Communities Model.

This essay argues that a process of convergence is taking place in Europe today. The dictatorial models have vanished or collapsed and within the democratic spectrum the 'extreme' separationist and establishmentarian models are moving closer to 'middle of the road' Endorsed Church or Recognized Communities models. The first model for discussion is theocracy – a state run by clerics according to religious law, where only one religion is legal and where minority religions and religious dissidents from the dominant religion are persecuted. 'Pure' theocracies have disappeared, though in some non-European countries like Iran, Sudan, Saudi-Arabia and Afghanistan semi-theocratic regimes still exist[1] In the past, European dictatorships like Franco's 'Confessional State' did have some theocratic features – an official State Religion, the provision that the laws of the state cannot contradict religious law, the representation of church dignitaries in the Councils of State and the denial of religious freedom to the religious minorities[2] – but today, none of Europe's regimes has any theocratic characteristics.

With the collapse of the totalitarian communist regimes of Eastern Europe, the secular-absolutist model, too, has disappeared. Formally these anti-religious regimes adhered to the separation of church and state

Benyamin Neuberger is Professor of Political Science at Israel's Open University.

(Lenin said: 'The state has no business in religion'),[3] but in reality there was no such separation. Communist ideology could not accept a separation, based on the view that religion is part of a man's private life and the state should be neutral in religious affairs. In fact, communist governments heavily interfered in religious and church affairs and they did so in an oppressive way. They saw to it that the church followed regime – friendly policies and that the leading clerics were communists or 'fellow travellers'. Religious activities were severely circumscribed; thousands of churches, mosques and synagogues were destroyed; religious institutions were closed; religious education in schools was abolished; and many believers were discriminated against and persecuted. Still, communist Eastern Europe was not monolithic. In Albania, religion was outlawed, all churches and mosques were closed, the possession of a Bible was a criminal offence and religious marriage was punishable by death. In Poland, on the other hand, a kind of *modus vivendi* existed between the communist government and the Catholic Church.[4]

In the democratic world, to which all European regimes of the late 1990s belong, states with an Established Church are on the religious extreme of the spectrum. In the Established Church States – England, Scotland, Denmark, Sweden, Finland, Norway, Greece and Cyprus – the state recognizes only one religion and one church as 'official' and 'national'. This 'establishment' of religion is institutionalized and the church is, in a sense, an organ of the state. The state is by law involved in church affairs and the church fulfills certain state roles and functions.

England is a prime example of an Established Church State. Since the Act of Settlement of 1701, the King or the Queen is the titular Head of the Anglican Church. His or her partner, too, has to be Anglican. In 1978, Prince Michael of Kent renounced any claim to the throne because he intended to marry a Catholic woman. Under the Coronation Oath Act of 1688, the King or Queen swear 'to maintain the Protestant Reformed Religion established by law' and proclaim to remain a faithful 'Defender of *the* Faith',[5] the faith being Protestant-Anglican. The leadership of the Church of England – the archbishops of York and Canterbury and twenty four bishops – serve ex officio as Lords Spiritual in the House of Lords. The King or Queen formally appoints the bishops of the church upon the recommendation of the Prime Minister and the 'measures' of the church have to be approved by Parliament. Thus, Parliament approved the recommendation of the church to appoint divorced men as clergy in 1992 and again in 1994 did so with regard to the appointment of women to the lower echelons of the clergy.

While England still has an Established Church – and in principle Crown and Parliament still determine the character of the 'national' church – in reality the establishmentarian character of the polity has weakened over the years. Parliament interferes less and less in church matters – the approval of the 'measures' is more of a formality and since the Enabling Act of 1919, Parliament has delegated the real power of approval to the Church's General Synod. The same is true with regard to church appointments. The real appointing agency is now the Church Appointments Committee and there has been an open understanding since 1977 that the King or Queen will appoint only those bishops on a list recommended by the church. According to the Education Reform Act of 1988, religious instruction in schools is 'in the main Christian' and the daily prayer is of a 'broadly Christian', not an Anglican ('establishmentarian'), character. In official ceremonies, the trend is to involve not only the dignitaries of the Established Church, but also those of other mainstream religions (e.g. Catholics and Jews). The State also finances private religious schools of all denominations and grants all of them free access to the public media. Lately, more and more non-Anglican religious dignitaries are being appointed to the House of Lords (although only the Anglican bishops have 'reserved seats'). More and more people talk about an Ecumenical Establishment, which would gradually replace the one Established Church. Significant for this ecumenical trend is also the Queen's participation in 1994 – for the first time since 1688 – in the centennial of the Catholic Westminster Cathedral. A final example of this ecumenical tendency is the outspoken wish of Prince Charles to be declared Defender of Faith, any faith, rather than Defender of *the* Faith.[6]

Another example of a weakened Established Church is Greece. The Greek Orthodox faith is part and parcel of Greek nationhood and the Greek Orthodox Church has been deeply identified with the modern Greek nation state. According to the Greek historian E. Skopeta, the nation has been the 'guardian of religion' and religion has been the 'guardian of the nation'.[7] The Greek monarchs who reigned until the 1970s were the titular Heads of the Greek Orthodox Church. Until 1988, all school teachers had to be Greek Orthodox and until 1952, the conversion of an Orthodox was prohibited. For any house of worship to be built, even those of non-Orthodox religions and denominations, the approval not only of the government but also of the local metropolit of the Orthodox Church was required. While according to the 1975 republican constitution, 'The prevailing religion in Greece is that of the Eastern Orthodox Church of Christ',[8] the process of disestablishing Greek Orthodoxy is well under way. The president now has to be Christian, not necessarily Greek-Orthodox. He is no longer sworn in before the Holy Synod of the Orthodox Church. The rule which prohibits non-Orthodox teachers from teaching in state schools has been modified and is applied (since 1988) only in small village schools that have no more than one or two teachers. The prohibition of conversion, which was discriminatory against non-Orthodox religions and denominations, now applies equally to all religions. In 1982, the option of civil marriage and divorce by mutual agreement finally became legal, thus further weakening the power of the Orthodox Church. That same year the State also introduced the possibility of civil marriage for those who were not allowed to marry by religious law ('mixed' religious marriages, fourth marriages, marriages of priests, etc.).[9]

An extreme example of the de-establishing trend is Sweden, where the state was disentangled in the 1980s from all involvement in matters of theology, liturgy, prayers, church appointments and missionary activity of the 'Church of Sweden.' Supervision in all these matters shifted to the General Synod of the Lutheran Church. Sweden has also decided that religious instruction in schools should consist of teaching all religions objectively, rather than inculcating an 'official' religion. In the 1990s Sweden finally decided that the establishmentarian status of the Lutheran Church should be abolished by the year 2000 and that a generally endorsing and sympathetic attitude to religion as such would continue to be followed without preference for the Lutheran Church.[10]

At the same time that the Established Church States have become less establishmentarian, the Separationist States have become less separationist. Generally, in separation regimes the state declares itself either 'secular' (in the sense of being non-religious, not necessarily anti-religious) or 'neutral', or it explicitly proclaims the principle of separation. In present-day Europe, France, the Netherlands, Russia, Albania, Serbia, The Czech Republic, Wales and the Swiss cantons of Geneva and Neuchatel can be regarded as separationist. Ireland, Spain and Poland, on the other hand, proclaim 'neutrality' and 'separation', but in reality fit the Endorsed Church model.

Historically, the separation of religion and state can be rooted either in a point of view sympathetic to religion (as in the United States) or in one that is hostile to religion (as in France). However, with time the 'sympathetic separation' may become less sympathetic and the 'hostile separation' may become less hostile. In all separation regimes, it is customary for governmental legislation to have secular goals and to avoid harming or giving preference to any religion. It is further agreed that the state must not be involved in religion or religious organization and that the latter must not intervene in political affairs.

Separation of religion and state does not always stem from sympathy to religion. Sometimes it originates in hostility to religion and a desire to clip its wings. France is an example of this. Whereas in the United States the separation was due, at least at first, to the multiplicity of churches and denominations and the desire to prevent one denomination from taking over,[11] in France one church was omnipotent and the idea of separation was directed against it. Unquestionably, one of the targets of the French Revolution of 1789 was the religious establishment, which together with the royal- aristocratic establishment made up the *ancien regime*. In pre-Revolutionary France, the King ruled by the grace of God, Catholicism was the state religion and religious minorities had an inferior status. The Revolution changed all that. It proclaimed freedom of religion, abolished the autonomy of the Catholic Church and replaced it with a church under the auspices of the state. Its priests had to swear fealty to the state. In 1791 the French government instituted civil marriage and secularized education. In 1795 it forbade the display of religious symbols in public and asserted that the Republic recognized no religion and would not finance religious services. A retreat from the separation concept occurred in 1801 when Napoleon signed a *concordat* with the Catholic Church, stating that Catholicism was the religion of the vast majority of the French people. With the return of the Bourbons to the throne, the church was given a new charter, declaring Catholicism the state religion. Except for insignificant modifications which lasted for only brief periods of time, this status did not change until 1905. At that time, all constitutional recognition of a religion or a church was abolished and complete separation was instituted between church and state. The state confiscated church property and stopped funding the church and its priests. The church regained its official status during the Vichy regime (1940–1944), but the constitutions of the Fourth and Fifth Republics (1946 and 1958 respectively) again stripped it of all official status and proclaimed state secularism. State secularism was demonstrated in the 1980s in the school system, when the *Conseil d'Etat* rejected petitions of Muslim girls to wear a veil in state schools on the grounds that religious symbols in school may be proscribed if 'by their ostentatious or assertive character' they amount to 'acts of pressure, provocation, proselytism or propaganda'.[12] The courts also rejected the petition of a Jewish boy to be exempt from Saturday classes. In all these cases, the judges of the *Conseil d'Etat* – the supreme judicial body for administrative affairs – ruled that the secularism of the state education system would not allow them to accede to the petitioners' requests.

Nevertheless, in the last decades strict separationism has receded and there is a gradual acknowledgment of the public role of religion. The secularist, anti-religious laicism was replaced by a *laicite positive*, by a state that is truly neutral and sees itself as a guarantor of freedom for all religions and denominations. Most church property, in the past confiscated by the state, has been returned to the church and churches are now exempt from paying taxes. The state even funds the maintenance of churches regarded as important historical and national monuments. State support for private religious schools continues and, following stormy mass demonstrations, President Mitterand's attempt (in the late 1980s) to cut aid to religious schools failed. State funding for religious services in hospitals, prisons and the army also indicates a slow retreat from extreme separationism. Religious instruction in schools is again allowed, provided it is upon the parents' request and is financed jointly by the parents and the church (but not by the state). Public radio and television also provide time for the broadcasting of religious services of the various religions and denominations. Symbolic for the new religion-friendly atmosphere is the fact that state ceremonies are conducted in churches. Thus, President Mitterand's state funeral took place in Notre Dame Cathedral although Mitterand had been a life-long secular socialist. In the 1990s the *Conseil d'Etat* declared as unconstitutional, discriminatory and contrary to the freedom of conscience, the expulsion of Muslim girls from school because they had worn head scarves (although the rule which prohibited wearing 'ostentatious distinguishing signs in clothing or otherwise' was maintained). France in the 1990s is indeed a far cry from the strictly separationist and militantly secularist France, of the 1790s or the early twentieth century.[13]

Another example of separation that originated in hostility to the church is the separation that prevailed in Italy from the time of its unification in 1860 until 1929. The source of this hostility was the opposition of the Papal State – which subsequently shrank and became today's State of Vatican City – to the unification of Italy. The separation regime collapsed completely with the signing of the Lateran Agreements between Mussolini and the Pope in 1929, which moved Italy from one extreme to the other, from complete separation to the establishment of a virtual state religion. After 1945, Italy's church–state relations changed again, but they did not return to the strict separationism of the early twentieth century.[14]

Holland is another Separationist State (the 1848 constitution prohibited, among other things, religious processions) that became religion-friendly and less 'separationist'. The 1983 constitution talks about 'respect for religion and faith'; private religious schools are fully financed by the state; optional instruction of religion is provided in all state schools; churches are exempt from taxes; religious services (financed by the state) are offered in all hospitals, prisons, old-age homes and army units; the state widely finances religious charities; and air-time is given to the various churches on public radio and television.[15]

In Russia, too, strict constitutional separationism is receding. Hostility towards religion under Communism became sympathetic separation under Boris Yeltsin. While the constitution says that 'no religion may be established as a state or mandatory religion' and that 'religious associations are separate from the state', in fact there is no solid 'wall of separation' between church and state. Thus the state funds the rebuilding of Orthodox churches destroyed under Stalin and the

Patriarch of the Russian Orthodox church fulfills a symbolic role in official functions (e.g., Patriarch Alexsij II played a semi-official role in the swearing-in of Yeltsin as President and in the 'unification' ceremony of Russia and fellow-Orthodox Belarus). Religious education may be provided in public schools upon the parents' demand and Orthodox priests may be invited to schools to teach religion. In the army, since 1995, priests have replaced the 'political commissars' of the former Red Army. In 1998, parliament also passed a law that empowers the government to fight 'foreign' missions and missionaries. Russia is thus slowly moving away from hostile separation, to sympathetic separation and from there to the Endorsed Church Model.[16]

A third model of church–state relations common in Europe is the Recognized Communities Model, or the 'German' Model. In the German Model, there is no 'official' religion or church. All the major religious communities recognized by law are for all intents and purposes, equal before the law. The German Model differs from the Established Church Model in the sense that the churches are not subjected to state interference, but it also differs from the Separationist States in the sense that religion is not 'privatized' and that co-operation between church and state covers wide areas, is institutionalized and is based on agreements between church and state. This model is sometimes described as 'mutual independence without separation'.[17] Relations between church and state are based on the Recognized Communities Model in Germany, Austria, Hungary, Belgium, Luxembourg, Alsace - Lorraine and some of the Swiss cantons.

Germany is the classic example of church–state relations based on recognized communities. Until 1918, Germany was a 'Christian State' and the Kaiser was titular head (*summus episcopus*) of the Lutheran Church. The Weimar Constitution of 1919 and again the West German (by now All-German) *Grundgesetz* (Basic Law) of 1949, say that there is no *Staatskirche* (State-Church). The Federal Government and the *Laender* Governments have written agreements with the Vatican (in the case of the Catholic Church), the *Landeskirchen* (in case of the Protestants) and the Jewish communities. While God is mentioned in the constitution (which talks about 'the responsibility of the German people before God'), there is no identification with one religion or church and the attitude of the state towards the recognized religious communities is based on equality. The state is neutral in ideological-theological matters and does not interfere in the internal affairs of the church, but there is no real 'wall of separation' between church and state.

In Germany, the religious denominations are regarded as public corporations and their relations with the state are based on close co-operation. The state finances the activities of the churches by levying a 'church tax' from all citizens, with the exception of those who declare that they do not belong to any religious community and have no interest in receiving religious services (baptism, communion, weddings, old-age homes, funerals, etc.). The revenues collected through the 'church tax' are distributed to the various religious communities according to the number of their tax-paying members.

In principle, the Recognized Communities States see the financing of religious services as a responsibility of the state, similar to health, education and other welfare services. In Germany many hospitals belong to religious denominations, though they are financed largely by the state. The same is true for old-age homes, day-care and rehabilitation centres. Religious services are also provided in the army, in prisons and in municipal and university hospitals. Religious instruction is offered in all public schools and teachers, though state employees, have to be approved by the church and to follow the church's theology. (In four of the new *Laender* of Eastern Germany there is a slightly different arrangement – in Thueringen, Sachsen and Sachsen-Anhalt pupils have to choose between the subjects Religion and Ethics, while in Brandenburg only one subject is taught, Ethics, in which all major religions are presented. Parents of children up to 14 can opt that their children will not attend religious instruction. The same is true for children aged 14 to 18. In the faculties of theology of the state universities, the appointment of faculty is handled jointly by church and state. Representatives of the major religious denominations sit on the boards of the public radio and television stations and receive air-time for religious services. Religion is also included in the official census, something which would be unacceptable in a Separationist State (where religion is 'privatized'). On the other hand, legal marriage and divorce are civil, not religious.

In Germany, a Recognized Community is defined by size and continuity, by having common institutions and by being faithful to Germany's democratic *Grundgesetz* (Basic Law). Until now the Muslim community has not gained recognition because it does not have a representative organization with common institutions and because its religious leaders refuse to recognize the constitutional right to conversion (according to Islam, conversion of a Muslim is punishable by death).[18] Other communities that did not gain recognition are Jehovahs Witnesses (who boycott elections and are thus regarded as hostile to the state and its democratic regime) and the Scientology Church (which is suspected of totalitarian tendencies).[19]

The other Recognized Communities States have slightly different arrangements. Belgium (since 1974) and Austria (since 1988), for instance, do recognize the Muslim Community.[20] Hungary has a more liberal approach than Germany in the sense that religious instruction in school is optional. In Germany it is compulsory although one may opt out; while in Hungary it is optional in the sense that one has to register for it. In addition, Hungary does not include religion in its census.[21]

The Endorsed Church State, which is becoming more and more attractive to former Established Church and Separationist Regimes, is still another model. In the Endorsed Church Model, there is a slight symbolic or real constitutional – legal preference for the dominant religion or church (Brasloff described post-Franco Spain as treating 'all religions as equal while discriminating in favour of Catholicism').[22] This 'slight' preference is very different from the institutionalized and highly visible 'superiority' of the Established Church and it is also different from the highly egalitarian Recognized Communities Model. The Endorsed Church Model is thus a middle of the road solution to the church–state dilemma between the Established Church and the Recognized Communities models. Today Italy, Spain, Ireland, Armenia, Poland, Bulgaria and Romania are Endorsed Church States, although in the past they were mostly Established Church States or Separationist States (or both at different points in history).

In Italy, where the 'Accordo di Villa Madama' of 1984 replaced the Lateran Agreements of 1929, there is no longer a state religion and the clause in the 1946 constitution that stated that 'The Roman Catholic Religion is the only religion of the Church', was abolished. Catholicism has, however, retained some symbolic and practical edge over other religious communities. Thus, the only church mentioned in the Constitution is the Catholic Church and it is mentioned on an almost equal footing with the State. The relevant constitutional clause says 'The State and the Catholic Church, each in its sphere, is independent and sovereign'.[23] Religious instruction is offered in the school system for all religious denominations, but the state finances only Catholic classes. The same is true for religious services in hospitals and other public institutions. As in the Recognized Communities Model, a state 'church tax' finances the activities of the Catholic Church and six other religious communities (Lutherans, Baptists, Seven Day Adventists, Tavola Valdese, the Assembly of God and the Union of Jewish Communities) who have agreements with the state. Thirty other smaller communities are recognized, but receive no funding and some (e.g., the Scientology Church) are not even recognized by law.[24]

Spain has similar arrangements – a far cry from Franco's 'confessional state' and the *regalismo* of traditional Spain. The 'endorsement' of Catholicism is based on the 1979 Partial Agreement with the Vatican and on the post-Franco constitution of 1978. The *concordat* commits the Spanish State to respect 'the feelings of Catholics'.[25] It also ensures that the state provide air-time for Catholic services on radio and television and access for the Catholic clergy to hospitals, prisons and the army. Though the constitution mentions the state's co-operation with the Catholic Church and other religions and churches, only the Catholic Church is mentioned specifically. In the schools, the arrangement is the same as in Italy – religious instruction is offered for all, but is free only for the Catholics. We find almost identical arrangements in Portugal after the overthrow of the Salazar-Caetano dictatorship.[26]

In Poland, another Endorsed Church State, the 1997 constitution talks about 'separation', but in fact there is no real separation in the American or French sense. The constitution talks about God as the origin of 'truth, justice, goodness and beauty' and about the 'Christian heritage of the Polish nation'. The constitution further says that 'relations of the Republic of Poland and the Catholic Church [the only one mentioned in the constitution – B.N] are based on the international agreement with the Holy See.'[27] In all state schools, the Catholic Church provides religious instruction, the school day starts with school prayers and there are crosses in all classes. As in Germany, the state universities have theological faculties in which professors approved by the church teach Catholic theology. And above all, according to the 1993 *concordat*, which defines the close links between the Catholic Church and the State, a particular body of state and church representatives tackles all the 'problems' in church and state relations. The existence of such a body highlights the importance of the Catholic Church in the Polish political system and is an indication of the close co-operation between church and state. The statement of Polish Minister of Education Andrzej Stelmachovsky, who said that, 'There is no such thing as separation of the state from religion',[28] represents this relationship better than the wording of the constitution.[29]

Armenia's solution to the Church and State problem is very similar to that of Poland. As in Poland, there is a close connection between nationhood, religion and the Armenian Apostolic Church. As in Poland, the law talks of 'separation' of church and state – in the Armenian case, even of 'absolute separation'. On the face of it there is separation, since the state does not interfere in church matters and does not finance the church's activities. But as in Poland, the Armenian Apostolic Church enjoys a legal and practical edge over other religions and denominations. The law defines 'the Armenian Apostolic Church as the national church of the Armenian people and an important bulwark for the edification of its spiritual life and national preservation'.[30] The 'national church' is allowed to use the official media and to perform religious services and ceremonies in all state installations. In addition to the Armenian Apostolic Church there are also a number of other recognized religious communities enjoying religious freedom and autonomy, but the many non-recognized communities are discriminated against in matters of finance, property rights, the use of state facilities, welfare services and the right to publish religious publications.[31]

Ireland is yet another example of an Endorsed Church State. The constitution does not specifically mention Catholicism, but it certainly endorses Christianity. The constitution speaks further about acknowledging 'the Irish people's obligations to our Divine Lord, Jesus Christ, who sustained our fathers through centuries of trial'. In paragraph 44 of the Constitution the state acknowledges that 'the homage of public worship is due to the Almighty God' and it commits itself to 'hold his Name in reverence' and 'to respect and honour religion'.[32] The 1937 Constitution also contained a clause which specifically mentioned the 'special position of the Catholic Church as the guardian of the Faith professed by the great majority of the citizens', but this clause about Catholicism as the faith of most Irishmen was annulled in 1972. Other 'religious clauses' (e.g. the 'divorce clause', which said that 'no law shall be enacted providing for the grant of a dissolution of marriage') were cancelled in the 1990s.

In Ireland, the churches are not directly funded. Nevertheless, the system is not 'separationist' because Christianity is endorsed in the Constitution and because most of the school system is denominational, with a large majority of schools controlled by the Catholic Church. There are almost no secular or pluralist schools and the 'primary school rule book' of the 1990s speaks about 'a religious spirit' which 'should inform and vivify the whole work of school'.[33]

All in all, the trend in Europe is clear. First of all, there is a trend away from the non-democratic and towards the democratic models. 'Pure' theocracies disappeared long ago from the European scene and the authoritarian semi-fascist states of Southern Europe (e.g., Franco's Spain), which exhibited some theocratic elements, finally disappeared in the 1970s. The communist secular-absolutist dictatorships collapsed in the late 1980s and early 1990s. Amongst the democratic states the Separationist States became less strict. Hostile separation has been replaced by friendly separation and more and more cracks have appeared in the 'wall of separation'. The 'soft' approach to separation leads the government to grant, albeit indirectly, financial aid to religious agencies and institutions. The Established Church Model is also steadily weakening. The state interferes less and less in church affairs. Furthermore, the trend is towards an Ecumenical Establishment, in which all major religious communities participate and in which the 'established' church gradually loses its 'official' status and superiority vis-à-vis the other religions and denominations. Most Established Church States are gradually moving towards the Endorsed Church Model (e.g. England and Greece). Communist states that were Established Church States in the pre-communist period (e.g., Romania, Poland and Hungary) did not return to the Established Church model after the collapse of communism. Most Separationist and Established

Church States have become more similar to the two middle of the road models –the Recognized Communities and the Endorsed Church States.

All the states in contemporary Europe are democracies with a basically positive attitude towards religion. All of them – whether enthusiastically or grudgingly – see religion as a legitimate part of the public and social sphere. The complete privatization of religion, which in the past was the ideal of strict separationism, seems difficult to obtain because of the nature of church and state. Gill says that, 'States frequently enter the domain of personal morality and seek transcendental justification for their actions. And for religions the moral proclamations of spiritual leaders often have the effect of either legitimating or challenging power relations in secular society'.[34] The Christian rule 'Render to Caesar the things that are Caesar's and to God the things that are God's' has not been completely realized by church and state after two thousand years of Christianity. All the states accept the rights of individuals and communities to 'freedom *of* religion', whether 'negative religious freedom' or 'positive religious freedom'. 'Positive religious freedom' means freedom from state oppression (e.g., freedom of belief and worship). 'Negative religious freedom' means freedom to have an impact as religious people (e.g., the right to organize politically; the right to religious education; the right to receive, directly or indirectly public funding for religious activities; and the right to media time for religious services). In addition, all democracies grant freedom *from* religion, defined as the freedom of every person not to observe religious precepts. In all European democracies, no religious institution, ceremony, ritual, declaration or commitment is forced on a person as a condition for the right to enjoy standard civil liberties, including human dignity, freedom of expression, freedom of conscience, freedom to marry and equality before the law. In the European states, no restrictions are placed on a person for religious reasons (except perhaps the requirement to close stores on religious holidays that are also official holidays, but it is doubtful whether this can be considered a 'restriction' imposed on a citizen).

It has been shown that freedom *of* religion also exists in countries that have separation of religion and state, even if this separation historically originated in hostility to religion. In the same way, freedom *from* religion exists even in countries in which one religion is officially given symbolic preference under the Established Church or Endorsed Church systems.

In all of Europe the infringement of equality before the law of religions, churches, denominations and of believers and non-believers does not apply to essential matters that relate to civil liberties. The proclamation of Christian holidays as official holidays in France (the Separationist Model), Great Britain (the Established Church Model), Germany (the Recognized Communities Model) and Italy (the Endorsed

Church Model) can be considered a minor infringement of equality because the vast majority of these countries' citizens are Christians. The inclusion of a cross in a country's flag (in Great Britain, Switzerland and the Scandinavian countries) and the fact that the monarch is the head of the Established Church detract from the equality of all citizens, but this infringement is mainly symbolic and does not detract substantially from their being equal before the law or from their basic freedoms.

It is also important to stress that only secular law counts in all European democratic countries. The rule of law in all these states is the rule of secular law, which is enacted by a democratic parliament and does not violate democratic principles. According to this definition, not only the Separation Model, but also the Established Church Model, the Endorsed Church Model and the Recognized Communities Model are democratically valid. We have also seen that the 'winning' models towards the end of the twentieth century are the Endorsed Church Model and the Recognized Communities Model. That means that in the future liberal democracy will not necessarily be based on a total contrast between the 'Heavenly City' and the 'Earthly City'.[35]

In Israel, most writers who deal with state-religion relations emphasize the 'exceptionalism' and the incomparability of the Israeli case.[36] I do not accept this point of view. Certainly there are some unique features in Israeli state-religion relations, as there are unique features in almost any state which has its own history, traditions and culture. There are, no doubt, differences between the European 'models' and the Israeli case, but the object of comparison is to demonstrate *both* similarities and differences. If everything is similar there is nothing to compare.

In Israel, there is a strong bond between religion and nationhood, but religion plays a similar role in Greece, Romania, Bulgaria, Serbia, Croatia, Poland, Russia, Slovenia and Lithuania and to a great extent also in Italy, Spain, France, Ireland, Sweden, Finland, Norway and Denmark. It is difficult to completely separate the nation-state from religion where the 'national' character of the state contains a religious dimension – this problem is common to Israel and to many other states in Europe.

The religious roots of some of Israel's state symbols – the flag, the 'Menorah', the public holidays – are similar to what we know in several European countries. Israel's educational system, which offers a choice between state-financed secular and Orthodox systems and a private state-financed Ultra-Orthodox system, is different from what we have in Europe; but the principle that the state provides at least the option of religious education in its school system is common to Israel (via the state Orthodox system and private but state-financed Ultra-Orthodox system) and to European countries who follow the Established Church, Endorsed Church and Recognized Communities Models in Church State relations (the Separationist State is different in this respect).

In Israel, the state finances religious services – the building, maintaining and running of synagogues and mosques, the salaries of the rabbis and kadis and the religious court system – but even this is not 'exceptional', as we have seen that many European States also regard religious services as another 'social' service they have to provide.

Relations between religion and state in Israel are very different from the Separation States (whether sympathetic or hostile), but they are in some ways close to the Recognized Communities and the Established Church Models. Israel is not different from the European democracies in its adherence to freedom *of* religion, the freedom of belief and worship. The individual's right to worship his or her God as he or she chooses, in private and in public, is based on a King's Order in Council from 1922, which states that 'all persons in Palestine shall enjoy full liberty of conscience and the exercise of their forms of worship subject only to the maintenance of public order and morals',[37] and on the Declaration of Independence, which promises 'freedom of religion, conscience, language, education and culture'. In terms of freedom *from* religion – that is, the individual's ability to choose not to be religious, not to observe religious precepts, not to be subject to religious laws and precepts and not to use the services of a religious authority to fulfill one's basic rights and freedoms (e.g. marriage, divorce and burial) – Israel does not meet the standards of Europe. There can be no doubt that the framers of the Declaration of Independence wished to maintain freedom in religious matters. The High Court of Justice, too, has repeatedly declared its support for liberal-democratic principles in religion-state relations. For example, the High Court ruled that, 'Based on the Declaration of Independence, every law and every power will be interpreted as recognizing freedom of conscience, faith, religion and worship'.[38] The High Court also ruled that all secondary legislation that contradicts basic concepts of freedom of religion or any other human right recognized as such by international law shall be deemed 'unreasonable and must be repealed'.[39] However, the State of Israel cannot achieve full religious freedom in religious matters, as is customary in the democratic West, because Jewish religious law is the law of the state in matters of personal status and because in several other issues religious legislation clashes with basic freedoms that are standard in democracies.

The gist of the problem is – as was said before – the distinction between freedom *of* religion, which does exist in Israel and freedom *from* religion, which does not. By law, all Israeli citizens are subject to the authority of the religious establishment in matters of marriage and divorce, a situation that runs counter to the liberal model. The Rabbinical Courts Jurisdiction (Marriage and Divorce) Law, 5713–1953, applies to all Jewish citizens and non-citizen Jewish residents, regardless of the person's preferences. According to the law marriages and divorces of Jews in Israel have to conform to the 'Halakhic tests of Jewish law'.[40] Supreme Court Justice Moshe Landau ruled unequivocally that religious restrictions on marriage and divorce that originate in religious law and are based on rabbinical judicial authority are not consistent with 'freedom of conscience and the freedom of action that this entails'.[41] In theory, civil marriage is not available in Israel and every couple that wishes to marry legally must do so in a religious ceremony conducted by a representative of a religious authority in accordance with the laws of the couple's religion.

The enforcement of Halakhic principles, even by state laws enacted legally by the Knesset, is problematic from the democratic perspective, just as any imposition of 'faith-based behaviour, such as participation in a religious ceremony'[42] runs counter to the standards and practices of Western liberal democracy. Unquestionably, this legal situation infringes substantially upon the freedom of conscience of non-believers.

The absence of a civil alternative to religious marriage is a blatant deviation from the standard practice in liberal-democratic Europe, which accepts Isaiah Berlin's assertion that 'In a liberal democracy there must be a legal right to civil divorce and civil marriage because subjection of these aspects of civic life to the supervision of a religious authority has always clashed with liberal principles'.[43]

The laws of personal status in effect in Israel under the religious *Status Quo* – as the compromise worked out by the political and religious establishments in the early years of the state is commonly known – infringe upon another basic freedom: Israeli law does not permit marriage between members of different religions (unless one of the couple converts) and does not stipulate appropriate marriage procedures for people with no legal religious status (for example, a person whose father is Jewish and mother is Muslim, is Muslim according to Jewish law and Jewish according to Muslim law and thus is neither Jewish nor Muslim). Thus, Israeli law infringes upon their right to marry and their equality before the law. No less sensitive and politically explosive is the prohibition imposed by Jewish law and consequently by Israeli law, on the marriage of certain categories of couples (a *Cohen* and a divorcee, a *Cohen* and a convert, a *Cohen* and a woman released from the requirement of levirate marriage, a couple who had an affair while the woman was married to someone else and a *mamzer* and a non-*mamzer*). These prohibitions violate both liberal-democratic norms and the Universal Declaration of Human Rights, which contains the following clause regarding the freedom to marry: 'Men and women of full age, without any limitation due to race, nationality or religion, have the right to marry and to found a family. They are entitled to equal rights as to marriage, during marriage and at its dissolution'. The High Court of Justice, too, has repeatedly expressed its dissatisfaction, in the name of liberal-democratic principles, with the fact that some people are Halakhically forbidden to marry. For example, regarding the ban on the marriage of a *Cohen* and a divorcee, the court ruled that 'for someone who does not believe, this prohibition is not only conscientious coercion, but also discrimination between a Cohen and an ordinary Jew on religious grounds'.[44] The Ministry of Religious Affairs maintains a 'blacklist' of unmarriageable people based on information gathered from marriage registrars, the Jewish Agency and government ministries; this is a severe infringement on the dignity of people who are blacklisted through no fault of their own. By means of these prohibitions, the religious status quo infringes not only upon the universal 'freedom to marry' but also upon the principle of equality before the law.

The democratic principle of equality before the law of all religions, denominations and sects is also violated by the exclusivity of the Orthodox Rabbinate in Israel in Jewish religious affairs and the state's refusal to give equal and parallel status to Conservative and Reform rabbis. Reform and Conservative rabbis are not licensed to conduct marriage ceremonies in Israel and do not sit on rabbinical court benches. Therefore, Jews affiliated with these movements (as well as non-believers) are forced to submit their personal affairs to Orthodox courts and judges that are not acceptable to them and that rule according to *Halakhah*, as interpreted by the Orthodox. Reform and Conservative Jews do not serve as army chaplains and so far they have been prevented – despite repeated decisions by the High Court of Justice – from serving on Religious Councils. Their rabbis do not receive salaries from the state and the state does not finance the establishment of synagogues for their congregations. The discrimination against the Reform and Conservative movements through denial of substantial governmental assistance for their congregations is not only a severe infringement of the principle of equality before the law, but also an indirect infringement of their freedom of religion and worship (since it is difficult to establish synagogues and pay the salaries of rabbis and cantors without budgets).

The constitutional-legal situation regarding religion and state also infringes upon equality for women. The Equal Rights for Women Law states: 'The law will treat women and men the same in any legal action; and any legal provision that discriminates against women *qua* women is not to be followed'. This principle is violated when religious laws of personal status are turned into state laws, because men and women are not granted equality in matters such as the right to a divorce (only men can grant a divorce) and the ability to remarry. A woman who was abandoned without receiving a divorce becomes an *aguna* (literally, an 'anchored woman') and cannot remarry. In contrast, a woman who refuses to accept a divorce is a 'rebellious wife' and her husband may receive a dispensation to remarry. In these matters, there is no symmetry between men and women. The disqualification of women from serving as witnesses in rabbinical courts also infringes upon the principle of equality before the law. True, the Equal Rights for Women Law gives legal *imprimatur* to the contradiction by asserting 'This law does not detract from the laws of prohibited and permitted matters regarding marriage and divorce'. The important point is that in reality women and men are not treated equally under the law.

Women are discriminated against because they are forbidden to serve as judges in rabbinical courts (in contrast to civil courts), despite their clear interests in the cases heard by the rabbinical courts. In the past, women were also deprived of the right to serve on Religious Councils and on the boards that elect the chief rabbis and the local rabbis; this rule was mitigated in the 1990s (on 21 February 1993, two women were included for the first time in the 150-member electoral board that elected the chief rabbis).

The Orthodox establishment's exclusivity in providing funeral services (*Hevra Kadisha*) is not consistent with the liberal principle of pluralism and freedom of choice. Liberal-democratic progress in this matter occurred with enactment of the Right to Alternative Civil Burial Law, 5756–1996, which stated that 'a person may choose to be buried in an alternative civil ceremony'. Implementation of the law is lagging, however and so far (as of May 1999) there is no real solution for citizens who want civil burial for ideological reasons or for citizens who need civil burial because they are not Halakhically Jewish (e.g., children of a Jewish father and a non-Jewish mother).

Other laws that are inconsistent with democratic principles restrict the raising of pigs (under the Pig Breeding Prohibition Law, 5722–1962); the marketing of pigs (under an amendment to the law passed in 1990, 'A person may not market and may not sell pigs, pork, or edible pork products and may not cause or permit them to be marketed or sold'); or the public display of leavened products during Passover (under the Passover Prohibition of Leavened Products Law, 5746–1986, 'The owner of a business will not display a leavened product in public for sale or consumption').

Many Israelis (Haredi, Orthodox and Traditional) accept these arrangements and argue that they are mandated by the nature of Israel as a Jewish State. Others regard them as contributing to national unity and to the prevention of a 'cultural war'. Even if these views have some substance to them (and this is debatable), it is not enough to justify the contradiction between these arrangements and the standards of liberal democracy.

Defining Israel as a Jewish and Democratic state, as was done in legislation for the first time in 1992 (Basic Law: Human Dignity and Liberty; Basic Law: Freedom of Occupation; and Political Parties Law,

5752–1992), does not solve the problem. There is a contradiction between Halakhic religious interpretation of the term 'Jewish' and the standard Western liberal interpretation of the term 'democratic'. Furthermore, certain arrangements in effect in Israel because of the Halakhic religious interpretation of the term 'Jewish' are inconsistent with liberal-democratic rules and practices that are standard in Western democracies.[45] The problem is not in the phrase 'Jewish and Democratic state', but in the Halakhic religious interpretation of the term 'Jewish'. There is not necessarily a contradiction between the term 'democratic' and the national-Zionist interpretation of the term 'Jewish': A state of the Jewish People, defined by a shared destiny, historical memory and a pluralistic cultural heritage; a state that upholds the Law of Return and gives official status to the 'National Institutions' (e.g., the Jewish Agency) that it shares with the Diaspora; a state whose symbols are national-Jewish, even if they have a religious origin. In the same way there is no contradiction between the term 'democratic' and the term 'Jewish' in the demographic sense: A *Judenstaat*, a 'State of the Jews', as envisiaged by Herzl, in which there is a Jewish majority that has a decisive influence on the language, the dominant culture and the immigration laws, in accordance with its free will and sovereign decision. There is also no contradiction between the terms 'Jewish' and 'democratic' if a 'Jewish State' means a state based on universal moral values that have Jewish roots (thus the Declaration of Independence speaks of a state based on 'freedom, justice and peace as envisaged by the prophets of Israel').

In Europe, the trend is away from the less democratic, less liberal and less egalitarian Separationist and Established Church Models. Increased religious legislation and the increased political strength of the Orthodox and Ultra-Orthodox in Israel seem to suggest that Israel is moving in a different direction.

NOTES

1. K. Boyle and J. Sheen, *Freedom of Religion and Belief – A World Report*, London: Routledge, 1997, pp.69–78, 416–427, 452–459.
2. A. Brassloff, *Religion and Politics in Spain – The Spanish Church in Transition 1962–1996*, London: Macmillan, 1998, pp.6–24, and I.C. Iban, 'Staat und Kirche in Spanien', in G. Robbers (ed.), *Staat und Kirche in der Europaeischen Union, Baden, Nomos, 1995*.
3. L. A. Morozova 'The State and the Church', *Russian Politics and Law*, Vol. 34, No. 5 (1996), p.44.
4. On Albania see Boyle and Sheen, *Freedom of Religion*, pp.260–265. On Poland see L. Kolakowsky, 'Church and Democracy in Poland', *Dissent*, Vol. 27, No. 3 (1980), pp.316–322; B. Steczek, 'Polish Jesuits Facing Communism and its Consequences', *Religion, State and Society*, Vol. 23, No. 4 (1993), pp.359–363; Z. Walaszek, 'An Open Issue of Legitimacy: The State and the Church in Poland', *The Annals of the American Academy of Political and Social Science*, Vol. 483 (January 1986), pp.118–134.
5. P. Cumper, 'Religious Liberty in the United Kingdom', in J. D. van der Vyver (ed.), *Religious Human Rights in Global Perspective*, The Hague: Martinus Nijhoff, 1996, p.215.

6. On England see S.V. Monsma and J. C. Soper, *The Challenge of Pluralism – Church and State in Five Democracies*, Lanham: Rowman and Littlefield, 1996, pp.121–154; Boyle and Sheen, *Freedom of Religion*, pp.314–329; Cumper, *Religious Liberty*, pp.205–241; P. Chadwick *Shifting Alliances–Church and State in English Education*, London: Cassell, 1997, and D. McClean, 'Staat und Kirche im Vereinigten Koenigreich', in G. Robbers (ed.), *Staat und Kirche*, pp.330–350.
7. V. Georgiadou, 'Greek Orthodoxy and the Politics of Nationalism', *International Journal of Politics, Culture and Society*, Vol. 9, No. 2 (1995), p.295.
8. Boyle and Sheen, *Freedom of Religion*, p.333.
9. On Greece see Boyle and Sheen, *Freedom of Religion*, pp.329–338; Georgiadou, 'Greek Orthodoxy and the Politics of Nationalism', pp.295–317; C. Papastathis, 'Staat und Kirche in Griechenland', in Robbers (ed.), *Staat und Kirche*, pp.79–98.
10. On Sweden see R. Schoett, 'Staat und Kirche in Schweden' in Robbers (ed.), *Staat und Kirche*, pp.319–332.
11. Monsma and Soper, *The Challenge of Pluralism*, pp.15–50, and S. Feldman, *Please Don't Wish Me a Merry Christmas – A Critical History of the Separation of Church and State*, New York: New York University Press, 1997.
12. Boyle and Sheen, *Freedom of Religion*, p.299.
13. On France see Boyle and Sheen, *Freedom of Religion*, pp.294–303; B. Basdevant-Gaudemet, 'Staat und Kirche in Frankreich', in Robbers (ed.), *Staat und Kirche*, pp.127–158; M. Larkin, *Religion, Politics and Preferment in France since 1890*, Cambridge: Cambridge University Press, 1995.
14. On Italy see S. Ferrari, 'Staat und Kirche in Italien', in Robbers (ed.), *Staat und Kirche*, pp.185–210.
15. On Holland see Monsma and Soper, *The Challenge of Pluralism*, pp.51–86, and S.C.V. Bijsterveld, 'Staat und Kirche in den Niederlanden', in Robbers (ed.), *Staat und Kirche*, pp.229–250.
16. On Russia see S.P. Ramet, *Nihil Obstat – Religion, Politics and Social Change in East Central Europe and Russia*, Durham: Duke University Press, 1998; H. Berman, 'Religious Rights in Russia at a Time of Tumultuous Transition: A History', in van der Vyver (ed.), *Religious Human Rights*, pp.285–304; P. Roth, 'Bericht ueber Russland', in H. Marre and D. Schummelfeder (eds.), *Essener Gespraeche zum Thema Staat und Kirche* (29), Muenster: Aschendorff, 1995, pp.111–121; M. Smirnow, 'Die Rolle der Russisch – Orthodoxen Kirche in der Gegenwaertigen Politischen Entwicklung Russlands (1993–1997)', *KAS – Auslandsinformationen* (January 1998), pp.95–121; G. Stricker, *Religion in Russland*, Guetersloh: Guetesloher Verlag, 1993; G. Stricker, 'Das Moskauer Patriarchat im Zeichen des neuen Nationalismus', *Osteuropa*, Stuttgart: Deutsche Verlagsanstalt, 1998, pp.268–281; G. Stricker, 'Die Orthodoxen Kirchen', *Internationale Kirchliche Zeitschrift*, Vol. 28, No. 1 (1998), pp.4–25.
17. R. Torfs, 'Staat und Kirche in Belgien', in Robbers (ed.), *Staat und Kirche*, p.37.
18. N. Lerner, 'Proselytism, Change of Religion and International Human Rights', *Emory International Law Review*, Vol. 12, No. 1 (1998), p.503.
19. On Germany see A.V. Campenhausen, *Staatskirchenrecht*, Muenchen: C.H. Beck, 1996; M. Heckel, 'The Impact of Religious Roles in Public Life in Germany', in J. D. van der Vyver (ed.), *Religious Human Rights*, pp.191–204; C. Link, 'Fuer verstaendige Zusammenarbeit geschafft', *Frankfurter Allgemeine Zeitung* (6.8.1998); J. Listl, 'Das Staatskirchenrecht in den neuen Laendern der Bundesrepublik Deutschland', in Marre and Schummelfeder (eds.), *Essener Gespraeche*, pp.160–218; H. Caygill and A. Scott, 'The Basic law versus the Basic Norm? The Case of the Bavarian Crucifix Order', *Political Studies*, No. 44, No. 3 (1996), pp.505–516; Monsma and Soper, *The Challenge of Pluralism*, pp.155–198.
20. On Belgium see Torfs, 'Staat und Kirche in Belgien', in Robbers (ed.), *Staat und Kirche*, pp.15–38, and on Austria see R. Potz, 'Staat und Kirche in Oesterreich', in Robbers (ed.), *Staat und Kirche*, pp.251–280.
21. On Hungary see Boyle and Sheen, *Freedom of Religion*, pp.338–344; P.Erdoe, 'Bericht ueber Ungarn', in Marre and Schummelfeder (eds.), *Essener Gespraeche*, pp.134–159; J. Luxmoore, 'Eastern Europe 1994: A Review of Religious Life in Bulgaria, Romania, Hungary, Slovakia, the Czech Republic and Poland', *Religion, State and Society*, Vol. 23, No. 2 (1995), pp.213–218; J. Luxmoore, 'Eastern Europe 1995', *Religion, State and*

Society, Vol. 24, No. 4 (1996), pp.357–365.
22. A. Brassloff, *Religion and Politics in Spain – The Spanish Church in Transition 1962–1996*, London: Macmillan, 1998, p.97.
23. S. Colombo, 'Religion and State in Italy Compared to Israel –Institutional Aspects', *Law and Government*, Vol. 4 (1997/98), p.203 (Hebrew).
24. On Italy see Colombo, 'Religion and State in Italy', pp.200–213, and Ferrari, 'Staat und Kirche in Italien', in Robbers (ed.), *Staat und Kirche*, pp.185–210.
25. Brasloff, *Religion and Politics in Spain*, pp.100–1.
26. On Spain see Brasloff, *Religion and Politics in Spain*, and Iban, 'Staat und Kirche in Spanien', in Robbers (ed.), *Staat und Kirche*, pp.99–126; On Portugal see V. Canas, 'Staat und Kirche in Portugal', in Robbers (ed.), *Staat und Kirche*, pp.281–302.
27. M.W. Eberts, 'The Roman Catholic Church and Democracy in Poland', *Europe–Asia Studies*, Vol. 50, No. 5 (1998), p.834.
28. Eberts, 'The Roman Catholic Church and Democracy in Poland', p.822.
29. On Poland see Eberts, 'The Roman Catholic Church and Democracy in Poland', pp.817–842; Luxmoore 'Eastern Europe 1994', pp.213–218, and 'Eastern Europe 1995', pp.357–365; A. Orszulik 'Bericht ueber Polen', in Marre and Schummelfeder (eds.), *Essener Gespraeche*, pp.90–110.
30. Boyle and Sheen, *Freedom of Religion*, p.268.
31. On Armenia see Boyle and Sheen, *Freedom of Religion*, pp.265–271.
32. Boyle and Sheen, *Freedom of Religion*, p.345.
33. On Ireland see Boyle and Sheen, *Freedom of Religion*, pp.344–351; Y. Casey, 'Staat und Kirche in Ireland', in Robbers (ed.), *Staat und Kirche*, pp.159–184; J. Coakley, 'Moral Consensus in Secularizing Society: The Irish Divorce Referendum', *West European Politics*, Vol. 10, No. 2 (1997), pp.291–296.
34. A. Gill, *Rendering unto Caesar – The Catholic Church and the State in Latin_America*, Chicago: University of Chicago Press 1998, p.1.
35. On church and state in democracies see Monsma and Soper, *The Challenge_of Pluralism*, pp.194–224.
36. The Israeli part of this paper relies on my *Religion and Democracy in Israel*, Jerusalem, Floersheimer Institute for Policy Studies, 1997.
37. A. Rubinstein, *Ha-mishpat Ha-konstitutzioni Shel Medinat Israel (The Constitutional Law of the State of Israel)*, Tel Aviv: Schocken, 1991, p.126.
38. High Court of Justice 292/83, in Rubinstein, *The Constitutional Law*, p.125.
39. High Court of Justice 103/67, in Rubinstein, *The Constitutional Law*, p.225.
40. H. Shelah, 'Freedom of Conscience and Religion in Israeli Law', in R. Gavison (ed.), *Herut Ha-matzpun Veha-dat (Freedom of Conscience and_Religion)*, Tel Aviv: Sifriyat Ha-poalim, 1990, p.106.
41. Quoted in Rubinstein, *The Constitutional Law*, 1991, p.133.
42. Shelah, 'Freedom of Conscience', p.65.
43. I. Berlin, 'Judaism and the Existence of Israel as a Democracy', *Secular Humanistic Judaism*, Vol. 2, Nos. 4–7 (1998), p.4.
44. High Court of Justice 103/67, in Rubinstein, *The Constitutional Law*, p.225.
45. For an extensive discussion of the issue see A. Rosen-Zvi (ed.), *Medina Yehudit Ve-democratit (The Jewish and Democratic State)*, Tel-Aviv: Ramot, 1996.

Conflict Management of Religious Issues: The Israeli Case in a Comparative Perspective

ELIEZER DON-YEHIYA

Problems of religion and state are among the most controversial issues in Israeli politics. They reflect profound differences in worldviews and ways of life in Jewish society in Israel. Nevertheless, the political system has generally managed to resolve conflicts over religious issues by peaceful means without undermining its basic stability, unity and democratic nature.

The Israeli case is, of course, not unique. Religious cleavages are to be found in almost every democratic country, and in some they have served as a source of heated political conflict. Nevertheless, in most cases religious controversies did not become a major factor of instability within democratic regimes. To a large extent, this can be explained by the patterns of conflict management in the religious area. In this essay, I will elaborate on this issue by comparing the resolution of religious conflicts in Israel and in some of the other Western countries. I will also compare patterns of conflict management in the religious area with those that are applied to other controversial issues in Israel.

Political scientists tend to deal with the issue of religious conflict and political stability within the more general framework of societal cleavages and the management of political controversies. For Robert Dahl and Arend Lijphart, religious controversies can be seen as part of a broader category of conflicts resulting from the division of society into rival sub-cultures.

Dahl argues that, 'In general, conflicts involving subcultures rarely seem to be handled – for long – by the normal political processes employed in other kinds of issues. For this sort of conflict is too explosive to be managed by ordinary parliamentary opposition, bargaining, campaigning, and winning elections'.[1]

What are the alternative ways to deal with conflicts involving rival sub-cultures? Dahl points to six methods that are actually used in the management of such conflicts. Lijphart integrates three of them into a

Eliezer Don-Yehiya is Professor of Political Studies at Bar-Ilan University.

special pattern of elite behaviour, which he terms 'the politics of accommodation'. This pattern is based on the willingness of political leaders representing rival groups to co-operate in a common effort to settle their differences on an agreed basis. The term 'accommodation' refers to the 'settlement of divisive issues and conflicts where only a minimal consensus exists'.[2]

The accommodationist solutions indicated by Dahl are proportionality, autonomy and 'mutual veto'. Proportionality is the allocation of public positions and resources among various groups in accordance with their relative numerical power. Autonomy is the recognized right of every subculture to conduct its own affairs and institutions, especially in educational and cultural matters, according to its values and way of life. Mutual veto is the recognized power of each of the contending parties 'to veto changes in the status quo involving his subculture'.[3] A fourth accommodationist practice, indicated by Lijphart, is the tendency to form grand coalitions in which all or most influential segments in society are represented. The 'politics of accommodation' explains the existence of a special kind of 'fragmented, but stable democracies', which Lijphart terms 'consociational democracies'.

To what extent and in what conditions have accommodationist practices actually been used in dealing with religious conflicts? Dahl cites cases from Holland, Belgium and the United States as examples for the application of such methods to the resolution of internal conflicts. However, he does not distinguish in this regard between various countries or areas of conflict.

Like Dahl, Lijphart does not differentiate between religious conflicts and other sources of controversy. Unlike Dahl, he does make a clear-cut distinction between different kinds of democratic regimes according to the nature of their social structure and patterns of conflict management. Thus, Lijphart sets aside a number of West European countries – Holland, Belgium, Austria and Switzerland – as 'consociational democracies'.[4] Later, Lijphart even further emphasizes the distinction between various sorts of democratic regimes in his new classification of Western democracies into two 'ideal types' of 'consensus' and 'majoritarian' political systems.[5] In contrast to his first model, this new one puts the emphasis on the formal structure of the regime, thereby focusing even more on the distinction between different kinds of democratic systems.

The Israeli case demonstrates that in studying patterns of conflict management, we should compare not only different countries, but also different sorts of conflict within the same country. Indeed, in recent years, Lijphart himself seems to turn his attention from the investigation of various kinds of regime to the exploration of a certain sort of conflict, namely ethnic conflict. However, he does not engage in a comparative study of ethnic and other sorts of conflict. In fact, he implies that the same methods that are used in resolving conflicts within consociational democracies are, or can be, applied to the management of ethnic conflicts. He terms these devices a 'power sharing system', but it is in fact a different name for 'consociational democracy'.[6] As my main concern here is with religious conflicts, I will point to the unique nature of these conflicts by comparing their management with the management of other controversial issues, especially in Israel.

Israel is not a consociational democracy in the full sense of the term. The consociational model has been applied only partially and inconsistently to most areas of controversy or group relations. True, in the pre-State Yishuv society, accommodationist methods were applied to most areas of conflict and group relations. Thus, the central organs of the Zionist movement and the Yishuv society were grand coalitions that included all Zionist groups except the Revisionists. Public resources were allocated on the basis of proportionality, known as the 'key-party system'. Autonomy was granted not only to religious education, but also to a Zionist socialist system of education – the 'Labour trend'.[7]

However, since the establishment of the State of Israel, there has been a marked decline in the use of accommodationist methods in most areas of conflict regulation and group relations. Thus, most Israeli governments were not based on grand coalitions, and the autonomous system of the Labour trend in education was canceled with the enactment of the Law of State Education in 1953.

There are also areas in which the consociational model has never been applied in a full and consistent way. This is clearly the case with regard to the Israeli Arab community. The Arabs have their own educational and cultural institutions, but they are not entitled to autonomy in the management of these institutions. No Arab was ever appointed a minister in an Israeli government and the Arabs are getting much less than their proportional share in the allocation of public resources. There has recently been a considerable improvement in this regard. However, the very definition of Israel as a Jewish state precludes the full integration of the Israeli Arab community into the politics of accommodation in Israel.[8]

The consociational model has been applied only in a limited and partial way to the area of inter-ethnic relations within Israeli Jewish society. Particularly salient is the fact that the autonomy principle, which plays an important role in the religious area, was not applied to the ethnic sphere. This situation has been changing in recent years. The most important development in this regard is the establishment and growth of an educational system affiliated with Shas, the party of religiously traditional Sephardim. This educational system and other ethnic institutions influenced by Shas have autonomous status and receive their proportional share of state financing. However, the application of the principles of autonomy and proportionality to Shas institutions is related to the fact that these institutions, like Shas itself, represent a combination of both the religious and ethnic cleavages in Israeli society. This combination of the religious and ethnic factors has also played a major role in the impressive electoral achievements of Shas. It should be noted that in contrast to the religious cleavage, the ethnic cleavage had been characterized by a low degree of political institutionalization before the establishment of Shas in 1983. This has been changed with the rise of Shas as a party, which represents both cleavages – religious and ethnic. To a large extent, then, it is the religious factor that legitimizes the political institutionalization of the ethnic cleavage, as well as the application of accommodationist practices to the area of ethnic relations.

The fact that ethnicity per se has rarely been a basis for the politics of accommodation has its origins in the Israeli version of the 'melting pot' ideology, which prevailed mainly in the early years of independence. This ideology was not willing to grant legitimacy to the ethnic divide, and therefore it rejected the use of accommodationist practices in dealing with ethnic issues. Instead, Israeli political leaders strove to confront these issues with a deliberate effort to blur the cultural distinctions between the various ethnic communities. This policy, which was initiated and directed by Ben-Gurion, set as its aim 'the blending of the exiles'.[9] It is the Israeli version of the 'assimilation' solution, which according to Dahl is one of the methods used in dealing with conflicts between subcultures.[10] Such a solution cannot, of course, be integrated within the consociational model, which assumes recognition of the legitimacy of differences between subcultures.

It can be concluded that religious issues constitute the main area in which consociational methods of conflict resolution continue to be applied in a consistent manner. The consociational model has been the main key to the success of the Israeli political system in peacefully overcoming the profound divisions in the religious domain and maintaining unity, stability, and the democratic nature of the system.

It has been noted that grand coalitions are not a common feature of Israeli politics. Nevertheless, accommodationist considerations did play a significant role in the formation of governmental coalitions. This has been clearly manifested in the pattern of the 'stable coalition' between secular and religious parties. According to Nordlinger, a 'stable coalition' that includes representatives of opposing sub-cultures is a salient method of resolving conflicts in 'deeply divided societies'.[11] In Israel, religious parties have been included in nearly all governmental coalitions. These parties were kept in the government, even when a winning coalition could be formed without their support.

Conflicts over religious education were resolved in Israel on the basis of granting religious schools a vast degree of autonomy in conducting their own affairs, and allocating them governmental resources according to their proportional share of students. The systems of religious education have retained their autonomy even after the enactment of the Law of State Education. Many other controversial issues in the area of religion and state, like legislation on marital matters or public observance of the Sabbath and the 'Who is a Jew' problem, have been resolved on the basis of the mutual veto principle, known in Israel as the 'status quo solution'.

The status quo principle reflects the attempt to neutralize the explosive political potential of controversial matters by avoiding a decision on these matters. In Israel, some of the practices that are preserved by the status quo principle were introduced in the pre-State area. A prime example is the authority of the religious courts in Israel in matters of personal status, which is based on the legal system introduced in Palestine by the Ottoman rulers and subsequently adopted by the British Mandatory government. In many cases, the status quo principle is used to preserve political accommodations reached in negotiations between religious and secular leaders.

In Israel, the status quo principle does not prevent conflicts over religious issues. In fact, the interpretation of the status quo may itself be a source of confrontation between rival parties. In many disputes between religious and secular political groups, both sides claim to be defending the status quo and argue that the other side is trying to violate it. This was the case in the disputes over Sabbath television broadcasts and the 'Who is a Jew' question. Nevertheless, the status quo principle is usually effective at dealing with confrontations over issues of religion and state. It helps mitigate the conflicts and makes it easier for the disputants to negotiate and to reach an agreement.

THE POLITICS OF ACCOMMODATION IN ISRAEL: THE DYNAMIC DIMENSION

One of the most important conclusions to be drawn from the Israeli case is that the consociational model as presented by Lijphart is too static, and more emphasis should be placed on the dynamic dimension of this model. Thus, the status quo principle, which serves as the cornerstone for the politics of accommodation in Israel, is really a dynamic principle that allows for development and change. In Israel, the status quo principle does not prevent changes in the existing situation; it merely limits them, restrains them, and prevents them from attaining public legitimacy and official validation by means of legislation. Therefore, the term 'status quo' is, in a way, a misnomer. It is essentially a flexible, dynamic system that adapts itself to new circumstances and conditions, but enables the parties involved to ignore de facto changes by withholding from them official recognition and public legitimacy.

The changes in the area of religion and state are due to various factors, and especially to demographic changes in the size and composition of the population and cultural changes in the values and ways of life of the society. In Israel, most of the changes in the religious area are marginal and gradual and do not involve explicit revisions of existing laws and regulations. However, sometimes the rival parties realize the need to introduce legal changes, which are based on compromises and can serve as a basis for a renewed status quo. Large-scale demographic changes caused by mass immigration in the early years of Israel's independence were the main factor behind the education crisis, which undermined the accommodations reached in this area during the Yishuv period. The crisis led to the establishment of new accommodations that were more in line with the new situation, and served as a basis for a renewed status quo in education, which holds to this day.

In this respect, Israel is different from the consociational democracies in Western Europe. These countries, too, were divided over the issue of religious education. However, unlike Israel, the West European countries have a fairly static population, the vast majority of whom have already been integrated in the various political sub-cultures. Therefore, the educational disputes in these countries were focused on government funding for religious schools and public supervision of them. In contrast, in the 'expanding society' of the Yishuv and the State of Israel, the competition between the political camps to recruit students for their schools was particularly important. This competition was most intense in the struggles over the education of immigrant children in the early years of the state.[12]

Pressures to change accommodations and practices in the religious domain in Israel were also exerted in recent years, since large numbers of immigrants arrived from Russia and the other countries of the former Soviet Union. The predominantly secular makeup of this wave of immigration is one of the main causes of the increase in violations of regulations regarding Sabbath observance and kashrut. Thus, many non-Kosher shops that sell pork were opened, in contradiction to local by-laws which forbid the selling of pork. Almost all the owners of these shops, and many of their clients, are Russian immigrants. The large percentage of non-Jewish persons among these immigrants also generated pressures on the status quo accommodations regarding marriage and divorce.

Demographic developments have also affected the emergence of changes in the religious status quo in the opposite direction. Thus, there are increased pressures to close roads to all kinds of traffic on the Sabbath and Jewish festivals. Most of the changes of this sort characterize the cities of Jerusalem and Bnei Brak and are the result of population fluctuations that have led to the 'haredization' of streets and residential areas.

Although demographic changes may affect processes of cultural and political change, these processes also have other causes, such as socioeconomic changes and outside cultural influences. These changes, too, may affect the religious status quo in different directions. For example, the closing of streets to traffic on the Sabbath is related to the greater willingness within Israeli society to accept ideological and social pluralism. This includes respect for the right of distinct groups in the population, such as observant Jews, to live in their own residential areas in accordance with their own values and ways of life. However, most of the changes in the status quo accommodations concerning Sabbath observance have been manifested in the growing opposition to regulations and practices that forbid public transportation on the Sabbath or the opening of cinemas and other places of entertainment on this day.

In many cases, this opposition leads to violations of regulations and by-laws designed for public observation of the Sabbath. To a large extent, changes of this sort reflect the growing impact of liberal and individual tendencies on Israeli Jews, manifested in their unwillingness to accept restrictions on individual freedoms for ideological or religious reasons. Other factors behind such changes are economic developments, changes in patterns of leisure culture, a rise in the standard of living, and increasing consumption of entertainment and recreational services. These processes bolster the unwillingness to accept the enforcement of restrictions grounded in the religious status quo agreements, especially those related to public observance of the Sabbath.

It can be concluded that changes in the role of religion in Israeli public life have been in various, and sometimes in opposing, directions. Some of them favour one of the contending sides while others favour its rival. This is related to one of the significant conclusions to be drawn from the Israeli case. This case demonstrates the substantial differences in the direction, scope, and pace of developments between different kinds of controversies regarding issues of religion and state. These differences concern the nature of the disputed subject, the distribution of opinions on the subject, the sources of power and influence of the various parties to the conflict, and the intensity of their positions.

The investigation of religious conflicts in Israel shows that the intensity factor is of special importance.[13] The more resolute and vehement a particular side is, the more likely it is to win. This in no way contradicts consociational principles, which are based not necessarily on reciprocity and symmetry, but rather on the political leaders' awareness of the dangers to the stability and unity of the system that would result from unrestrained conflict. This awareness is shared by the leaders of the different groups and motivates them to conduct dialogue and to co-operate in an effort to achieve consensual accommodations. However, the side with the more intense position has an edge in the bargaining process because its adversary is more willing to compromise and make concessions.

Intensity is affected by various factors. Especially important is the sense that one is standing guard and waging a defensive campaign against threats to sanctified values and ways of life or to its status and vital interests. This can explain the success of the religious circles in defending religious education and in preventing the conscription of yeshiva students and religious women. It also explains the success of the opponents of Orthodoxy in issues that they consider especially important, such as the struggle by the Reform and Conservative movements against the amendment of the 'Who is a Jew' clause.

The changes that occurred in the religious sphere frequently involved the eruption or intensification of disputes and conflicts in this area. Recently, such conflicts have also to do with signs of growing antagonism in the overall pattern of relations between the religious and secular Jews in Israeli society. This is manifested in various ways, such as acrimonious condemnations of religious people and religious institutions in the mass media, public protest against the establishment of synagogues and religious schools in predominant secular neighborhoods, etc. One of the main factors behind this development is the fact that many secular Jews are worried about what they perceive as the growing social and political power of the religious groups.

The great electoral achievement of the religious parties in the 1996 Knesset elections (in which they increased their parliamentary share from 16 to 23 Knesset seats), was in itself one of the major sources of the secular Jews' anxiety. The electoral success of the religious parties has been perceived as an indication of the growing impact of religion on wide circles in Israeli society. It is interesting to note that the further increase in the overall electoral power of the religious parties in the 1999 elections to the 15th Knesset did not have a similar effect on the secular groups in Israel. The reason is that although the religious parties increased their parliamentary representation by 4 Knesset seats to 27 Knesset members, their power has been actually weakened due to the electoral failure of their political ally, Benjamin Netanyahu, who lost the premiership to Ehud Barak.

Other factors that exacerbate relations between religious and secular Jews are the 'expansionist' activities of religious groups within territorial areas or segments of population that had been considered as predominantly non-orthodox. Of special importance in this respect are the activities of Shas within the Sephardic sector and the deep penetration of the 'repentance movement' into this sector. There is also the growing involvement of the Haredim in Israeli politics and their territorial expansion into previously non-Haredi environments. All this has resulted in confrontations over living space and allocation of resources in the local and national sphere.

A special factor that has increased animosity between the Haredim and secular Jews is the continued exemption of Haredi yeshiva students from military service. Although this has been a controversial issue for many years, secular opposition to this arrangement has been growing in recent years. This is due to two main factors. The first is the growing number of yeshiva students who are exempted from military service. The second factor is the growing share of the Haredim in the allocation of public resources, while they continue to be exempt from what most Israelis perceive as the prime national obligation of military service.

The developments presented above put much stress on the prevailing system of political accommodation in the area of religion and state in Israel. In the last elections to the 15th Knesset, this was manifested in the electoral success of Meretz and Shinui – two parties that challenge the politics of accommodation in the religious sphere. Especially remarkable is the electoral achievement of Shinui – a new party, which ran its election campaign under the banner, 'Stop the Haredim', and won 6 Knesset seats.

RELIGION AND STATE IN ISRAEL: THE SURVIVAL OF CONSOCIATIONALISM

There are students of Israeli politics who argue that the changes that occurred in Israeli society and politics indicate that the consociational model is no longer applicable for the management of religious conflicts in Israeli politics. These authors claim that Israel has been moving in recent years from 'the politics of accommodation' in the religious sphere to 'the politics of decision'.[14]

It is, however, significant to distinguish between changes within the prevailing system of political accommodation (or the exertion of pressures on its operation), and the breaking of this system and its replacement by an alternative system of conflict management. At this point, the dynamic nature of the religious status quo should be reiterated. The 'politics of accommodation' are not 'politics of immobilism'. Demographic changes as well as other sources of social and political change exert heavy pressures on the prevailing system of political accommodation in the religious sphere, and may cause changes in certain arrangements and practices in this area. These changes, however, do not amount to the breaking down of the system, as long as they are not comprehensive and radical and they do not preclude the continuity of dialogue and co-operation between the contending parties.

This is partly explained by the fact that pressures from one side frequently counter pressures on the prevailing system from the other side. These may be the products of social and political processes of change in the opposite direction or the result of deliberate efforts to counterbalance the pressures on the system. Thus, the mass immigration from the former Soviet Union has increased the share of the secular segment in Israeli society. However, it did not result in a far reaching change in the balance of power between religious and secular Jews in Israel, which might have seriously threatened the accommodationist system in the religious area. The reason is that the increase in the Israeli secular population due to the Russian immigration has been countered by social and political changes within the veteran population that greatly increased the power of the religious sector. This is evident by the impressive electoral achievements of the religious parties in the 1996 and 1999 Knesset elections.

True the political achievements of the religious sector, and particularly its Haredi wing, did become one of the factors in the worsening of relations between religious and secular Jews in Israeli society. This development, which has been indicated above, may put pressure on the system of political accommodation in the religious sphere. However, a distinction should be made in this regard between relations on the mass level and on the level of the political elite. Tensions and animosities between social groups should not necessarily preclude political co-operation and compromises between political elites representing different and hostile social groups. On the contrary, sharp tensions grounded in societal cleavages may well serve as a motivating force for dialogue and co-operation in the political sphere in order to counter the destabilizing effects of the fragmented social structure. Indeed, this combination of social fragmentation and political co-operation is, according to Lijphart, the essence of the consociational model.

There are, of course, limits to the willingness and ability of political leaders to accommodate their differences in the face of deep divisions and growing tensions within society. However, it is evident from the Israeli experience, as well as that of other nations, that the political elites of opposing groups can co-operate in a common effort to overcome or neutralize the divisive potential of the fragmented social structure.

There are, to be sure, in Jewish Israeli society those who are willing to overturn the prevailing system of conflict management in the religious sphere. If they had their way, they would have replaced the accommodationist politics in this sphere with the 'politics of decision', even if it were to lead to a severe social and political crisis. The results of the 1999 elections indicate that there has been, indeed, an increase in the electoral and parliamentary base of these circles in Jewish society. This is manifested in the electoral achievements of Shinui, and to a lesser extent, of Meretz. However, even in the newly elected 15th Knesset, the anti-accommodationist approach has received the support of only a minority of Knesset members.

There are also indications that following the elections, there has been a kind of retreat to a more conciliatory style of politics in the religious sphere and other areas of contention. Prime Minister-elect, Ehud Barak, declared his intention to be the 'Prime Minister of all'. Other political leaders of the religious and secular groups also voiced public declarations in this 'spirit of accommodation'. The accommodationist pattern of politics has also been manifested in the process of coalition formation. Barak expressed his willingness to form a broad coalition and leaders of religious and secular parties showed much interest in getting into such a coalition. It may well be that despite his efforts, Barak will not be able to form a broad coalition. However, it seems that even a narrowly based coalition will not change the religious status quo in a radical way.

At this point it should be mentioned that even the Labour-led coalition formed after the 1992 elections did not introduce far-reaching changes in the religious status quo in favour of the secular position. On the other hand, the impressive electoral achievement of the religious parties and the concomitant increase in their bargaining power after the 1996 elections did not result in the introduction of new religious legislation.

There have indeed been significant changes in the Israeli legal and political systems and also in the patterns of conflict and co-operation that characterize these systems. One of these changes is the enactment in 1992 of the two Basic Laws: 'Human Dignity and Liberty'[15] and 'Freedom of Employment'.[16] These laws are unique in the sense that any regular law considered by the Supreme Court to be incompatible with them is denied legal validity. Indeed, the adoption of the 1992 Basic Laws was interpreted as an indication that Israel has been moving from its flexible consociational system to a more rigid and formal system of decision making. This means that it is becoming more and more difficult to resolve conflicts on the basis of negotiation, bargaining and informal agreements.[17]

This claim is based mainly on the interpretation of Supreme Court Chief Justice Aharon Barak, who insists that the introduction of the 1992 Basic Laws signifies a 'constitutional revolution' in the Israeli legal and political system.[18] By this he means that these laws should be considered as essential first components of a written constitution, which is in the process of being drafted. The politics of accommodation in the religious sphere were indeed one of the main causes for the lack of a formal constitution in Israel. This is because in the face of deep differences regarding the identity of the state and society, and the role of religion in public life, the strategy adopted was to avoid as much as possible making decisions on fundamental issues in this area. Therefore, the adoption of a formal constitution could have indicated the decline of consociationalism.

Nevertheless, the view that Israel is in the process of a 'constitutional revolution' has been forcefully challenged by some of the leading figures in the Israeli legal profession.[19] Recent developments have had the effect of supporting and strengthening this view. Contrary to Barak's expectations, the 1992 Basic Laws were not followed by other laws of the same sort. Moreover, one of these laws, the Basic Law: Freedom of Occupation, was amended so as to enable the Knesset to pass laws which are incompatible with the Basic Law, provided that this incompatibility will be stated explicitly in those laws.

This legal amendment was designed to overcome a Supreme Court ruling that the Knesset law forbidding the import of non-Kosher meat is incompatible with the Basic Law: The Freedom of Occupation. The legal measures that were meant to protect the prevailing status quo from interference by the Supreme Court were supported by a vast Knesset majority of right-wing and left-wing representatives. Moreover, from the very beginning, the adoption of the two Basic Laws by the Knesset was based on the understanding that they would not infringe on the religious status quo. This was explicitly stated in the case of the Basic Law: Human Dignity and Liberty'. Paragraph 10 of the law maintains that, 'This Basic Law can not invalidate any law that was in power before its introduction'.

From all of the above, we can conclude that the developments in the legal area did not lead to a radical change in the patterns of conflict management and decision making in the area of religion and state. This is true even in regard to a significant structural change such as the introduction of direct election of the prime minister in the new Basic Law: The Government, which was adopted in 1992 and first came into effect in the 1996 elections.

Writing before the Knesset decided to adopt the proposed electoral reform, Lijphart had argued that such a radical change would signify Israel's moving from a nearly pure type of 'consensus democracy' to a more 'majoritarian' system of government.[20] There are two points to be made in this regard. First, Lijphart referred to an earlier version of the law, which would have concentrated far more power in the hands of the prime minister and made it practically impossible for the Knesset to vote him out of office. In contrast, according to the law currently in effect, the Prime Minister is still dependent on the support of a winning coalition in order to keep his office. This leaves much power in the hands of the smaller parties, and especially the religious parties.

The second and more important point is that 'consensus democracy' is not the same as 'consociational democracy'.[21] The first term refers mainly to the structural-formal characteristics of the political regime, such as proportional elections, multi-party system and coalition government. In contrast, the term 'consociational democracy' places the emphasis on informal agreements that result from deliberate efforts of political leaders to settle the differences between the sub-cultures they represent in a peaceful way.

The informal features of consociational politics account for the fact that consociational politics may characterize a certain area of conflict and decision making, while being largely absent from other areas. Thus, in Israel, the politics of accommodation are mainly applied to issues of religion and state, while in other controversial areas decisions are often made according to the principle of majority rule. A case in point is the policies of the Rabin government. This government used its one vote majority to impose a unilateral decision on the very controversial issue of the Oslo Accords. This kind of behaviour clearly deviated from the pattern of accommodationist politics. However, there is no room for the conclusion that the Rabin government violated consociational principles 'in every conceivable way'.[22]

It should be noted that differences and controversies on foreign and defence issues are especially difficult to handle by accommodationist practices. Thus, the autonomy principle is not applicable to the management of internal conflicts in this area. The application of the proportional method to the resolution of conflicts over matters of policy making is possible in theory, but quite difficult in practice. Even more problematic is the application of the status quo principle to the management of internal controversies over matters of foreign and defence policy. The main problem here is the need to respond to pressures exerted from the dynamic international environment. Changes in this environment may pose new external threats to national security, exacerbate existing ones, or create new opportunities for attainment of peace. All this might make it very difficult to avoid making decisions in order to overcome internal differences. It may also turn out to be a barrier against the making of decisions based on compromise and mutual concessions.

Admittedly, for the religious opponents of the Oslo agreements, the issue at stake was not only political, but also religious. It is also true that for this reason, they regarded the policies of the Rabin government as a blunt violation of the consociational tradition in the religious sphere, which was one of the main factors behind their fierce opposition to that government. Nevertheless, the issue was not perceived in this way by the initiators and supporters of the Oslo peace process. In contrast to their religious opponents, the Labour leaders perceived the peace process in purely political terms and dealt with it in very different way than with issues of religion and state. While they were determined to continue with the peace process without any consideration to the criticism of right wing parties, the Labour leaders were responsive to the claims of the religious parties regarding violations of the religious status quo through Supreme Court rulings.

All of this notwithstanding, the differences over the territorial issue did play a significant role in the worsening of relations between the religious community and the left wing circles in Israel. The tension has been further aggravated by the political support that was lent to the right wing camp and its leader Benjamin Netanyahu by almost all of the Israeli religious community. However, this overlapping of the religious and ideological cleavages should not be taken as indicating a severe crisis of consociational politics in Israel. It should be noted that Lijphart developed the consociational model in order to account for the existence of overlapping and mutually reinforcing cleavages in certain stable democracies. As the political leaders of the rival groups realize the divisive potential of the societal cleavages, they engage in a deliberate effort to counteract the destabilizing effects of the fragmented social structure by means of co-operation, negotiation and compromises.

It can be concluded then that the application of the consociational model in the area of religion and state in Israel has been exposed to heavy pressures, but by and large consociationalism in this area has managed to survive. This is not the case in other areas of controversy within Israeli society and politics. In most of these areas there has been a marked decline in consociational patterns of conflict management and decision making. In this regard, the Israeli case is quite similar to those of some West European countries in which consociationalism, too, is in a process of decline. The main cause for this decline in Israel, as well as in Western Europe, is not the exacerbation of tensions and controversies between different segments of society, but rather the mitigation and moderation of differences and controversies. This can account for the fact that while consociational practices have declined in most areas of Israeli society and politics, they have largely survived in the sphere of religion and state. The reason for this is that with the probable exception of the territorial issue, the religious cleavage is the only one to retain its highly divisive potential, and therefore it especially needs management by consociational methods.

Two main questions arise in this regard. The first one refers to the difference between the religious factor and other sources of cleavage and division in society. The second question has to do with the fact that contrary to the situation in Israel, the decline of consociationalism in West European countries has also been salient in the religious area. In order to deal with the above questions, we have to discuss in general terms the unique nature of the religious issue in Israel.

THE RELIGIOUS CLEAVAGE AND OTHER SOURCES OF CONFLICT

The politics of accommodation is not limited to the religious domain. Accommodationist practices are quite frequently applied in the area of ethnic relations. In Israel, as in other countries divided along ethnic lines, the ethnic factor plays a considerable role in the allocation of public resources and representation in governmental positions. However, the consociational model tends to be applied in a wider and more consistent manner in the religious area. In this area, not only problems of representation and allocation of resources, but also other important issues are resolved on the basis of negotiations and compromises. Most important in this respect are the status quo principle and other strategies of avoiding explicit and clear-cut decisions, particularly when they involve the enactment of parliamentary laws. This is especially the case in a country like Israel, where problems of religion and state continue to be a central controversial issue.

This centrality can be explained by the nature of religious conflicts, which are inclined to involve fundamental values and basic beliefs of an absolute nature, and therefore it is very difficult to resolve them through unilateral decisions. True, adherents of 'secular values' may also claim an absoluteness to their positions. However, often the main adversary of such 'secular religions' is traditional religion. Therefore, the clashes over values and attitudes of a secular nature may also have the dimension of religious conflict.

In Israel, during the Yishuv period, Zionist socialism was a comprehensive system of values and symbols that sought to replace traditional Jewish religion as the main source of solidarity and unity for the Jewish people. This kind of 'civil religion' served as a basis for a community of believers – the Zionist Labour movement – that established a very developed network of institutions in all spheres of activity and especially in the educational and cultural domain.[23] The Labour movement claimed and achieved for its educational institutions the same autonomous status and proportional allocation of resources that was granted to the religious system of education. However, this did not prevent clashes between the Labour movement and the religious camp over the mobilization of students to their rival systems of education. The conflict greatly intensified during the early years of Israel's independence, due to the fierce competition between the two communities of believers over the political socialization of the mass immigration.

The Israeli case demonstrates another reason for the fact that the politics of accommodation is especially prevalent in dealing with religious conflicts. The fierce conflict over the education of the immigrants' children was resolved by a political arrangement that led to the abolition of the autonomous system of Labour education, while the religious educational systems largely retained their autonomy and their proportional share in the allocation of resources. One of the reasons for this development was the decline of Zionist socialism as a kind of secular religion. The abolition of the 'Labour trend' in education further enhanced this decline of Zionist socialism.

The Israeli case, and others as well, seem to indicate that the survival capacity of secular religions tends to be lower than that of traditional religions, which have been proven more successful in retaining the devotion and loyalty of their adherents. This is especially true in democratic regimes, in which secular religions cannot rely on the political power of a totalitarian system of government to preserve their hold on society. The declining role of secular religion or 'total ideology' in Western democratic countries means that there is no vital need to resort to accommodationist devices in order to settle intensive ideological conflicts.

There has also been a marked decline in the intensity of conflict over religious issues in many Western countries, which is due in part to processes of secularization. As a result, there has been a considerable weakening of sub-cultural loyalties based on support or opposition to traditional religion. This process of 'de-pillarization' led, in turn, to a marked decline in the role of accommodationist politics in the consociational countries of Western Europe.[24] However, the decline of religious conflicts in these countries can be attributed, to a large measure, to the application of consociational methods to the management of conflicts in the religious sphere. In this way, the success of consociationalism was actually a significant factor in its own decline in Western Europe. It is instructive at this point to compare patterns of conflict management of religious issues in Israel and in some of the Western countries.

ISRAEL AND WESTERN EUROPE

Israel has not been exposed to secularization to the same extent as Western Europe. In some respects there is even a counter trend of de-secularization in this country. This is one of the reasons for the significant difference between Israel and the West European countries in terms of the role of religion in their political systems. Most important in this respect is the fact that in Israel there is a much wider use of accommodationist devices in religious politics. In contrast to Western

European countries, a solution to the education problem in Israel was not enough to calm tensions between the religious and secular camps. Other issues involving the role of religion in state and society remain a source of intensive conflict in Israeli politics.

Lijphart presents the educational agreement in Holland as the cornerstone for politics of accommodation in that country, and a key factor in stabilizing the relations between the various segments that differ in their religious attitudes. 'The relative peace among the religious blocks in Holland... must be attributed, to a large extent, to the pacific settlement of the school issue'.[25]

There are definite similarities between the political conflicts over education and religion in Israel and in West European countries, especially Holland and Belgium. For instance, the methods commonly used to resolve such conflicts in Israel and in such other countries are based on the principles of autonomy, proportional funding, and the status quo. Like in Western Europe, resolution of the educational issue in Jewish society was a precondition for peaceful coexistence and political co-operation between the secular and religious segments. The issue of religious education was the first major area of controversy at the inception of the Zionist movement, and later it became the first controversial issue to be settled by accommodationist methods. Conflicts over religious education played a major role in the establishment of religious parties in Jewish society, as well as in Holland and Belgium.

The dispute over education in Israel is not merely over ideological principles; it also reflects a power struggle between political camps over the socialization of citizens within their organizational frameworks. In this respect, too, Israel resembles consociational democracies such as Holland and Belgium.

There are also marked differences between the political role of the education issue in religious conflicts in Israel and in the West European countries. The education issue was a decisive factor in the relations between the religious and secular camps in Belgium, Holland and France. Therefore, resolution of this issue substantially diminished the conflict between the political camps, and even served to weaken the basis for their continued existence as distinct and organized political sub-cultures. According to John Frears, in France 'the notion of Catholicism as a separate and hostile sub-culture would have disappeared long ago, were it not for the periodic disputes about state aid to Church schools'.[26] Lorwin maintains that the Belgian Schools Pact of 1958 impaired the political consolidation of the Catholic camp there, despite state recognition and funding of Catholic schools, because it 'removed the strongest argument for separate Catholic political action and for Catholic political unity'.[27] Lijphart notes that 'Once this question [of religious schools] is resolved, religious cleavages lose much of their political salience'.[28] Though religious issues continue to be a factor in Dutch politics, they are not divisive enough to undermine political stability. 'Other differences have not disappeared, but they are only minor irritants'.

In contrast to other Western countries, within Israeli Jewish society there have been many other issues besides education that have become a source of major conflict between the religious and secular political camps. Therefore, the resolution of the education question in Israel has not significantly reduced the salience of the religious factor in Israeli politics.

This unique role of religion in Israeli society and politics reflects the special nature of the Jewish religion. Unlike other religions, Judaism includes a large number of practical precepts, aspires to guide all aspects of individual and public life, and has a historical affinity between religious and national existence. Therefore, many religious issues besides education are subjects of heated controversy in Israeli politics. Among them, there are problems unique to Israel, such as the 'Who is a Jew' question, matters of Kashrut and Sabbath observance, conscription of yeshiva students and religious women, the status of non-orthodox Jewish movements and the role of Jewish law in Israeli legislation. Since the Six Day War, the religious dimension has also been prominent in debates over issues of foreign and defence policy, particularly those related to the Arab–Israeli conflict, such as the question of the occupied territories and the peace process.

The self-definition of Israel as a Jewish state and the central role of religion in Jewish history and culture would make it very difficult for many Jews to identify with Israel were it to become a completely secular state, cut off from any attachment to the Jewish religious tradition. Many people who are not strict about observing religious precepts in their private lives recognize the need to give religion a position of influence in the country's public life. These people wish to express and give content to the Jewish identity of Israel by maintaining the important role of religious values and symbols in its national culture and political life.

Consequently, religious parties in Israel, unlike those in Western Europe, do not limit themselves to a defensive role in issues of religion and state. Therefore, they cannot settle for autonomous status and government funding for religious institutions, services, and education. The aim of these parties is to ensure a central role for religious tradition in shaping Israeli society and to leave the imprint of religious Judaism on the state as a whole.

ISRAEL AND THE UNITED STATES

The claim that accommodationist methods of conflict management are especially appropriate to dealing with issues of religion and state raises the question: How do we account for the fact that such methods have generally not been applied to the management of religious issues in some Western democracies? In this regard the most obvious example seems to be the way religious issues are confronted in the United States.

The interesting point is that despite very marked differences, there are certain common elements in the ways that the United States and Israel deal with religious differences within their societies. To a large degree, these common elements are also shared by the consociational democracies of Western Europe. The most striking similarity between the patterns of conflict management in Israel and in the United States is the tendency in both countries to avoid direct political confrontations over religious issues as much as possible, by taking these issues out of the regular political process. This is done in three major ways:

* A national agreement to stabilize and consolidate existing arrangements in the religious sphere;
* The formulation of differing attitudes in this area in non-ideological terms as disagreements over matters of interpretation and application;
* The non-involvement of national political institutions in the management and resolution of controversial religious issues.

The tendency to stabilize and consolidate political arrangements in the religious sphere, thereby avoiding the need to reopen them for a debate and decision, is manifested in both the status quo solution in Israel and the First Amendment to the American Constitution. It is true that the First Amendment is part of a formal constitution, while many of the status quo accommodations do not have even the legal status of a regular law. However, in Israel the religious status quo does have the status of a basic constitutional principle, although this position does not rely on the legally binding power of a written constitution.

It should be noted that the consensus in American society on the religious articles of the first amendment is based to a large extent on the willingness of the Americans to accept constitutional principles and to avoid opening them up to debate and criticism.[29] In this way, the American practice is not so different from the mutual agreement to avoid introduction of changes in the religious status quo in Israel. The difference is that the status quo in Israel has been generally acknowledged as an accepted means for avoiding religious conflict, while the first amendment fulfills this same function in the United State largely due to the broader consensus on the American Constitution.

Just as the agreement on the religious status quo in Israel does not preclude the rise of conflicts in this area, so the consensus on the religious articles of the First Amendment in the United States does not preclude conflicts over issues of religion and state.[30] However, in the United States, like in Israel, controversies over the role of religion in public life have been largely neutralized by formulating them in legal, constitutional terms that reflect differing interpretations of the constitution, or the status quo.

There is still a marked difference in this respect between the United States and Israel. The formulation of religious issues in legal terms has been greatly enhanced and made much easier in the United States through the recognition of a supposedly non-political institution – the judicial system, particularly the Federal Supreme Court – as the authorized interpreter of the constitution, including its religious articles. In this way, the Supreme Court has assumed the role of an arbiter in controversial issues of religion and state, thereby taking these issues, in a way, out of politics.

In Israel, as well as in the consociational democracies of Western Europe, political institutions at the national level may also avoid involvement in controversial religious issues by delegating them to local authorities, administrative bodies, or ad-hoc committees. However, such practices can be much more effective if they are based on wide public agreement to treat them as legal issues to be decided by the judicial system, as is generally the case with regard to issues of religion and state in the United States. By contrast, there has been no such agreement concerning the management of religious issues in Israel. Instead, controversies in this area, which often involve differing interpretations of the status quo, are resolved by deliberations, bargaining and agreements – many of them of an informal nature – between representatives of the opposing parties at the national or local level.

True, the Israeli Supreme Court has also been involved in controversies on religious issues. In certain cases, this involvement played a role in neutralizing the political impact of religious issues. However, in many of the cases, the intervention of the Israeli Supreme Court in religious affairs resulted in the intensification and further politicization of the conflict, rather than its resolution. This has to do with a basic difference between the two political systems. In the United States, the role of the Supreme Court in the resolution of religious controversies is based on its recognition as the authorized interpreter of the constitution. In the absence of a written constitution in Israel, the Court's decisions on religious matters are open not only to criticism but also to challenge and counteraction on the side of dissatisfied parties, who seek to abolish the Court's verdicts by resorting to parliamentary legislation.

Even more important is the fact that in contrast to the United States, in Israel the involvement of the Supreme Court in religious issues is not based on a widely accepted legal norm or practice that is recognized as the guiding principle in this sphere. Moreover, in Israel, the decisions of the Supreme Court on religious matters often stand in open contradiction to the accepted guiding principle for dealing with religious issues in the Israeli polity, which is the status quo. It should be noted that the Supreme Court is not willing to grant recognition and legitimization to the status quo, unless it is grounded in a parliamentary legislation. As many of the status quo arrangements are based on informal agreements or secondary legislation, the intervention of the Supreme Court has quite often resulted in the abolition of these arrangements. This, in turn, gave rise to the reopening of conflicts and to attempts at legislation that is aimed at restoring the original status quo, which had been harmed by the intervention of the Supreme Court.

There is a basic difference between the role of the Supreme Court in the United States and in Israel. While not all Americans agree with the way the Supreme Court interprets the religious clauses of the constitution, most of them accept his authority on these matters. By contrast, in Israel the very legitimacy of judicial involvement in the religious sphere has been put into question and has turned into a controversial issue.[31]

All of this is related to the most fundamental difference between the American and the Israeli systems, which is their contrasting concepts of the proper relationship between religion and the state. While the notion of separation of religion and state is not explicit in the American Constitution, a consensus has been formed on interpreting the First Amendment as implying this notion. This process has been greatly enhanced by decisions of the Supreme Court, but it also has reflected the growing acceptance of separation as the most appropriate solution for religious conflicts within American society.

In the American case, religious conflicts are avoided, or resolved, on the basis of the agreement to treat religious concerns and institutions as private matters of the individual, or voluntary community, to be kept separate from the public sphere of government, legislation and politics. Therefore, controversies over the actual implementation of the separatist model are treated as constitutional issues, to be resolved by the judicial system. By contrast, most Israeli Jewish citizens consider religion an essential component of national life, which must not be limited to the private sphere. This means that, in Israel, separation cannot be an agreed solution to religious controversies.

CONCLUSION: MODELS OF MANAGEMENT OF RELIGIOUS CONFLICTS

The American model of separation has not been accepted in Israel, nor in most West European democracies. In these countries, relations between religion and state are resolved on the basis of various kinds of accommodations. Nevertheless, there are also differences in this regard between Israel and the West European countries, as well as among these countries themselves.

We propose a distinction between two 'ideal types' of separation and accommodation, which leaves room for another subdivision between an active and comprehensive system of accommodation and a more passive and limited form of it. The first kind is best exemplified by the Israeli case, while the consociational democracies of Western Europe are good examples of the other kind of political accommodation. In the West European consociational democracies, the accommodationist practices have been efficient to the point that they have generally prevented the need for an active use of conflict regulation methods in order to resolve or restrain intensive controversies on religious issues. To a large extent this is related to processes of secularization and de-pillarization within these countries. In Israel, on the other hand, there has been a continued active resort to various methods of political accommodation in order to resolve or restrain conflicts over religious issues. This has to do with the special nature of the religious issue in Israel – a point discussed above.

How can we account for the difference between the American model and other patterns of dealing with religious conflicts in Western democracies? It can be argued that religious divisions in the American population did not give rise to the formation of distinct and well-organized subcultures; therefore, it was not necessary to accommodate the different values and interests by way of agreements based on proportionality, autonomy and status quo.

However, this begs the question as to why religious divisions in the United States did not result in the formation of distinct and segmented subcultures, like in Israel and a great part of West Europe. Students of West European systems have noticed that the segmented structure of some of these countries is the result, rather than the cause, of intensive conflicts, mainly on issues of religion and education.[32] To a large extent, the same can be said of the formation of segmented religious subcultures in the Yishuv, which was a kind of defensive reaction to the processes of secularization and modernization in the general society, and particularly to the danger of secular education.

Why, then, did conflicts of this kind not arise in the United State or not give rise to the formation of religious parties with distinct subcultures? This issue has been a subject for much discussion in the academic literature. There are those who point to the difference between countries with a large Catholic population and those with a dominant Protestant one, as was the United States in its early years. To this we should add the nature of the United States as a pluralistic new nation of immigrants from various countries and ethnic origins, who affiliate with different religious denominations. In this situation, the only way to form an integrated nation was by avoiding identification of the American state with any of its various religious or ethnic groups. This goal was efficiently served by the separation of religion from the state.

In this respect, the Israeli situation is diametrically opposed to that of the United States. This is because the self-definition of Israel as a Jewish state has been a major motivating force in the use of the Jewish religion as a source of national solidarity and political legitimization. In this way, the religious status quo in Israel can also be seen as reflecting a basic consensus among the Jewish population on the Jewish identity of Israel and the need to assert it by granting the Jewish religion a role in the public life of the state.

This argument notwithstanding, there are also fairly large circles in Israel that advocate the separation of religion and state. Even many who reject this idea disagree with the religious parties and their supporters on the desired nature and extent of the link between religion and state and the means of preserving the Jewish identity of Israel. This is the reason that while the status quo and other accommodationist devices are based on a basic sense of Jewish solidarity, they also serve as a means to avoid or restrain conflicts resulting from differing interpretations of Judaism.

NOTES

The central arguments of this article are largely based on the conclusions of a 1999 study, *Religion and Political Accommodation in Israel*, sponsored by the Floersheimer Institute for Policy Studies.

1. Robert A. Dahl, 'Some Explanations', in R.A. Dahl (ed.), *Political Oppositions in Western Democracies*, New Haven: Yale University Press, 1966, p.358.
2. Arend Lijphart, *The Politics of Accommodation*, Berkeley: University of California Press, 1968, p.103.
3. Dahl, 'Some Explanations', p.358.
4. Arend Lijphart, 'Consociational Democracy', *World Politics*, Vol. 21, No. 2 (1969), pp.207–225.
5. Arend Lijphart, *Democracies: Patterns of Majoritarian and Consensus Democracy in Twenty-One Countries*, New Haven: Yale University Press, 1984.
6. Arend Lijphart, 'The Power-Sharing Approach', in Joseph V. Montville (ed.), *Conflict and Peacemaking in Multiethnic Societies*, New York: Macmillan, 1990, pp.107–114. There are, nevertheless, authors who make a distinction between 'consociationalism' and 'power-sharing'. See Paul Dixon, 'Consociationalism and the Northern Ireland Process: The Glass Half Full or Half Empty?', *Nationalism and Ethnic Politics*, Vol. 3, No. 3 (1997), pp.21–23.
7. See Eliezer Don-Yehiya, 'Conflict and Cooperation between Political Camps: The Religious Camp and the Labour Movement and Education Crisis in Israel', Ph.D. dissertation, The Hebrew University of Jerusalem, 1977 (Hebrew).
8. See Sammy Smooha, 'Ethnic Democracy: Israel as an Archetype', *Israel Studies*, Vol. 2, No. 2 (1998), pp.198–241; Eliezer Don-Yehiya and Bernard Susser, 'Nationalism vs. Democracy: Israel as a Deviant Case', *Tarbut Democratit*, Vol. 1, No. 1 (1999), pp.9–22.

9. See Eliezer Don-Yehiya, 'Political Religion in a New State: Ben-Gurion's Mamlachtiyut', in Noah Lukas and Ilan Troen (eds.), *Israel's First Decade of Independence*, Albany: State University of New York Press, 1995, pp.171–192.
10. Dahl, 'Some Explanations', p.358.
11. Eric Nordlinger, *Conflict Regulation in Deeply Divided Societies*, Cambridge: Harvard University Press, 1972, pp.21–33.
12. See Don-Yehiya, *Conflict and Cooperation*.
13. On the importance of the intensity factor for democratic theory, see Robert A. Dahl, *A Preface to Democratic Theory*, Chicago: University of Chicago Press, 1956, pp.48–49.
14. Asher Cohen and Bernard Susser, 'From Accommodation to Decision: The Transformation of Israel's Religio-Political Life', *Journal of Church and State*, Vol. 38, No. 4, 1996, pp.817–839. See also the article by Reuven Y. Hazan in this volume.
15. *Sefer Ha-hukim* (Book of Israeli Laws), Jerusalem, 1992, p.150.
16. *Ibid.*, p.114.
17. Cohen and Susser, 'From Accommodation to Decision', pp.826–830.
18. Aharon Barak, 'The Constitutional Revolution: Protected Human Rights', *Mishpat u-Mimshal*, Vol. 1, No. 1 (1992), pp.9–35.
19. See Ruth Gavison, *Ha-mahapeha Ha-hukatit (The Constitutional Revolution)*, Jerusalem, Israel Democracy Institute, 1998.
20. Arend Lijphart, 'Israeli Democracy and Democratic Reform in Comparative Perspective', in Ehud Sprinzak and Larry Diamond (eds.), *Israeli Democracy under Stress*, Boulder: Lynne Rienner, 1993, pp.107–123.
21. Arend Lijphart, 'Democratic Political Systems: Types, Cases, Causes and Consequences', *Theoretical Politics*, Vol. 1, No. 1 (1989), pp.39–40.
22. Cohen and Susser, 'From Accommodation to Decision', p.838.
23. Charles Liebman and Eliezer Don-Yehiya, *Civil Religion in Israel: Traditional Judaism and Political Culture in the Jewish State*, Berkeley: University of California Press, 1983.
24. On the decline of consociationalism in Holland and Belgium, see A. Bax, *Modernization and Cleavage in Dutch Society*, Groningen, Rijsk Universiteit, 1988; Kris Deschouwer, 'The Decline of Consociationalism and the Reluctant Modernisation of Belgian Mass Parties', in Richard S. Katz and Peter Mair (eds.), *How Parties Organize: Change and Adaptation in Party Organizations in Western Europe*, London: Sage, 1994, pp.80–108.
25. Lijphart, *The Politics of Accommodation*, p.118.
26. John Frears, 'Conflict in France: The Decline and Fall of a Stereotype', *Political Studies*, Vol. 20, No. 1 (1972), pp.31–41.
27. Val R. Lorwin, 'Segmented Pluralism', *Comparative Politics*, Vol. 3, No. 2 (1970/71), pp.141–175.
28. Lijphart, *The Politics of Accommodation*, p.118.
29. According to Dahl, 'An understanding quickly developed that all controversies, particularly constitutional controversies, must take for granted the overriding legitimacy of the constitution and the superiority of American institutions'. Robert A. Dahl, 'The American Oppositions: Affirmation and Denial', in Dahl (ed.), *Political Oppositions in Western Democracies*, p.37.
30. See among others, William H. Marnell, *The First Amendment: The History of Religious Freedom in America*, Garden City, Doubleday, 1964; A. James Reichley, *Religion in American Public Life*, Washington: Brookings Institute, 1985, pp.115–167.
31. A noted example is the huge demonstration against the Supreme Court held in 1999, which was attended by more than 300,000 religious Jews.
32. Brian Barry, 'The Consociational Model and its Dangers,' *European Journal of Political Research*, Vol. 3, No. 4 (1975), pp.407–408.

Religion and Politics in Israel: The Rise and Fall of the Consociational Model

REUVEN Y. HAZAN

INTRODUCTION: ISRAEL AND THE CONSOCIATIONAL MODEL

Consociational theory has had a significant impact on the comparative study of European democracies. There are, however, a few countries outside Europe that have received attention from scholars of consociational democracy and have been identified as consociational at some point in their history, among them Lebanon, Colombia, Malaysia and Uruguay. Regretfully, consociational practices in most of these countries were unable to fulfil their basic role – maintaining political stability amid a deeply fragmented political culture.

In the somewhat meagre amount of literature devoted to consociationalism in Israel, the relationship between the main social segments has been termed quasi- or semi-consociational. This article seeks to assess the extent to which consociational theory can truly be applied to the dynamics between the dominant power blocs in Israel. In doing so, it will elaborate the political sociology of the major power blocs in the country and the political behaviour of their elites, in order to show that two encapsulated and hostile political subcultures existed within the dominant religious group and that the gap between them was bridged by the accommodating practices of the elites.

This essay delineates the presence of consociationalism in Israel and elaborates its subsequent decline, as in Europe. This article then suggests that consociationalism was replaced by another European model during Israel's first post-independence phase and by yet a third European model during the current period. In other words, the analysis of the dynamic interplay between the dominant sub-cultures in Israel is developed using key political concepts adopted from the European context.

The focus of this essay is the most central aspect of consociationalism in Israel, namely, the role of the parties and the party system. The parties

Reuven Y. Hazan is a Lecturer in the Department of Political Science at the Hebrew University of Jerusalem, Israel.

in Israel were the mechanism that linked the two dominant sub-cultures and their elites and the party system allowed accommodationist practices to take place.

THE RELEVANCE OF POLITICAL PARTIES IN ISRAELI DEMOCRACY

The parties in Israel continued, or inherited, their tradition of political activity from the pre-state period. The parties that functioned in the voluntary organizations of what was then a state-in-the-making penetrated practically every aspect of society in a manner much more intensive than was acceptable in most democracies. Soon after its establishment, Israel was described as a 'party state' by Akzin, who wrote that in Israel, the political parties represented the single most influential political institution, fulfilled a more important role and were more influential than in any other country, apart from a few of the one-party states.[1]

According to Akzin, the party system that developed in Israel was characterized by intensive ideological differences between the political parties. As a result, the political parties attempted to influence, and politicize, almost all spheres of life. Individually, or as a bloc, the parties in Israel stood at the apex of networks that covered education, culture, sports, youth movements, trade unions, employment agencies, housing, agricultural and industrial co-operatives, transportation authorities, periodicals and publishing companies, health organizations, urban development and more.

The intensity of party activity, coupled with the broad range of areas into which the parties penetrated, expanded the role of the Israeli parties almost to the point of becoming all-embracing. Therefore, the central forces in the nascent, but comprehensive, political activity of Israel were the political parties and the party system. As Galnoor posited:

> It would therefore not be an exaggeration to say that, in the first 20 years of the state, domestic affairs were based on the functioning of the parties. Parties were not merely involved in the classical political function of interest aggregation and articulation, since their activities extended into most aspects of social and economic life.[2]

ACCOMMODATION VERSUS EXCLUSION

Israeli society is divided along four major cleavages, the first two cover the entire population, whereas the second two cover only the Jewish majority. The divisions are: (i) socio-economic; (ii) Jews and Arabs; (iii) secular and religious Jews; and (iv) Ashkenazi–Sephardi ethnic divisions. The first cleavage has strengthened the remaining cleavages. That is, the differences between Jews and Arabs, between secular and ultra-orthodox Jews, and between Sephardi Jews of Mediterranean extraction and Ashkenazi Jews of Central and Eastern European origin also cut, to a significant extent, along socio-economic lines.[3]

While the national and ethnic cleavages (ii) and (iv) did not bring about the creation of politically segmented and co-operative sub-cultures, the remaining two cleavages – religion and class – did create both social segmentation and political pillarisation. It is due mainly to this fact that this essay is devoted solely to these two latter divisions, which possessed both the social and political institutional infrastructures to establish consociational ties. The ethnic divisions were addressed in a manner that can be better described as a combination of clientelism and patronage, of the politically-established Ashkenazi group toward the Sephardis, while the national divisions were treated by a pattern of exclusion and control, by the Jewish political establishment toward the Arabs – a model quite contradictory to that of accommodation.

Israel, therefore, cannot be described as a consociational democracy, because the mechanisms that describe this type of regime are absent in substantial segments of the Israeli polity, specifically the Arab minority. The definition of Israel as a Jewish state thus creates a problem concerning the application of accommodative practices at the systemic level. While civil and political rights are, officially, extended to all its citizens, Israel has institutionalized control over the state and the party system by the Jewish majority. Due to the social and political predominance of the Jewish majority, there are those who have attempted to classify it as an 'ethnic democracy' or even an 'ethnocracy'.[4] These concepts strive to reconcile, in the case of the former, or to make a contradiction, in the case of the latter, between Jewish predominance and democracy.

Such classifications, however, do not make the consociational concept inapplicable in the Israeli context. On the contrary, Israel can contribute to the comparative theoretical debate by being a model wherein consociationalism can characterize not only entire political systems, but also particular behaviour within a political system. In other words, the consociational model has been used to differentiate between different types of democracies (and this is partially the reason why Israel has been termed semi- or quasi-consociational), but it can be also be adopted at a lower level of analysis to distinguish between different patterns of political behaviour across various dimensions or cleavages within democracies.

This article argues that the dynamic relations within the dominant Israeli 'ethnicity' are better described by the consociational model than by any other conceptual tool. Moreover, the development of these relations during the first fifty years of Israel's existence can be analyzed and assessed using the theoretical counterparts of the consociational model – consensualism and majoritarianism – in a method unrivalled by any other political classification or typology. Furthermore, from the party system perspective, the consociational model and its counterparts provide the key to understanding not only the accommodation of religious conflicts in Israel, but also the success and stability of the entire Israeli political system.

SOCIAL SEGMENTATION, RELIGION AND POLITICS IN ISRAEL

The socio-economic divide in Israel produced only one sub-culture, rather than two. During the pre-state period, as well as in the first decades of Israel's independence, the socio-economic cleavage was decidedly one-sided, with the socialist camp predominant over the bourgeois group. Indeed, it was the institutional segmentation of the socialist camp that drove the religious sub-culture to emulate it, and quite successfully. Although the bourgeois group attempted to do likewise, it never reached the level of social segmentation and institutionalization that the other two camps enjoyed.

Ever since the pre-state period, the inclination of the political leadership – a majority of whom were both socialist and secular – to court the religious groups and include them in the nation-building and coalition-making processes has had its price. The religious groups made their participation and support contingent upon receiving full control of many aspects of personal status, such as marriage and burial. Therefore, in order to appease the orthodox religious groups and to keep them from being alienated from what was becoming a secular (independent) state, the civil authorities accepted religious norms in their orthodox interpretation and forced them upon the population at large. The social conflict that this development created is due to the fact that only a small minority, approximately 20 per cent of the Israeli population, adheres to orthodox Judaism.

Nonetheless, Jewish identity in Israel is not necessarily secular. Although a small minority identify themselves as orthodox, only a slightly larger minority – approximately 25–30 per cent – describe themselves as secular. The majority of the Israeli population is characterized as traditional, i.e., those who observe some religious practices. Yet, this group does not perceive Jewish practices as adherence to God's commandments, but rather as a way of maintaining Jewish customs and tradition. Therefore, a majority in Israel favours some aspects of Judaism in Israeli public life and some relationship between religion and state in Israel.[5] Israeli and Jewish identities thus tend to overlap and religion plays a prominent role in the expression of Israeli identity.

The separation of religion and state in Israel is, therefore, unlikely. The principle of separating between religion and state means, among other things, that direct state support for religious services is prohibited. In Israel, most of the political parties support the continued funding of religious institutions and only a minority of the population questions this principle. The contemporary debate in Israel is not the separation of these two factors, but rather how much state support will be given to which religious institutions and how much supervision of religious organizations will the state be granted in exchange. In short, the present condition is neither total integration nor total separation. It is a complex situation that does not entirely satisfy either side, but which will undoubtedly continue into the foreseeable future.

Dan Horowitz and Moshe Lissak correctly pointed out that 'the religious–secular cleavage divides the dominant group in Israeli society, but also serves as a basis of political mobilisation and social and cultural separatism'.[6] The religious–secular cleavage has, therefore, severe conflict potential for Israeli society and politics. Nonetheless, the political system has, thus far, managed to resolve religious conflicts by peaceful means, while preserving Israel's stability and democracy.

The religious camp in Israel is divided between religious Zionist parties and religious non-Zionist parties. The former came to terms with Zionism – the Jewish national movement – and its goal of creating a Jewish homeland, which they perceived as the beginning of the process of salvation. The latter parties, on the other hand, opposed the establishment of a Jewish State prior to the arrival of the Messiah. The religious Zionist parties co-operated with the secular Zionist parties in the process of state-building, worked towards a unified society and participated in the pre- and post-independence national institutions. The religious non-Zionist parties adopted an isolationist approach, sought autonomy from the rest of society and boycotted the national institutions.

The co-operation between the secular Zionist and religious Zionist parties brought about a moderate and pragmatic position concerning religion from both sides, whereas the isolationist rift created by the religious non-Zionist parties produced an extremist and non-compromising religious stand. These processes were buttressed by the fact that the religious Zionist movement was less extremist concerning religion to begin with, while the religious non-Zionists were ultra-orthodox in their religious outlook, seeking to achieve full compliance with religious tenets in all aspects of life. The clearest example of the difference in attitudes toward the state is that the religious Zionists had always participated in elections to the pre-state institutions and since independence have always sought to participate in government in order to gain support for their interests. The religious non-Zionists, on the other hand, boycotted elections in the pre-state period and after independence participated in elections and coalitions in order to gain access to government funding and influence policy-making, but largely refused to become members of the government of a secular Jewish state.

Despite the differences in the two religious groups in Israel, both share the recognition that the religious authority has the right to influence the decisions and activities of the religious parties. In this respect, the religious parties in Israel are quite different from most important religious parties in Europe, where autonomy and mutual non-intervention is usually the defining characteristic of religion–party relations. Moreover, the Israeli religious parties' electoral support comes almost exclusively from the religious electorate, contrary to most relevant European religious parties, who both attempt to attract and receive support from voters who do not have a clear attachment to religion.[7] The basic similarity between religious parties in Israel and Europe is the socio-economic makeup of their electorate. In both cases, the religious voters come from various social standings and hold differing views on socio-economic policies. In this respect, the religious parties in Israel are socially pluralistic, similar to their European counterparts.

In other words, the religious parties in Israel are quite different from Christian Democratic parties in Europe because the former are parties whose primary concern is religion, whereas the latter are parties who identify with religion and religious principles, but their preoccupation with religion is not prevalent. The European religious parties might, therefore, be described as parties that strive to defend religion, while the Israeli religious parties seek to advance and expand the role of religion. Neuberger has gone as far as saying that the kind of religious parties found in Israel are similar to the religious parties found in some Muslim countries, rather than those found in Europe.[8]

CONSOCIATIONALISM IN ISRAEL: THE EARLY YEARS

Israel, during its pre- and immediate post-independence period, can be said to have exemplified consociational mechanisms in a manner approaching those states – Austria, Belgium, The Netherlands and Switzerland – that have been used as the primary models for consociational theory. In Israel, as well, both the formal governmental institutions and the party system have been structured to acknowledge and reinforce the ideological or religious cleavages, in addition to the socio-economic ones. The result has been – and continues to be, albeit at a lesser level – a combination of social segmentation and political stability, similar to the consociational democracies of Europe.

McRae's synthesis of consociationalism points to three basic factors: (i) a social structure, segmented in a manner sufficiently intense and durable to give members of the respective groups a different orientation and outlook; (ii) a pattern of behaviour by the elites, who recognize the dangers of fragmentation, are committed to maintaining the system, are willing to work with other elites and are capable of compromise; and (iii) a political culture, whose underlying characteristic is based on a tradition of accommodation arising from historical circumstances.[9] Israel, in its formative and early years, exhibited all three factors.

The religious–secular cleavage has managed to maintain its force and passion throughout the first half-century of Israeli independence. The success of the religious community in forging and maintaining a distinct sub-culture only strengthens this cleavage. Indeed, as Gutmann stated: 'It is a fact that the religious population is becoming more and more isolated from the non-religious, primarily as a consequence of policies deliberately followed with this aim in mind. As a result, the cleavage between these two separate segments of the population is ever widening'.[10]

The socio-economic cleavage was already strong enough to establish the main and dominant, secular socialist sub-culture of the pre-independent Jewish community in British Mandatory Palestine. Unlike the religious–secular cleavage, which is still strong, this divide has reduced its intensity with time. Yet, it was the pioneer in the process of social segmentation and the most successful in its achievements, without which the tradition of accommodationist practices of the pre-state period would have been practically impossible.[11]

A tradition of accommodation was developed by the elites of two main camps – socialists and religious – who established a pattern of behaviour that recognized the dangers of separation and, through compromise, showed a commitment to the survival of the system. One of the main reasons for this is that given the voluntary nature of the pre-state institutions, which lacked any sovereign powers and existed in the midst of massive immigration waves, any predominance by one camp could be only relative. The position achieved by the socialist camp, over a decade before the establishment of the state, made it the major player – but not without the need for coalition partners in order to rule. Moreover, the need for institution-building within a voluntary framework elicited a strong emphasis on internal solidarity. That is, due to the necessity of working together, broad solidarity was sought among the different movements in order to legitimize authority.

The socialist-secular leadership attempted to court both the religious Zionists and the religious non-Zionists. The relationship that developed between the socialists and the religious Zionists has been called the 'historical partnership'. By the early 1900s, the religious Zionists participated in power-sharing arrangements in the voluntary institutions of the Jewish community. Following virulent confrontations over issues such as education, a tradition of compromise began to develop, exhibited by the creation of dual educational institutions, one secular and one religious. As Gutmann wrote:

> There is a very deep understanding between the leadership of the two camps, which are constantly exposed to pressure from their supporters who demand a less compromising policy and who exhibit less understanding of the necessity, which need not be condemned, for reaching compromises as the price of enjoying the fruits of government.[12]

Eliezer Don-Yehiya goes a step further, pointing to two motivating factors for the socialists in establishing the historical partnership:

> First, there is a recognition of the need to grant both expression and representation to the 'religious sub-culture'. Second, there is a tendency to overcome the divisive potential concerning the different outlooks on religion by negotiation and compromise with the political elite of the religious camp.[13]

This pattern carried over to the British Mandate period between the two world wars and into the first thirty years of Israel's independence. The partnership was based on a coalition between the main socialist party and the main religious Zionist party, even when the latter was not needed. Thus, the religious Zionists participated continuously in government, except for very brief interludes. Explicit elite arrangements backed this coalition, such as the proportionate division of jobs and other benefits.

The relationship between the socialist leadership and the religious non-Zionists, is based on a letter that became known as the status quo agreement. In June 1947, the socialist leadership of the Jewish community attempted to reach out to the religious non-Zionist leaders, prior to the arrival of the United Nations' Special Committee on Palestine (UNSCOP), in order to unite behind the goal of establishing a Jewish State. A letter was sent offering a number of promises with respect to public control of religious matters, attempting to assure the leadership of the religious non-Zionists that the principle arrangements regarding religion–state relations would be maintained in the newly-established state – hence the term status quo, which has come to identify this letter and its resulting accommodation.[14] The status quo became the principle for co-operation between these two elites and later served as the basis of the resolution of religious questions that arose. Moreover, these principles had already been accepted by both sides prior to the issuing of the letter and hence the status quo was an affirmation of what had become accepted by the two elites and a confirmation between them of what would continue. The status quo was, therefore, a dynamic solution, its provisions changing according to alternations in the balance of power and to new circumstances. In short, it was a pragmatic resolution of religious–secular tensions that facilitated and fostered elite accommodation.

The two dominant sub-cultures in Israel, in the pre- and immediate post-independence period, thus exhibited the three main elements of consociationalism, similar to the smaller European countries. Furthermore, the specific factors and facilitating conditions of consociationalism concerning the elites of the sub-cultures, as developed by its major theorist, Arend Lijphart, were also present in Israel at that period. The socialist and the religious elites had the capacity to accommodate the divergent interests and demands of their sub-cultures, the ability to transcend cleavages and co-operate with the rival sub-culture, a commitment to the cohesion and stability of the system and an understanding of the perils of fragmentation. The result was that religious affairs were dealt with at the elite level through alliances among the political parties. As Gabriel Sheffer argues:

> Maintaining political unity in the face of enormous policy problems could only be accomplished – given the ideological cleavages within the society – by the use of elite bargaining and accommodation as the main instruments of policy formation. Through these processes Israel came to reflect the politics, political arrangements and policies of a full-fledged consociational democracy.[15]

This is in accordance with Lijphart's definition of consociational democracy as 'government by elite cartel designed to turn a democracy with a fragmented political culture into a stable democracy'.[16]

The deliberate joint effort by the elites to stabilize the system was later defined by Lijphart in terms of four characteristics: government by a grand coalition of all significant segments of the plural society; mutual veto as a protection of minority interests; proportionality in elections, appointments and allocations; and autonomy for each segment to run its internal affairs.[17] Once again, Israel initially exhibited all the characteristics of consociationalism.

Governing coalitions in Israel have rarely been grand coalitions, but they also have rarely been minimum winning ones, especially during the first two decades of Israel's independence.

As Table 1 shows, an overwhelming majority of the governing coalitions between 1949 and 1967 included more than 61 of the 120 MKs (Members of Knesset). Moreover, of the only two coalitions that approached this majority threshold, the third government coalition

TABLE 1
GOVERNING COALITIONS IN ISRAEL, 1949–67

Knesset	Government Coalitions	Years	Number of MKs in Coalition	Number of Religious MKs in Coalition	Religious Balancing Position
I	1–2	1949–51	73	16	Yes
II	3	1951–52	65	15	Yes
	4–5	1952–55	84	10	No
	6	1955–55	63	10	Yes
III	7–8	1955–59	80	11	No
IV	9	1959–61	86	12	No
V	10–12	1961–66	68	14	Yes
VI	13	1966–67	75	13	No

lasted for only 14 months and included parties above the minimum winning requirement, while the sixth government coalition was truly a minimum winning coalition but lasted for less than five months. In other words, minimum winning coalitions existed in Israel for only four months out of the first 18 years, or just slightly less than two per cent of the time. In short, while grand coalitions are rare in Israel, the inclusion of parties – specifically religious ones – above and beyond the minimum winning requirement is not only common but actually prevalent. As long as the Labour Party was dominant, the 'historical partnership' with the NRP (National Religious Party) was stable, even though Labour could have often formed a governing coalition without the latter's support. Therefore, as Don-Yehiya pointed out:

> The almost permanent participation of the NRP in governmental coalitions was not due to arithmetic considerations of coalition formation. Rather, it reflected the application of the consociational model in Israel to the management of religious conflicts.[18]

The Israeli system allowed mutual veto rights through what became known as the status quo agreement. The acceptance of this framework by the diverging sides enabled the political system to dodge crises by solving or shelving explosive and controversial issues. That is, the status quo principle, based on the explicit or implicit consent of the parties involved, was used to maintain and preserve political agreements by granting either side veto power to block any changes in the existing framework that involved vital sub-cultural interests. Therefore, neither side could force a controversial decision on the other, even if it was backed by a majority in power. The maintenance of such a fluid solution was based on the fact that both sides perceived it to be more important to continue the ongoing process, than to gain a specific advantage on a particular issue. The most blatant manifestation of mutual veto can be found in the lack of a written constitution in Israel. Despite the fact that Israel's Declaration of Independence states that the soon-to-be-elected constituent assembly would enact a constitution, its first piece of legislation was to transform itself into a regularly-elected legislature and thereby to relegate its constitution-making function to a lower level of importance. This step was due mainly to the fundamental conflict over the source of legitimacy of such a document in the newly-established Jewish State: on the one hand, popular sovereignty; and on the other, theological principles. The religious parties have always opposed enacting a constitution that would abrogate the special role played by religion in Israel, rejecting the likely separation of religion and state that would be embodied in the constitution; and due to their possession of veto rights, they have kept Israel in the small category of democratic states – along with Britain and New Zealand – that do not have a formal, written constitution.[19]

A proportional system of representation, of appointment to public positions and of allocation of public funds were all present in Israel. The electoral system, which had a rather meaningless threshold set at only one per cent, with the entire country serving as one constituency, was tied with that of The Netherlands – one of the archetypes of consociationalism – in terms of extreme proportionality. The same kind of electoral system had been utilized before independence for various voluntary organizations, as well as after independence for various quasi-governmental institutions and agencies. The proportionality principle was also applied among the sub-cultures in other spheres, such as the allocation of ministries, patronage, the allotment of financial resources, access to state lands, etc. This method of proportionality, a highly refined version of *proportz* known in Israel as the 'party key', distributed public goods and benefits according to the relative strengths of the parties. In other words, proportionality was extended beyond the electoral system and applied to the method of public allocation in general.

Segmental autonomy was, in practical terms, granted to the religious sub-culture with regard to the internal management of its affairs. The severe conflict potential of the secular–religious cleavage was abated by the acceptance of the autonomy principle, for both the religious Zionist and religious non-Zionist camps. For example, one of the most volatile conflicts was over the control of education – similar to the history of Europe – which, in accordance with the autonomy principle, resulted in the creation of two state school systems, one secular and one religious (for the religious Zionists), as well as a third, state-funded, independent religious school system (for the religious non-Zionists). Similar autonomous compromises extend to an entire network of religious institutions, including even a separate court system. Moreover, the state also granted additional autonomy concerning particularistic issues for the religious sub-culture, such as the exemption of religious women and male theological students from compulsory military service.

Galnoor summarized the existence of these four characteristics of consociationalism in Israel:

> The religious parties were the main beneficiaries of these arrangements. The proportional system allowed them to retain approximately 13 per cent in all centers of power. They enjoyed effective veto power on core religious issues, thus the political struggle was over questions on the margins of the status quo. The religious camp enjoyed a high degree of autonomous control over such institutions as the chief rabbinate, the ministry of religious affairs and the local religious councils. The inclusion of the religious parties, particularly the NRP, was the main reason why government coalitions in Israel were usually not 'minimum winning coalitions'.[20]

Furthermore, several of Lijphart's favourable conditions for consociationalism, which are conducive to elite co-operation and stable non-elite support, were exhibited by Israel in that period:[21] a multiple balance of power, based on three main segments, with the largest short of a majority; the small size of the country and the serious external threats to its existence; the multi-party nature of Israel's party system; strong overarching loyalties producing a commitment to the survival of both Judaism and Israel; distinct lines of cleavages and segmental isolation, mainly of the orthodox religious sub-culture; and a prior tradition of elite accommodation developed during the Zionist movement and expanded in the pre-state period. All of these conditions led Lijphart to conclude that: 'Israel fulfils almost all of the conditions that are conducive to consociational democracy; in fact these are so strongly favourable that they should have been able to sustain a much higher degree of consociationalism than has actually been developed'.[22]

THE DISSOLUTION OF CONSOCIATIONALISM: THE RISE OF CONSENSUALISM

Consociationalism declined in Israel not because it failed, but more precisely because it succeeded. Two extremely divergent sub-cultures, mutually exclusive in virtually every aspect, were able to co-operate and overcome their segmentation due to elite accommodation and the utilisation of characteristically accommodationist mechanisms. Here, too, Israel resembles European patterns, as seen in the success and subsequent decline of segmental pluralism in The Netherlands.[23] The major reason for the demise of the consociational model in Israel is the fact that the newly-established state authorities took over many of the functions once performed by the sub-cultural voluntary organizations.

More precisely, the leadership and sub-cultural institutions of the main secular socialist camp became the official state leaders and agencies when independence was achieved, while the religious sub-culture remained relatively intact, but became financially dependent on the state.

Therefore, while it was still important to maintain the illusion of consensus as much as possible in the new state, segmental autonomy was reduced to one particular sub-culture – a minority religious camp – while the dominant sub-culture slowly gave way to statehood. This change did not occur overnight, but was a gradual process over many years. Nonetheless, the more stringent requirements of consociation- alism, which according to Lijphart 'demands segmental autonomy',[24] could no longer be met. Moreover, as the new state began to emphasize formal–institutional devices, instead of the informal practices of the previous period, consociationalism began to give way to consensualism, the former being a 'stronger form' of the latter.[25]

Consensus democracy, much like consociationalism, aims to restrain majority rule by sharing, dispersing and limiting political power. It is defined by Lijphart based on two separate dimensions, the executive–parties dimension and the federal–unitary dimension.[26] Israel's position in the top left-hand corner of Figure 1 means that it was highly consensual on the first dimension – approximately as consensual as Switzerland and The Netherlands – but quite the opposite on the second dimension.

The executive–parties dimension is made up of five variables. The first variable, executive power-sharing, is measured by the percentage of minimal winning coalitions. The lower this percentage is, the higher the level of executive power-sharing. In Israel's first two decades, between 1949 and 1967, the percentage of time that minimal winning coalitions existed was less than two per cent. Executive–legislative balance, the second variable, is measured by cabinet durability, in months. Israel's average for the first 20 years was 28. The existence of a multi-party system, the third variable, is verified according to the 'effective number of parties',[27] which was above five in Israel for that period. The fourth variable, a multi-dimensional party system, is assessed according to the number of issue dimensions, which in Israel included not only the socio-economic but also the religious and the foreign policy dimensions. The last variable of the executive–parties dimension, proportional representation, is measured according to electoral disproportionality, which in Israel was the lowest of any country, surpassed only by The Netherlands since 1956. The results of these five variables identified Israel as highly consensual. Table 2 presents a comparison between Israel's scores and those of one of the most outstanding case of consensualism, Switzerland and also those of the average of 25 democracies.

FIGURE 1

TWENTY-FIVE DEMOCRATIC REGIMES PLOTTED ON THE TWO
CONSENSUAL-MAJORITARIAN DIMENSIONS

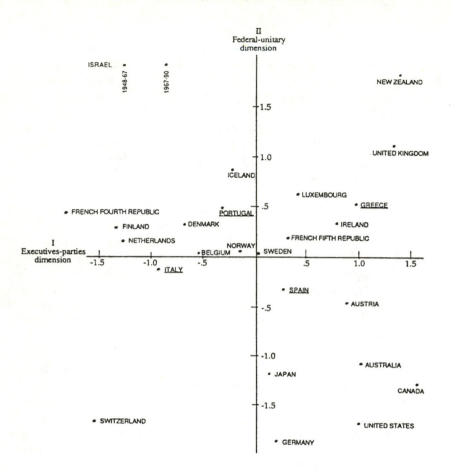

Source: Lijphart, 'Israeli Democracy and Democratic Reform in Comparative Perspective',
        p.108.

TABLE 2

EXECUTIVE-PARTIES DIMENSION VARIABLES

	Israel	Switzerland	Average
executive power-sharing	2	0	68
executive-legislative balance	28	30	52
multiparty system	5.1	5.0	3.3
multidimensional party system	2.5	3.0	2.6
proportional representation	0.8	1.5	3.9

Source: Elaborated from Lijphart, 'Israeli Democracy and Democratic Reform in Comparative Perspective', pp. 111, 118.[28]

The federal–unitary dimension has three variables and presents a problem for Israel, because on all three variables it ranks as non-consensual. On the first variable, federal and decentralized government, which is measured by the government's share of total tax receipts, Israel ranks at 96 per cent. Strong bicameralism, the second dimension, which is measured on a five-point scale, places Israel on the edge due to its unicameral parliament. The last variable, a written and rigid constitution, which is measured on a four-point scale, places Israel close to the end because it lacks a written constitution. Table 3 shows the contrast between Israel's position and that of consensual Switzerland and the average of 25 democracies.

TABLE 3

FEDERAL-UNITARY DIMENSION VARIABLES

	Israel	Switzerland	Average
federal and decentralized government	96	41	78
strong bicameralism	5.0	0.0	2.4
written and rigid constitution	3.0	1.0	0.9

Source: Elaborated from Lijphart, 'Israeli Democracy and Democratic Reform in Comparative Perspective', pp. 111, 118.[29]

Two of these three measures, it could be argued, misrepresent the Israeli case. The first neglects to reflect informal decentralisation, which takes such forms as official recognition and subsidisation of private religious associations and has been called a 'quasi-federalist' aspect of Israeli society.[30] The third variable does not recognize the existence of several 'Basic Laws' that are the building-blocks of an ongoing constitution-making process in Israel, some of which are quite difficult to amend due to the requirement of a special majority. Moreover, Lijphart himself gave the best reason for discounting this entire second dimension, when he concluded that countries such as Belgium, The Netherlands,

Luxembourg and Israel, which are 'characterized by non-territorial autonomy... should not be expected to be consensual on Dimension II'.[31]

In conclusion, the dissolution of consociationalism in Israel and its replacement by consensualism, was due to the establishment of legitimate state authorities – which were based on the agencies of the dominant sub-culture – and the continued opening up of the system with time. As the dominant sub-culture converted into a pluralist state, the distance between it and the rest of the secular society diminished, while the minority religious sub-culture continued to distance itself from Israeli society. During this period, consociational practices were sustained, but the infrastructure for consociationalism ceased to exist. The result was a 'less strong' form of consociationalism, namely consensualism, which began to manifest itself in Israel in the 1950s and expanded with time. The main players were still the dominant socialist secular party and the religious Zionist and non-Zionist parties. Moreover, the 'historical partnership' between the socialists and the religious Zionists continued throughout this period. Thus, despite the retraction of segmental isolationism into one sub-culture, the characteristics of mutual veto, proportionality and autonomy continued to function. Perhaps this is why those who have written about consociationalism in Israel prefer to call it a semi- or quasi-consociational democracy. However, a more appropriate terminology for this second period would be consensualism.

Since the attributes of consensualism began to appear in the years immediately after independence and some persist until today, this 'transitional' phase of consensus politics covers the overwhelming majority of Israel's existence as a state. It was preceded by a period of consociationalism, which identified the pre- and immediate post-independence period and is currently being supplanted by elements of majoritarianism.

THE DECLINE OF CONSENSUALISM: THE ADVENT OF MAJORITARIANISM

Majoritarian politics appeared in Israel for four main reasons: (i) the Six Day War and its territorial consequences (ii) the appearance of a two-bloc party system that altered party relations and systemic mechanics; (iii) changes within the religious sub-culture; and (iv) a new electoral reform law that transformed the entire regime. These changes extend over a period of 32 years, from 1967 to 1999, thus representing a gradual shift toward majoritarianism and away from consensus politics. This shift is by no means over and Israel cannot yet be termed majoritarian, but it has taken significant steps away from consensualism and towards majoritarianism.

The 1967 Six Day War reopened the ideological debate, which had been either frozen or accommodated, on the goals of Zionism and the ways and means to obtain them. The quick victory by Israel, despite the massive forces allied against it, was perceived by certain elements of the religious camp as 'miraculous'. The territories captured during the war were considered by many on the right-wing of Israeli politics to be a much awaited correction of the dismal border situation since independence. Zionism, which some perceived to be manifested by Jewish settlement in the entire Land of Israel, now had a new opportunity for expansion. The result was the emergence of a new cleavage in Israeli politics, focused on the territories, where the left (minimalist Zionists) became identified as those willing to exchange captured territories for peace and the right (maximalist Zionists) as those unwilling to part with them. This new cleavage would soon become the dominant dimension of party competition in Israel.[32]

The dominance of one camp for almost thirty years and specifically one party within that camp, characterized the Israeli party system, which resembled the Italian one of the same period. However, unlike its Italian counterpart, Israel's one-party dominance ended already in the 1970s. The first election results after the 1967 Six Day War showed the gap between the two opposing camps narrowing significantly and within less than a decade it would reach parity, ending the dominance of the socialist camp forever. As Figure 2 illustrates, elections began to result in two parties equal in size – Labour and Likud – though both were short of a majority.

FIGURE 2

SEAT PERCENTAGE OF LABOUR AND LIKUD COMPONENTS,
KNESSET ELECTIONS, 1949–1996

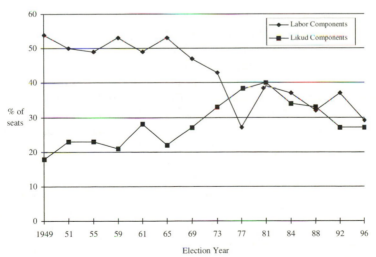

The Israeli party system thus shifted to a competitive bipolar structure, leaving the centrally-located religious parties as the brokers of political power. The 'historical partnership' came to an end, since the religious parties were now able to grant either side the necessary majority to form a coalition. While the two major parties competed ferociously for the support of the smaller religious parties, these, in turn, successfully played one off against the other – and not only demanded a much higher fee for their inclusion, but continuously threatened to bring down the government while constantly increasing their demands.

Within the religious camp itself, a metamorphosis took place. The religious Zionist party (NRP) which had dominated the religious camp until then began to decline. Simultaneously, it became involved with non-religious aspects of Israel's political life; and as its younger leadership took over the party, it became more closely associated with those opposed to territorial concessions – the right wing in Israel. The NRP also became more extremist concerning religious matters and more militant in its demands concerning these issues.[33] At the same time, the religious non-Zionists began to take positions on non-religious issues, as well. Although not as dramatically as their Zionists counterparts, they, too, moved to the right and adopted nationalistic principles. The result was a closing of the gap between the two types of religious parties. As Charles Liebman argued, the religious extremists became more nationalized, while the religious nationalists became more extremist.[34] However, unlike the religious Zionists, the religious non-Zionists increased their representation, which served to exacerbate the tensions surrounding religious issues. Shas, an orthodox ethnic party that appeared in the 1980s, also broke the isolationist political practices of the religious non-Zionists and has participated not only in the coalition but in government as well, thus raising both the influence and the visibility of ultra-orthodox religious elements in Israeli politics.

As previous political partnerships and arrangements collapsed, even the status quo agreements were reopened for debate and conflict. The result was that fragile coalition agreements became the norm and minimal winning coalitions became more frequent. Religious confrontation started to become more closely linked both to ethnic cleavages and to the dominant division over the future of the territories. Because of the extreme demands made by some of the religious parties in the mid-1980s, the two big parties reached a point where they could no longer enter into a coalition with such parties, due to the backlash expected from the secular electorate. This produced a period of 'national unity' governments, from 1984 through 1990. Unlike the grand coalition governments of the consociational model in Europe, these were 'last ditch' efforts to maintain a system that had already passed the point of instability. Since 1967, therefore, coalition governments in Israel have been either too small or too large. By the end of the 1980s, it was apparent to all concerned that the system was in need of reform.

On the heels of these developments, in 1992, the Knesset enacted a new 'Basic Law: The Government', which provides Israel with the distinction of being the only country to have direct popular election of its Prime Minister (beginning with the 1996 election). This new Basic Law not only effectively altered the electoral system, but also changed the entire political system in Israel.[35] The tenure of the Prime Minister is concurrent with that of the Knesset and they are elected simultaneously. The Prime Minister is elected according to the two-ballot system, requiring an absolute majority of the voters.[36] Moreover, the parliament can oust the Prime Minister by a vote of no-confidence, which requires only a bare majority of 61 of its 120 members. The removal of the Prime Minister brings about the dissolution of the Knesset as well, meaning that new elections will be necessary for both. In short, the electoral and political reforms appear to have decidedly shifted Israel towards a majoritarian form of democracy, both by the way its Prime Minister must be elected and by the requirements for maintaining the Prime Minister in, or removing him from, power.

The need to win an absolute majority of the vote in order to win the first directly-elected prime ministerial race in 1996 forced the two major parties – whose candidates were the only ones running – to woo the religious voters. However, by 1996, the religious sub-culture had moved largely to the right, adopting a clear position on the predominant secular issue over which the campaign was waged – the peace process. The result was that most of the religious parties openly backed the candidate of the right and campaigned for him. Surveys show that over 90 per cent of the religious voters cast their ballot for Prime Minister for Netanyahu.[37] Benjamin Netanyahu's victory, with 50.5 per cent of the vote, shows that: (i) Israeli society is divided into two equal camps; (ii) the religious sub-culture clearly belongs to one of these camps; and (iii) the majoritarian electoral system serves only to strengthen the two previous factors. That is, the adoption of majoritarian elections produced a clear winner and in the process made the social division both apparent and measurable. Moreover, majoritarian elections forced the religious camp to take sides – as opposed to the previous proportional electoral system, which had managed to maintain a semblance of consensualism by allowing the religious parties to play a pivotal role in a party system lacking a clear winner. Cohen and Susser state,

> As became clearly visible in the 1996 elections, the fault line dividing political 'hawks' and 'doves' is more or less identical with the line dividing the religious from the secular. Both the national religious [Zionists] and the Ultra-Orthodox [non-Zionists]

communities have come down in massive numbers on the hawkish side of the divide It is indeed paradoxical that the religious parties, once the main beneficiaries of consociational accommodation, are today – especially after the 1996 elections – adopting a majoritarian politics of decision and outright victory.[38]

The electoral reform thus pushed the religious bloc to openly side with the right wing in Israel, a natural alliance in light of its voters' positions on most issues, but one that would deprive it of a pivotal role in Israeli politics and exacerbate already enflamed domestic tensions. Indeed, already prior to the 1996 elections, public opinion polls showed that 36 per cent of the population thought that progress in the peace process would increase secular–religious conflicts, while only 11 per cent thought it would lessen this friction.[39] By 1998, opinion polls showed that conflicts within Israeli society were thought to be much more dangerous (60 per cent) than foreign conflicts with, for example, the Palestinians (30 per cent). Of the domestic conflicts, the religious–secular one was ranked first (63 per cent), followed by hawkish–dovish (22 per cent), ethnicity (three per cent) and economic gaps (two per cent). However, this does not necessarily mean that religious tensions were three times more important than the peace process, but that the 'first conflict dimension already encompasses, to a large extent, the second one as well'.[40]

The religious–secular cleavage in Israel thus came to practically overlap with the hawkish–dovish dimension. As Shamir and Arian stated, 'Religion has become closely intertwined with nationalism, especially since 1967'.[41] Throughout the 1990s, particularly after the signing of the Oslo agreements, public opinion polls exhibited this pattern on several issues related to the peace process. The strongest opposition to the peace process was expressed by the ultra-orthodox respondents. Only 20 per cent among the ultra-orthodox supported the peace process, while the supporters among the orthodox group were double that, 43 per cent and among the traditional and secular groups it was double that again, 80 per cent. Of the opponents of the peace process, only eight per cent expressed this opinion in the secular and nine per cent in the traditional groups, while 45 per cent of orthodox Jews opposed the peace process, as did 54 per cent of the ultra-orthodox. These results led the survey team to report that:

> Contrary to the widely-held belief that the ultra-orthodox public is relatively moderate in its opinion on foreign and defense affairs ... this public, in effect, is very hawkish indeed with regard to all aspects of the peace process ... These findings support the claim ... to the effect that the secular–religious and dovish–hawkish rifts are, to a great extent, superimposed. It would seem that this overlapping

deepens the rift between the camps and lessens the chance of coming up with a feasible political formula that could bridge the gap between them and help to mobilize continued nationwide support for the process.[42]

In a later survey, when other cleavages were added (such as ethnicity or income levels), the religiosity of the respondent remained the most significant and driving factor in explaining the respondent's opposition to the peace process.[43] When asked to classify themselves as right, left or centre, 100 per cent of the ultra-orthodox placed themselves on the right, while 81 per cent of the orthodox, 50 per cent of the traditional and only 20 per cent of the secular Jews did so.[44]

After Netanyahu's election and subsequent meetings with Arafat, it was the religious voters who wanted to harden Israel's position more than any other sector. 85 per cent of Yahadut HaTorah voters, 88 per cent of Shas voters and 89 per cent of NRP voters wanted the new government to take a harsher position on the peace process, while only 75 per cent of Likud voters supported this position.[45] Opposition to an independent Palestinian state can be found in 92 per cent of the ultra-orthodox community, 81 per cent of the orthodox, 71 per cent of the traditionalist and 58 per cent of the secular Jews. A compromise on Jerusalem is opposed by 84 per cent of the ultra-orthodox, 74 per cent of the orthodox, 58 per cent of traditional and 49 per cent of secular Jews.[46] The Wye River Accord, signed in October 1998, was supported by 76 per cent of the secular Jews, 69 per cent of the traditionalists, 45 per cent of the orthodox and only 33 per cent of the ultra-orthodox.[47]

The religious–secular cleavage expresses itself not only on the peace process, but on issues of Israeli democracy and the rule of law as well. For example, after the ultra-orthodox community organized a mass rally against the High Court of Justice (Israel's Supreme Court, which acts as the highest instance of appeal), polls showed that 89 per cent of secular Jews and 78 per cent of traditional Jews thought that the ultra-orthodox claims were unjustified. Of orthodox and ultra-orthodox Jews, on the other hand, 60 per cent and 100 per cent, respectively, thought that the assertions were justified. Moreover, 88 per cent of secular Jews and 70 per cent of the traditional Jews thought that religious influence was too strong, while 74 per cent of the orthodox Jews and 65 per cent of the ultra-orthodox Jews thought it was either appropriate or rather weak.[48] Surveys also show that the ultra-orthodox public is more supportive of violent opposition to governmental decisions (14 per cent) than other sectors (seven per cent of orthodox, six per cent of traditional and four per cent of secular Jews).[49]

The significance of these surveys, coupled with the majoritarian electoral system adopted in Israel, can be seen both in the election results and in a survey conducted after Netanyahu's defeat. The election

FIGURE 3

RELIGIOUS OBSERVANCE AND VOTING FOR PRIME MINISTER, 1999

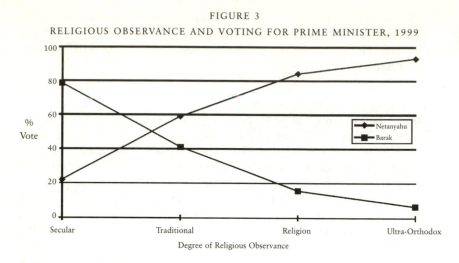

Degree of Religious Observance

Source: Dahaf poll, 19 June 1999.

results show a clear, practically linear, relationship between voting for the prime ministerial candidate of either the right or the left and the degree of religious observance, as depicted in Figure 3.

After the 1999 elections, a survey showed that 68 per cent thought the elections had either kept the country divided as it was before, or actually made it worse.[50] However, in the post-election atmosphere, there was also much optimism on all fronts, except for one. A larger percentage thought that the peace process, the economy, relations between society and government and left-right tensions would improve. The only area in which the population expressed pessimism – exhibited by a larger percentage thinking that the situation would continue to worsen rather than improve – was the religious–secular cleavage.[51]

Indeed, Ehud Barak's 1999 campaign, unlike Shimon Peres' in 1996, did little to attract the religious vote. Other than the inclusion of the moderate orthodox Meimad in the One Israel list headed by Labour, Barak seemed to have discounted the religious vote from the outset. His campaign promises focused on reducing the financial benefits allotted to the ultra-orthodox, in exchange for a more egalitarian distribution and the drafting of Yeshiva students into the military.

The almost latent – at least in the 1990s – ethnic cleavage also erupted in 1999. The virulent campaign of the Russian immigrant Yisrael B'aliyah party, targeted at Shas and the rise of the anti-ultra-orthodox Shinui party, both served to rally the secular Ashkenazi Jews, whether native or immigrant, against the ultra-orthodox Sephardis. The close alliance between Shas and Netanyahu throughout the 1999 campaign, despite the conviction of Shas' political leader, drove the Russian immigrant voters – who had supported Netanyahu in 1996 – toward the left in record numbers. In other words, the majoritarian electoral system, in only its second implementation, seems to have had a coalescing effect on many of the major cleavages in Israeli society. However, this coalescence is not toward accommodation and compromise, but rather in the direction of dividing the country into two groups based on almost overlapping cleavages.

According to Lijphart, the conditions for majoritarian democracy are precisely the inverse of those that identify consensual democracy; and a shift away from consensualism can be seen in every variable in contemporary Israel. Executive power has become more concentrated, as exhibited by the increase of both minimal winning and 'last ditch' grand coalitions. After both the 1984 and 1988 elections, the exorbitant demands of the religious parties made even a minimal winning coalition practically impossible, even though Labour and Likud were in a dead heat. The resulting grand coalitions were thus not a sign of executive power-sharing between sub-cultures, but rather an attempt by the two major secular parties to co-operate in order to concentrate executive power and diminish the influence of the religious sub-culture. When this arrangement ceased to function, the resulting coalitions in 1990 and 1992 were both minimum winning coalitions. From 1993, however, the government was a minority coalition – a new phenomenon in Israeli politics – with the outside support of the Arab parties, resulting in a minimum winning parliamentary 'bloc'. As Table 4 shows, the six years prior to the 1996 elections were characterized by minimum winning coalitions, or blocs and exhibited a sharp decrease in executive power-sharing.

In 1996, the Netanyahu government was not a minimum winning coalition, even though his victory with just 50.5 per cent is as close to a minimum winning result as possible. However, after the early departure of David Levy's Gesher party, the coalition became minimum winning. This helped bring it down prematurely and forced new elections in 1999. Barak's government, after his decisive victory, was based on 75 MKs, far beyond the minimum winning threshold.

Prior to the first implementation of the direct election of the Prime Minister in 1996, average cabinet durability in Israel, reflecting executive dominance, increased significantly to 38 months, an increase of over one-third compared to the pre-1967 period. Multi-partism, measured by the 'effective number of parties', declined from over five to less than four in the latter period. Multi-dimensionality, expressed by the number of issue dimensions in the party system, increased after 1967 with the rise of the security dimension. However, due to the growing involvement of the religious parties in non-religious politics, the

TABLE 4
GOVERNING COALITIONS IN ISRAEL, 1967–99

Knesset	Government Coalitions	Years	Number of MKs in Coalition	Number of MKs in Coalition	Religious Balancing Position
VI	1–2[a]	1967–69	108	13	No
VII	3	1969–74	101	12	No
VIII	4–5[b]	1974–77	65	10	Yes
IX	6	1977–81	77	16	No
X	7–8[c]	1981–84	67	13	Yes
XI	9–10[d]	1984–88	97	12	No
XII	11	1988–90	95	16	No
	12	1990–92	62	13	Yes
XIII	13	1992–95	62	6	Yes
	14[e]	1995–96	58	0	No
XIV	15	1996–99	66	23	Yes
XV	16	1999–	75	27	Yes

[a] The first government came to an end due to the death of the Prime Minister. The second government, headed by a Prime Minister from the same party as the previous government, was reconstituted with all of the same parties except for one minor party, and continued to function according to the guidelines of the previous government. The two governments, for the purpose of cabinet durability, are thus considered as one.

[b] The fourth government came to an end due to the resignation of the Prime Minister. The fifth government, headed by a Prime Minister from the same party as the previous government, was reconstituted with all of the same parties, including two minor additions. The two governments, for the purpose of cabinet durability, are thus considered as one.

[c] The seventh government came to an end due to the resignation of the Prime Minister. The eighth government, headed by a Prime Minister from the same party as the previous government, was reconstituted with all of the same parties. The two governments, for the purpose of cabinet durability, are thus considered as one.

[d] The grand coalition agreement included a rotation of the Prime Minister between the two major parties; the ninth and tenth governments were, therefore, based on the same parties. The two governments, for the purpose of cabinet durability, are thus considered as one.

[e] The fourteenth government was formed following the assassination of Prime Minister Rabin in November 1995, continuing a minority government based on the same two parties, which was in place since 1993, after the sole religious party split from the coalition. A small faction of two members that had joined in 1994 remained as well. This and the previous government, for the purpose of cabinet durability, are thus considered as one.

TABLE 5
EXECUTIVE-PARTIES DIMENSION VARIABLES IN ISRAEL

	1949–67	1967–95
executive power-sharing	2	18
executive-legislative balance	28	38
multiparty system	5.1	3.9
multidimensional party system	2.5	2.0
proportional representation	0.8	1.8

religious dimension came to practically overlap with the dominant security dimension. Simultaneously, a decline in the socio-economic dimension occurred. Proportional elections, of which Israel was an extreme example, are now relegated to the parliamentary elections alone. The overall shift is presented in Table 5.

The direct election of the Prime Minister – along with mayors and heads of local authorities – by majoritarian electoral methods has already had significant ramifications on all the variables associated with the executive-parties dimension. For example, the durability of the first directly elected Prime Minister was quite short, while multi-partism increased substantially, as did multi-dimensionality – the latter two aspects intensified further in the 1999 elections.[52] These results are, however, due more to the adoption of a majoritarian electoral reform that has missed its goals, rather than to a reversal of the majoritarian trend on the executive–parties dimension.

In short, while Israel has moved little on the federal–unitary dimension – where it already occupied a majoritarian position – it has changed its position significantly on the executive–parties dimension by moving away from extreme consensualism and towards majoritarianism.

It is interesting to note that Lijphart strongly recommended against any radical moves toward a majoritarian form of democracy in Israel, recognising that what was then a reform plan alone was indeed strongly majoritarian.[53] The electoral and political changes that were, none-theless, implemented induced the following changes in the executive: they introduced a majoritarian electoral system for the chief executive; they reduced the prime ministerial election to two candidates; they focused on one dominant issue dimension; they disengaged the executive from the legislature; and they concentrated executive power.[54] It appears as though Israel, in the late 1990s, is no longer interested in restraining majority rule by either sharing, dispersing or limiting political power.

CONCLUSION: THE DEMISE OF PARTIES IN ISRAEL?

In the span of about fifty years, the Israeli party system has evolved from one that aimed at precluding simple majoritarian decision-making in the pre- and immediate post-independence period, to one that is embracing majoritarianism. In the process, Israeli democracy has exhibited consociational practices, then consensual characteristics and was now manifesting majoritarian behaviour.

The political parties, which were the key co-ordinating factors during the first phase of consociationalism, saw their functions slightly reduced during the period of consensualism, but more recently are no longer able

to carry out their accommodating functions. As Israel has become a more
pluralistic and open society, social tensions have become less
'manageable' politically, the elitist nature of Israeli politics has weakened
and social cleavages are now finding different outlets within the political
system. The ability of the political leadership to make accommodative,
binding decisions has thus been adversely affected. As Galnoor stated,
'The inability of the parties to perform their mediating roles discreetly
contributes to political instability'.[55] In other words, the contemporary
Israeli political system exhibits a marked decline in the ability to produce
compromises. For example, in the previous periods, the participation of
the religious parties in the governing coalitions was perceived as an
accommodative and stabilising factor, whereas their more recent
inclusion has become a disruptive ingredient. Moreover, the religious
parties, in contrast to their earlier behaviour, are making a significant
effort to impose their doctrines on the majority and to advance issues of
principle rather than particular demands, which in the 1999 elections
created an electoral backlash from the secular community.

Furthermore, the erosion of the fundamental consensus in Israel on
many issues, including the meaning of Zionism and the demarcation of
the country's borders, has weakened the ability of the political system
even further in the production of functional coalitions based on
compromise and accommodation. Other branches of government have
already begun to fill the void – most prominently the judiciary,
intervening in what has until now been an exclusively political domain.
One must remember that judicial decisions are based on legal aspects of
right and wrong – not politically-produced compromises that are meant
to accommodate both sides – and thus are, in essence, zero-sum and can
be seen as contributing to the majoritarian trend of Israeli politics.

In conclusion, after its fiftieth anniversary, Israel finds its political
system having crossed the threshold toward majoritarianism. This
majoritarian trend in Israeli politics hides the consensual underpinnings
which still characterize the value structure of much of the Israeli
electorate, whose views are more shared than discrete.[56] Paradoxically,
as Israel embraces majoritarian methods, while discarding
consociational and consensual practices, the rise of religious issues to the
forefront comes at a time when the party system would have been much
better off had the accommodative patterns of the previous periods not
been swept away by social changes and electoral reforms. The transition
to majoritarianism can thus only serve to exacerbate and polarize the
imminent crisis in Israeli politics, which has been successfully
accommodated for generations.

NOTES

The author would like to thank the Jerusalem Van Leer Institute and the Volkswagen Foundation for their generous funding in support of this project.

1. B. Akzin, 'The Role of Parties in Israeli Democracy', *Journal of Politics*, Vol. 17, No. 4 (1955).
2. I. Galnoor, 'The Israeli Political System: A Profile', in K. Kyle and J. Peters (eds.), *Whither Israel? The Domestic Challenges*, New York: St. Martin's, 1994, p.92.
3. Arabs make up approximately 15 per cent of the Israeli population, and are the largest national minority in a state that is over 80 per cent Jewish. Within the Jewish population, the Ashkenazis dominated in numbers during the pre-state period, but after independence there began an influx of Sephardi Jews that slowly brought the ratio to its current state of near parity.
4. The concept of Israel as an ethnic democracy was first articulated by Smooha. For a recent overview of this concept see S. Smooha, 'Ethnic Democracy: Israel as an Archetype', *Israel Studies*, Vol. 2, No. 2 (1997). The term ethnocracy was elaborated by Yiftachel, partially as a critique of ethnic democracy. For an application of this concept see O. Yiftachel, 'Israeli Society and Jewish–Palestinian Reconciliation: "Ethnocracy" and its Territorial Contradictions', *Middle East Journal*, Vol. 51, No. 5 (1997). For an Arab perspective on Israel as an ethnic state see N. Rouhana, *Palestinian Citizens in an Ethnic Jewish State: Identities in Conflict*, New Haven: Yale University Press, 1997.
5. C. Liebman and E. Don-Yehiya, *Religion and Politics in Israel*, Bloomington: Indiana University Press, 1984.
6. D. Horowitz and M. Lissak, *Trouble in Utopia: The Overburdened Polity of Israel*, Albany: State University of New York Press, 1989, p.51.
7. It is interesting to note that the ultra-orthodox community votes in very high percentages, estimated at over 90 per cent, and does so largely in accordance with the decisions of their religious leaders. Furthermore, the members of the Council of Torah Sages represent the leadership of most of the ultra-orthodox sects, and a division between two important Rabbis can lead, and has led, to the creation of a new party and a split in the ultra-orthodox vote.
8. B. Neuberger, *Ha-Miflagot Be-Israel (Political Parties in Israel)*, Tel Aviv: Open University Press, 1991.
9. K. McRae, 'Introduction', in K. McRae (ed.), *Consociational Democracy: Political Accommodation in Segmented Societies*, Toronto: McClelland and Stewart, 1974, pp.5–13.
10. E. Gutmann, 'Religion and Its Role in National Integration in Israel', in M. Curtis (ed.), *Religion and Politics in the Middle East*, Boulder: Westview Press, 1981, p.203.
11. Indeed, Horowitz and Lissak contend that all of the pre-state politics need to be understood in consociational terms. In their subsequent study on the period of statehood, they claim that despite the abandonment of many of the consociational practices, religion and politics remain a striking exception, and are still governed by consociational mechanisms. See D. Horowitz and M. Lissak, *Origins of the Israeli Polity*, Chicago: University of Chicago Press, 1978; and *Trouble in Utopia*.
12. E. Gutmann, 'Religion in Israeli Politics – A Unifying and Dividing Factor', in M. Lissak and E. Gutmann (eds.), *Ha-maarechet Ha-politit Ha-Israelit (The Israeli Political System)*, Tel Aviv: Am Oved, 1979, p.410.
13. E. Don-Yehiya, 'Cooperation and Conflict between Political Camps: The Religious Camp and the Labor Movement and the Education Crisis in Israel', PhD Dissertation, Hebrew University of Jerusalem, 1977, p.271 (Hebrew).
14. The letter promised that the Sabbath would be set aside as a national day of rest; that dietary laws would be observed by all state institutions; that religious courts would maintain exclusive jurisdiction over personal status laws; and that the existing autonomous religious educational system would be recognized by the state.
15. G. Sheffer, 'Elite Cartel, Vertical Domination, and Grassroots Discontent in Israel', in S. Tarrow, P. Katzenstein and L. Graziano (eds.), *Territorial Politics in Industrial Nations*, New York: Praeger, 1978, p.68.
16. A. Lijphart, 'Consociational Democracy', *World Politics*, Vol. 21, No. 2 (1969), p.216.
17. A. Lijphart, *Democracy in Plural Societies: A Comparative Exploration*, New Haven: Yale University Press, 1977, pp.22–44.

18. E. Don-Yehiya, 'The Resolution of Religious Conflicts in Israel', in S. Cohen and E. Don-Yehiya (eds.), *Conflict and Consensus in Jewish Political Life*, Jerusalem: Bar-Ilan University Press, 1986, p.204. For a discussion on how the accommodative process in Israel actually rests on the structural features of the coalition system, see K. Paltiel, 'The Israeli Coalition Cystem', *Government and Opposition*, Vol. 10, No. 4 (1975).
19. For a fuller discussion, see E. Gutmann, 'Israel: Democracy without a Constitution', in V. Bogdanor (ed.), *Constitutions in Democratic Politics*, Aldershot: Gower 1988.
20. I. Galnoor, 'Israeli Democracy in Transition', in P. Medding (ed.), *Israel: State and Society, 1948–1988*, New York: Oxford University Press, 1989, p.139.
21. Lijphart, *Democracy in Plural Societies*, pp.53–103, 129–34.
22. Lijphart, *Democracy in Plural Societies*, p.132.
23. V. Lorwin, 'Segmented Pluralism: Ideological Cleavages and Political Cohesion in the Smaller European Democracies', *Comparative Politics*, Vol. 31, No. 2 (1971).
24. A. Lijphart, 'Democratic Political Systems: Types, Cases, Causes, and Consequences', *Journal of Theoretical Politics*, Vol. 1, No. 1 (1989), p.41.
25. A. Lijphart, 'Democracies: Forms, Performance, and Constitutional Engineering', *European Journal of Political Research*, Vol. 25, No. 1 (1994), p.3.
26. A. Lijphart, *Democracies: Patterns of Majoritarian and Consensus Government in Twenty-One Countries*, New Haven: Yale University Press, 1984.
27. M. Laakso and R. Taagepera, '"Effective" Number of Parties: A Measure with Application to West Europe', *Comparative Political Studies*, Vol. 12, No. 1 (1979).
28. Israel results cover 1949–67, Switzerland and Average cover 1945–1980. My measure for Israel differs from that presented by Lijphart for the first dimension.
29. Israel, Switzerland and Average results cover 1945–1980. My measure for Israel differs from that presented by Lijphart for the second dimension.
30. S. Eisenstadt, *Israeli Society*, London: Weidenfeld and Nicolson, 1967, p.410; L. Fein, *Politics in Israel*, Boston: Little Brown and Co., 1967, p.100; Paltiel, 'The Israeli Coalition System', p.405.
31. Lijphart, 'Democratic Political Systems', p.42.
32. M. Shamir and A. Arian, 'Collective Identity and Electoral Competition in Israel', *American Political Science Review*, Vol. 93, No. 2, (1999).
33. S. Sandler, 'The National Religious Party: Towards a New Role in Israel's Political System?' in S. Lehman-Wilzig and B. Susser (eds.), *Public Life in Israel and the Diaspora*, Jerusalem: Bar-Ilan University Press, 1981.
34. C. Liebman, 'Religion and Democracy in Israel', in E. Sprinzak and L. Diamond (eds.), *Israeli Democracy Under Stress*, Boulder: Lynne Rienner, 1993. This finding has recently received support by statistical analyses of voting patterns. See Shamir and Arian, 'Collective Identity and Electoral Competition in Israel'.
35. R. Hazan, 'Presidential Parliamentarism: Direct Popular Election of the Prime Minister, Israel's New Electoral and Political System', *Electoral Studies*, Vol. 15, No. 1 (1996).
36. A majority of the vote is necessary to elect the Prime Minister in the first round; if that is not obtained, then two weeks later a second round is held in which only the two candidates with the highest vote in the previous round can participate. The Knesset, however, continues to be elected by a fixed list system of proportional representation, with the entire state serving as one constituency and the legal electoral threshold set at only 1.5 per cent.
37. Survey conducted by A. Arian and M. Shamir, Israel Democracy Institute, May 1996.
38. A. Cohen and B. Susser, 'From Accommodation to Decision: Transformation in Israel's Religio-Political Life', *Journal of Church and State*, Vol. 38, No. 4 (1996), pp.817–839.
39. Survey conducted by the Tami Steinmetz Center for Peace Research, Tel-Aviv University, February 1995.
40. Survey conducted by the Tami Steinmetz Center for Peace Research, Tel-Aviv University, January 1998. Similar results were reported in the February 1999 survey.
41. Shamir and Arian, 'Collective Identity and Electoral Competition in Israel', p.271.
42. Survey conducted by the Tami Steinmetz Center for Peace Research, Tel-Aviv University, August 1997.
43. Survey conducted by the Tami Steinmetz Center for Peace Research, Tel-Aviv University, November 1997.
44. Survey conducted by the Tami Steinmetz Center for Peace Research, Tel-Aviv University, October 1997.

45. Survey conducted by the Tami Steinmetz Center for Peace Research, Tel-Aviv University, June 1996. Three months later, similar results were reported: 53 per cent of secular Jews thought the new government's positions were too harsh, while only 26 per cent of the religious and 10 per cent of the ultra-orthodox thought so (September 1996 survey).
46. Survey conducted by the Tami Steinmetz Center for Peace Research, Tel-Aviv University, January 1999.
47. Survey conducted by the Tami Steinmetz Center for Peace Research, Tel-Aviv University, October 1998.
48. Survey conducted by the Tami Steinmetz Center for Peace Research, Tel-Aviv University, February 1999.
49. Survey conducted by the Tami Steinmetz Center for Peace Research, Tel-Aviv University, December 1997.
50. Survey conducted by the Tami Steinmetz Center for Peace Research, Tel-Aviv University, May 1999.
51. Survey conducted by the Tami Steinmetz Center for Peace Research, Tel-Aviv University, May 1999.
52. R. Y. Hazan and A. Diskin, 'The 1999 Knesset and Prime Minister Elections in Israel', *Electoral Studies*, forthcoming.
53. A. Lijphart, 'Israeli Democracy and Democratic Reform in Comparative Perspective', in Sprinzak and Diamond, *Israeli Democracy Under Stress*.
54. R. Hazan, 'Executive–Legislative Relations in an Era of Accelerated Reform: Reshaping Government in Israel', *Legislative Studies Quarterly*, Vol. 22, No. 3 (1997).
55. Galnoor, 'The Israeli Political System', p.97.
56. Shamir and Arian, 'Collective Identity and Electoral Competition in Israel'.

PART III
PARTY SYSTEM CHANGE

Rethinking De Swaan (1973): A Note on Closed Coalitions, Uni-Dimensionality and the Role of Sectarian Political Parties

ABRAHAM DISKIN

Twenty-five years ago, in his famous book *Coalition Theories and Cabinet Formations*, Abram de Swaan empirically examined the applicability of different coalition theories in nine multi-party democracies.[1] De Swaan employed in his study a uni-dimensional ordinal scale on which he placed all relevant political parties in the systems examined. The object of this paper is to demonstrate that a slight modification of the uni-dimensional ordinal model considerably improves the predictive power of the 'closed coalition theory'.[2]

De Swaan summarizes his examination of the Israeli case as follows:

> Israel is a difficult country for the theories. Most of them score below their average over all countries. The closed coalition proposition performs best, the closed coalition version of policy distance theory comes second, but neither theory achieves a significant level (26 per cent and 31.7 per cent respectively).[3]

De Swaan examined 16 Israeli coalition formations. The political parties that did not fit the 'closed coalition proposition' are Agudat Israel (seven deviations), Rafi (a single deviation), and the 'State Party' (two deviations). One may claim that all three parties were artificially placed on De Swaan's Israeli uni-dimensional model.

Agudat Israel was the most extreme ultra-orthodox party in Israel. At the same time, it did hold middle-of-the-road positions on many issues. Both Rafi and the 'State Party', were led by David Ben-Gurion. Ben-Gurion, the first prime minister of the state of Israel, defected from his party, Mapai, in 1965 because of harsh differences with Levi Eshkol, who succeeded Ben-Gurion as prime minister and leader of Mapai. Due to these differences, and in spite of the proximity of his positions on

Abraham Diskin is the Chairman of the Israel Political Science Association.

most issues to Mapai's positions, Ben-Gurion could not join any governmental coalition headed by Eshkol.

The question that arises from the examination of the Israeli case is whether equivalent deviations of such 'irregular' political parties also reduce the applicability of the closed coalition theory in other cases.

The modeling of any reality causes a problematic conflict between two tendencies. On the one hand, one is interested in presenting as simple a model as possible. Simple models are more elegant. They draw the attention to the core of the reality examined. On the other hand, simple models often miss some elements. This weakness of simple models is quite obvious when one examines social problems. People and human organizations can never be fully represented by dots fixed in a uni-dimensional, or even in a multi-dimensional, space. The challenge of a social theorist is usually to present a complicated reality through the employment of a simple model without missing important features of that reality.

More than forty years ago, Downs[4] suggested in his *An Economic Theory of Democracy* a conservative–liberal single dimension as a proper representation of party systems in competitive Western democracies. Many criticized this representation, claiming that political cleavages are multi-dimensional and that the positioning of political parties on policy scales could never be accurate. Others, however, successfully demonstrated the power of left–right or liberal–conservative uni-dimensional models.

A majority of parties in most democracies can be placed on a single ideological spectrum without any major difficulty. Thus, in most West-European systems, a Communist Party would be placed left of a Socialist Party; Social Democrats would be placed right of Socialists; Liberals tend to be more centrist than Nationalists or Conservatives, etc. At the same time, Sartori[5] and a number of other scholars demonstrated that some political parties do not focus on issues associated with the 'regular' left–right policy scale, but rather on other issues. Such are religious political parties (Re), national-minority and ethnic-minority parties (M), 'special-issue' parties (SI, e.g., agrarian, anti-immigrants, 'economic', or green parties) and 'single-person' parties (SP, e.g., political parties established in order to promote an individual politician). Hereafter, we shall refer to such (Re, M, SP and SI) actors as 'sectarian' political parties. This article suggests that when sectarian parties are excluded from de Swaan's uni-dimensional models, almost all parliamentary coalitions do tend to be fully 'closed', in spite of the employment of a simple, uni-dimensional, ordinal scale.

It should be emphasized, however, that in the past only a minority of European political parties tended to be of a sectarian nature. Usually, the proportion of seats controlled by such parties was quite low. During the last few decades, a number of 'new-politics' sectarian parties have emerged.[6] In several West-European political systems, an opposite development took place: Sectarian political parties transformed into 'regular' ('left-right') parties. When such a development occurs, these parties should be included in the model. The latter phenomenon refers, for instance, to Centre Parties (formerly Agrarian Parties) in Scandinavian countries, and to the Zentrum in the Weimar Republic.[7]

De Swaan defined a 'closed coalition' as 'a coalition that contains actors whose positions on the policy scale are adjacent. A coalition that "skips" an actor along the policy scale is "open"'.[8]

Table 1 represents a hypothetical political system in which A, B, C and D are political parties that should be placed, in this order, on a single left-right dimension. S represents a sectarian political party that does not 'naturally' belong to the left-right continuum. Nevertheless, S is imposed on the model and placed between C and D. Either the participation or the non-participation of S in a parliamentary coalition can cause the 'openness' of a coalition, in spite of its basic 'closed' nature. This is depicted in Table 1 below. In this table, the word 'member' depicts the membership of an actor in a given coalition formation. In example 1 of this table, C is 'skipped over' because of the very inclusion of S in the uni-dimensional model and its participation in the coalition. In example 2, S itself is skipped over while the 'regular' parties to its left and right do participate in the coalition.

TABLE 1
'OPENNESS' OF COALITIONS CAUSED BY THE INCLUSION OF A SECTARIAN
PARTY IN A UNI-DIMENSIONAL POLICY SCALE

Example/Political Party:	A	B	C	S	D
example 1: participation of S	member	member		member	
example 2: non-participation of S		member	member		member

De Swaan examined in his book 203 coalition formations in the following political systems: the Weimar Republic; the French Fourth Republic; Italy; the Netherlands; Israel; Finland; Sweden; Denmark and Norway. The results of the original de Swaan uni-dimensional model and the modified 'excluding sectarian parties' model are depicted in Table 2. According to de-Swaan's original model, 24 per cent of the formations examined are not closed. The French Fourth Republic leads the list: 52 per cent of its parliamentary coalitions are open. A large proportion of open coalitions also existed in Weimar (45 per cent), Israel (44 per cent), Finland (25 per cent) and Norway (22 per cent). Only in four cases – the Netherlands (14 per cent), Sweden (12 per cent), Italy (seven per cent) and Denmark (five per cent) – was there a relatively small number of open formations.[9]

This picture, however, changes dramatically when the relatively few sectarian parties are excluded from the calculations. Under such a modification, only five (2.5 per cent) of the coalitions examined remain open. The Weimar exception in the modified model occurred when the Democrats were skipped over, while the SPD to their left and the Zentrum to their right participated in the initial Bauer coalition in June 1919. (The Democrats joined the Bauer coalition in July 1919). The two Italian exceptions were caused by the non-participation of the Republicans (PRI) in De Gasperi III – 1947, and De Gasperi V – 1947. (The PRI did participate in De Gasperi I, 1946. It did not regain representation in the 1948 elections.) One Finnish exception was caused by the Agrarian–Conservative coalition of Kallio II (December 1925). This coalition, which lasted for approximately one year, skipped over the Progressive Party (and the Swedish People's Party). Another Finnish deviation occurred when the large coalition of Fagerholm III (August 1958) skipped over the small, new 'Social Democratic League of Workers and Small Farmers'. It could be argued that even these few cases involved sectarian political parties. Furthermore, most of these exceptions took place only a very short period after the introduction of democracy to the systems examined.

The failure of the regular closed coalition model in Weimar was caused by the Bavarians (four cases), by the 'economic' Wirtschaftpartei (2.5 cases) and by the Agrarian–Conservative Land (1.5 cases) parties. The implementation of the regular model to the French Fourth Republic

TABLE 2

'OPEN' COALITIONS IN NINE MULTI-PARTY DEMOCRACIES EXAMINED BY DE SWAAN

Case	Period	Number of coalitions examined	Number (%) of open coalitions	Number (%) of open coalitions when sectarian parties are excluded
Germany	1919-1930	20	9 (45%)	1 (5%)
France	1945-1957	21	11 (52%)	0 (0%)
Italy	1946-1972	28	2 (7%)	2 (7%)
Netherlands	1918-1973	22	3 (14%)	0 (0%)
Israel	1949-1970	16	7 (44%)	0 (0%)
Finland	1919-1972	48	12 (25%)	2 (4%)
Sweden	1917-1969	17	2 (12%)	0 (0%)
Denmark	1918-1971	22	1 (5%)	0 (0%)
Norway	1933-1971	9	2 (22%)	0 (0%)
Total		203	49 (24%)	5 (2.5%)

failed in most cases because of the inclination of Gaullist-oriented parties not to participate in parliamentary coalitions. In one case (Borges Mannoury – 1957), the Catholics were skipped over, but they continued to support minority government through abstention. In another semi-open case (Mollet 1956), the Catholics supported the coalition in parliament despite their non-participation.

In both the Netherlands and Israel, all open coalitions were caused by the non-participation of religious parties (the Protestant Dutch ARP and the ultra-orthodox Aguda in Israel). In three of the Israeli cases, splinter, short-lived parties led by Ben-Gurion (Rafi and the State Party) shared responsibility for 'openness' with the religious Aguda.

Three of the deviations in Finland were caused by non-participation of the Swedish People's Party in governmental coalitions. Conversely, in seven other cases, the Swedish People's Party caused openness by its participation. The two Swedish deviations from the regular uni-dimensional model were caused by non-participation of the Agrarian Party long before it became a Center Party (Eden – 1917 and Branting III – 1924). Most governmental coalitions in Denmark tended to be very small and very stable. In 1957, the Hansen/Kampmann minimal winning coalition skipped over the traditional right-wing parties when the Social Democrats and the Radicals joined forces with the 'Single-Tax' Justice Party (a typical SI and SP party). The two Norwegian deviations were caused by the Social Democrats–Agrarian coalitions of Nygardsvold–1935 and Nygardsvold–1936, which left the Liberals in opposition. This is so because de Swaan placed the Liberals between the Agrarians and the Social Democrats. The nature of the sectarian parties that caused openness in the de Swaan study is summarized in Table 3 below.

It could be argued that the diverse nature of the relatively few, and usually weak, sectarian parties does not justify the employment of more than one dimension on the regular policy scale. It should be noted,

TABLE 3

THE NATURE OF SECTARIAN PARTIES IN OPEN COALITIONS
(DE SWANN MODEL)

Case	Re	M	SI	SP
Germany			Bavarians Wirtschaftp. (Land)	
France	Catholics			Gaullists
Italy				
Netherlands	Protestants			
Israel	Agudat Israel			Rafi/State Party
Finland		Swedish PP		
Sweden			Agrarian Party	
Denmark			(Justice Party)	(Justice Party)
Norway			Agrarian Party	

however, that sectarian parties can be placed on 'rays' connected to the pivotal (median) point of the 'regular' uni-dimensional model. The connection of sectarian parties to the centre makes sense for three reasons: A. Sectarian parties frequently do not have any position on 'regular' political issues; B. Pivotal parties may prefer the inclusion of sectarian parties in governmental coalitions because they leave greater 'maneuvering space'; C. In several cases, sectarian parties transformed into 'centre'-pivotal parties.

In some cases, several parties can be placed on the same 'ray'. The latter can be demonstrated by the three Israeli religious parties during the period 1949–1967. The National Religious Party (Mafdal) was considered the most moderate religious party during that period. Hence, it should have been placed close to the pivotal point of the system. The Agudah was considered the most extreme (and hence the most distant). The Poalei Agudah (a non-actor in de Swaan – 1973) should have been placed between the NRP and the Aguda. It is interesting to note that all Israeli coalitions were closed even *vis-à-vis* this group of parties. The pivotal (median) party (Mapai, and later the Labour Party) never joined forces with the Agudah without the participation of the two other religious parties. It also never included the Poalei Agudah in a coalition without the participation of the Mafdal. The Israeli modified uni-dimensional model is depicted in Figure 1. In this figure, Poalei Agudah is added to de Swaan's list. De Swaan's notation is used for all other actors. In cases of splits or unifications, the names of the smallest possible components are mentioned. Similar models can be used in other multi-party systems.

FIGURE 1

A MODIFIED UNI-DIMENSIONAL MODEL OF ISRAEL

RAFI/STP

CPI   SOCL   AGAV   SOCD   PROG   ZION   HRUT

MAFD

Poalei Agudah

AGDH

STP – State Party
CPI – Communist Party of Israel
SOCL – Mapam
AGAV – Ahdut Ha'Avodah
SOCD – Mapai/Labour
PROG – Progressive Party
ZION – General Zionists
HRUT – Herut
MAFD – Mafdal (National Religious Party)
AGDH – Agudat Yisrael

It seems that the predictive power of a modified uni-dimensional model is much higher than the predictive power of the original uni-dimensional model. At the same time, the configuration of the modified model is not too complicated, while the number of and power of sectarian actors is usually low.

The ideas on which this essay is based were elaborated in a series of conversations with Emanuel Gutmann in 1976. It has never been published because of our will to update the original version. Such updating is even more necessary today. Thus, one should relate to coalition formations in multi-party systems since 1973. The role of the many new European parties should be examined, as should the interdependence between the role of sectarian parties and the durability and stability of governmental coalitions.[10] I can only express my hope that such questions will be addressed to within the framework of a larger study.

NOTES

1. Abram de Swaan, *Coalition Theories and Cabinet Formations*, Amsterdam: Elsevier, 1973.
2. It should be mentioned that one of the first who suggested this theory was Robert Axelrod, *Conflict of Interest*, Chicago: Markham, 1970. De Swaan was not the first to empirically examine coalition theories. See, for instance, Eric C. Browne, *Coalition Theories: A Logical and Empirical Critique*, Beverly Hills: Sage, 1973. Browne, however, focused on 'size theories'.
3. De Swaan, *Coalition Theories*, p.237.
4. Anthony Downs, *An Economic Theory of Democracy*, New York: Harper and Row, 1957.
5. Giovanni Sartori, *Parties and Party Systems: A Framework for Analysis*, Cambridge: Cambridge University Press, 1976; *The Theory of Democracy Revisited*, Chatham: Chatham, 1987.
6. For a quantitative analysis see, Michal Shamir, 'Are Western European Party Systems "Frozen"?', *Comparative Political Studies*, Vol. 17, No. 1 (1984), pp.35–79. For systematic information on the subject see, Thomas. T. Mackie and Richard Rose, *The International Almanac of Electoral History*, London: Macmillan, 1991, (Third Edition). For an updated analysis see, Arend Lijphart, *Electoral Systems and Party Systems*, Oxford: Oxford University Press, 1994.
7. See, Reuven Y. Hazan, *Centre Parties: Polarization and Competition in European Parliamentary Democracies*, London: Pinter, 1997.
8. This definition is taken from de Swaan's 'Glossary', *Coalition Theories* (see also pp.117–118). Axelrod suggested the term 'connected' instead of 'closed', *Conflict of Interest*, p.170.
9. A comprehensive and more updated analysis can be found in Michael Laver and Norman Schofield, *Multiparty Government: The Politics of Coalition in Europe*, Oxford: Oxford University Press, 1990. Additional information on these countries can be found in Gordon Smith, *Politics in Western Europe*, Aldershot: Gower, 1994 (Fifth Edition).
10. See, for instance, Paul V. Warwick, *Government Survival in Parliamentary Democracies*, Cambridge: Cambridge University Press, 1994.

Political Change and Party System Transformation

GABRIEL SHEFFER

THE MAIN ISSUES

The recent profound social and political changes that have occurred in various Western democracies prompt practitioners, analysts and laymen to re-examine accepted views, assertions and theories about these regimes. Among other issues, the perennial question of the relationship between general systemic social and political change on the one hand and the transformation of party systems, as well as particular parties thereof, on the other, have been reconsidered. For similar reasons these questions have also been on the agenda of Israeli politicians, scholars and laymen.

Each of these observers has been interested in a different aspect of such changes and their ramifications. Most scholars dealing with these matters in Israel have mainly been concerned with the Israeli case *per se*. This approach has stemmed from an exceptionalist view of Israel, its regime and patterns of behaviour.[1] Therefore, only a few Israeli analysts have examined this system from a comparative perspective and considered the theoretical implications of these developments. This approach is changing now. Recently there has been greater interest in the possible application and potential contribution of the analysis of the Israeli case to the general field of comparative politics and theory development and vice versa.

This essay falls into this category and, as such, it has two goals. The first is to re-examine the relationship between changes in the structure and operational arrangements in the Israeli political system on the one hand and in the structure, composition and behaviour of the party system, as well as of particular parties thereof, on the other. The second purpose is to suggest that findings about the Israeli case can contribute to comparative and theoretical development.[2]

To accomplish these goals, the essay begins with a review of the main structural and operational systemic changes that have occurred in the Israeli polity. This part includes also an analysis of the transformation of the party system and of the organization and functions of particular

Gabriel Sheffer is Professor of Political Science at the Hebrew University of Jerusalem.

parties. The second part evaluates the comparability of the Israeli case and its possible contributions to comparative studies in this sphere. The last section briefly presents certain implications that demonstrate the potential inherent in the inclusion and application of the findings about the Israeli case for theory development.

SOCIAL AND POLITICAL CHANGE IN ISRAEL[3]

Israeli and foreign analysts have not expressed doubts about the nature of the Israeli regime – most of them regard it as the 'only democracy between Rome and Delhi'. They postulated that it has been a stable system and that at most it has been characterized by 'conservative dynamism' – that is, by structural stability and gradual moderate changes in processes.[4] As much as several observers criticized the Proportional Representation electoral arrangement, they noted that the Israeli democracy suffered not so much from structural deficiencies, but rather from operational 'imperfections'. Some of these analysts have attributed these 'flaws' to the exceptional history of Israel that has been caused by the Jews' protracted experience in 'exile'; the impact of the Holocaust; the unprecedented influx of Jewish immigrants to the country during very short periods; the security situation and the constant external threats.[5] Other analysts have attributed them to the youth of the Israeli system, arguing that more experience would eventually eradicate these flaws.[6] To illustrate their claims, these analysts have noted, for example, the negative ramifications of the problematic treatment of the Palestinians within the Green Line and consequently also in the territories.[7] Similarly, such analysts have mentioned the maltreatment of Jewish immigrants, particularly from Asia and North Africa, and its later influences on the treatment of Ethiopian and Russian Jews.

Their criticisms of certain operational aspects notwithstanding, most observers were impressed by the capacity of Israeli democracy to survive and function in its multiple hostile environments. Moreover, most analysts have regarded Israeli democracy as a stable polity that despite all difficulties and pressures has performed reasonably smoothly. In other words, although this democracy has faced domestic, regional and international crises and upheavals, which contributed to or were responsible for those imperfections, there has been substantive consensus about the continuity, regularity and stability of the regime, including its party system and its various parties.[8]

As noted above, recently there has been a shift in the focus of the inquiries into Israeli democracy and its politics. Scholars pose tougher questions about this political system and its performance. This has occurred in light of the rapid and strenuous process of regime change that has been accompanied by noticeable difficulties in the system's performance, such as difficulties in coalition formation and the toppling of incumbent governments. Moreover, this new trend among students of Israeli politics is a reflection of a growing realization that Israel is becoming a 'normal' democracy. Thus, more scholars are inclined to examine Israeli society, politics and economy within a comparative and developmental framework.[9] As noted, like these studies, the present essay emphasizes both the comparative and developmental perspectives.

In this context, it is important to note that the most recent shift to direct election of the Israeli prime minister and the resultant outcomes of the 1996 and 1999 elections, are not the first systemic change since Israel's establishment in 1948. In fact, this is the second transformation that has altered the nature of the Israeli polity during these fifty years.

The first transformation, which gradually unfolded during the late 1960s and early 1970s, was essentially a structural shift from a consociational to a liberal corporatist political arrangement.[10] While few observers would debate the fact that the Israeli system is in the midst of a second transformation, the direction of this change is far from being clear or agreed upon. Therefore, in order to understand the current transition, a brief historical review of political development in Israel since 1948 is necessary.

THE FIRST PHASE OF POLITICAL DEVELOPMENT IN ISRAEL

Israeli democracy inherited the main features of its social and political systems from the Jewish community in pre-state Palestine (the Yishuv) and through it, from the Zionist movement. In fact, the essential features of the political arrangements preceded the emergence of the Yishuv and Israeli party system and parties.[11] While there is an ongoing debate about the scope and the meaning of Israeli consociationalism, after the establishment of the Jewish State in 1948, the system, especially in the Jewish sector, clearly demonstrated such arrangements.[12] Thus, from the late 1940s until the mid-1960s, the Israeli political arrangements resembled some essential aspects of the consociational mode of operation that had been evident in countries such as Holland, Belgium, Austria and Switzerland. These countries, however, better suited the formal consociational model as suggested by Lijphart and other consociationalists, which emphasized the fact that consociationalism was an answer to the needs of certain culturally deeply-segmented societies.

In the Israeli case, the social cleavage configuration, which is a core property of the consociational model, was characterized by the existence of three distinct, vertical ideological camps, rather than by clear ethnic or religious sub-cultures, as in the other consociational countries mentioned above. Although one of the Israeli system's 'pillars' – the

Labour camp – was predominant, (the seats that this camp, excluding the Communist Party, held in the Israeli Parliament (the Knesset) were: in the first Knesset (1949) – 67 seats; in the 2nd (1951) – 62; the 3rd (1955) – 53; 4th (1959) – 68; 5th (1961) – 62; 6th (1965) – 75; 7th (1969) – 60; 8th (1973) – 57; and in the 9th Knesset (1977) – 49), the lack of continuous consensus within this camp and the relative size and electoral strength of the two other camps, required broadly based parliamentary coalitions that included religious and centre parties. However, because of deep ideological segmentation (highlighted by David Ben-Gurion's 'principle' – 'Governing coalitions without Herut (later the Likud) and the Communists' – until 1967) there was no possibility of establishing grand coalitions as in other 'classical' consociational systems. Because of the results of the various elections to the Knesset, the various coalition parties had mutual veto power.

The consociational arrangement guaranteed that whoever formed the coalition could not disregard the most vital interests and needs of the other blocs and parties. Other important attributes of this system were the arrangements for the allocation of national resources according to the proportional principle; the avoidance of uncontrolled conflicts (but when such conflicts occurred, usually the blocs' elites could manage them) and the assurances that the autonomy of the major blocs would be maintained. It is important to note that these consociational arrangements were mainly applied in the Jewish sector, with very few principles of this system applied to Israeli Arabs.[13] Though this segment enjoyed formal equal political rights, it was discriminated in most areas and in regard to most issues.

Because Israeli society was deeply segmented, it was prone to rifts that led to spontaneous clashes at the grassroots level. Foremost among these cleavages and tensions was the Jewish–Arab divide. Yet the Jewish sector itself was also deeply segmented. Maintaining the well-established social structures of the Yishuv after independence in 1948, the Jewish segment in Israel was characterized by a number of superimposed ideological, social and economic cleavages. These cleavages separated the three major camps – the Labour, the religious and what was known as the Civic Bloc. The Labour bloc and its small senior elite, which dominated all coalitions and their governments until the late 1970s, tried hard to foster full cultural and social integration of the different Jewish groups and factions. They hoped to attain this through the promotion of the *etatist* approach (Mamlachtiut), intended to implement a melting pot strategy. Despite these efforts at integration, the main social segmentation patterns remained almost intact, the result being the persistence of the three socio-political camps.

The *raison d'être* of these three loosely federated blocs was their divergent ideologies. Although regarded as a Socialist camp and by some bitter opponents as 'Bolsheviks', the mainstream in the Labour bloc followed a nationalist Social-Democratic, rather than an orthodox Socialist, ideology.[14] This ideological inclination was responsible for the introduction of an elaborate welfare system, which in turn contributed to the emergence of a highly centralized state, tightly controlled by a relatively small elite.

The main groups in the loosely organized Civic bloc adopted a liberal economic and social platform. Some of these parties also developed a hawkish nationalist ideology in regard to the protracted Arab–Jewish conflict. (This bloc controlled 26 Knesset seats in the 1st Knesset (established in 1949); 32 seats in the 2nd Knesset (1951); 33 in the 3rd Knesset (1955); 31 in the 4th Knesset (1959); 34 in the 5th Knesset (1961); 31 in the 6th Knesset (1965); 30 in the 7th Knesset (1969); 43 in the 7th Knesset (1973); and 44 in the 8th Knesset (1977)

The third bloc was based on a highly mobilized and devoted membership adhering to various shades of religious and ultra-religious dogmas. The leaders of these parties and their members and voters were determined to follow the orthodox Halakhic (Jewish orthodox law) tradition. (The bloc's seats in the Knesset: 16 in 1949; 15 in 1951; 17 in 1955; 18 in 1959; 18 in 1961; 18 in 1965; 15 in 1973; and 17 in 1977).

Like in other consociational democracies, cultural, social, economic and occupational gaps were superimposed on these diverse ideological beliefs. These gaps defined the borders of the various vertical political pillars (or blocs) and determined their goals, political orientations, strategies and main patterns of action.

An important aspect of this structure was that, again like in other consociational democracies, each of the blocs was well organized. Each bloc provided its members with solid social support and supplied most of the services to cater for their needs. In return for the sense of belonging, services and benefits that members received from and through their blocs and constituent parties, they were expected to show loyalty and obedience to these blocs and their leaders. Firm loyalty and discipline were required for two reasons: to prevent defection, since maximal membership guaranteed a maximal proportional share of national resources; and to prevent spontaneous and uncontrolled clashes between members of the various blocs at the grassroots level, which could rock the entire boat and harm the interests of each group whether in coalition or in opposition.

During the first two decades following the establishment of Israel, members at the grassroots level, indeed, showed both electoral and daily loyalty to their respective camps and parties. Since these camps, parties and leaders were capable of maintaining impressive levels of loyalty and discipline, which prevented undesired conflicts and clashes, they gained respect and prestige and exerted great influence over their members.

These arrangements explain the overall systemic stability, reflected in the electoral results throughout the Yishuv period and during the first two decades after 1948. During that period the level of electoral volatility was relatively low.[15]

Again like other consociational regimes, Israel was a pure *proporzdemokratie*.[16] Basically, this meant that in addition to a proportional electoral arrangement, national resources were allocated strictly in accordance with the principle of proportionality. Since this arrangement met the basic needs of all blocs and their constituent parties, Israel preserved the pure Proportional Representative (PR) electoral system that had been practiced by the Zionist Movement and the Yishuv that this movement created.

To avoid sparks that might have caused undesired spontaneous public clashes between the various blocs, the Israeli parliament was designed as a weak partner in national-level policy making. And since parties and parliaments are intimately related, the Knesset's weakness adversely influenced the status and role of the parties. Consequently, the entire system was firmly controlled by a strong elite-cartel and a central and centralized government. The result of that form of power sharing among the elites dictated most of the internal social, political and economic developments.[17]

Thus, for example, there was wide consensus about the need for vast Jewish immigration and the patterns of its absorption (these patterns reflected the proportional arrangements), the predominance of defence calculations in resource allocation and the allocation of national resources, such as the reparations from Germany (thus, economic enterprises that were connected to traditional opposition parties, such as the Likud, have benefitted too from these reparations).

Most of the parties that constituted the three blocs were mass, or branch, parties. These were parties that represented distinct social-ideological groups; had large card-carrying memberships; were partly financed by membership dues; demonstrated an elaborate organizational structure; and were led by small groups of leaders. Through those active branches, these parties performed almost all the 'classical' functions that parties were expected to perform. These functions included social and political socialization; interest articulation and aggregation; mobilization of members and voters; representation of members and voters in the legislative and executive political bodies; and selection, mobilization and promotion of leaders. As can be noted, from this list of traditional party functions certain functions are missing: formulation of party platform; and policy making both at the party and national levels. These two functions were the prerogative of the senior political leaders. As can be expected of parties in such a consociational system, these organizations served as important channels for information dissemination and resource transfer from the centre to the various geographical, social and political peripheries and for feedback from the rank and file. The parties and their branches were also responsible for the provision of various services to party members and voters, such as access to cheap housing, jobs, education, health, cultural and social events, etc.

The ideological blocs and their constituent parties were firmly controlled by these small elites.[18] These oligarchic elites both formulated and implemented public policies, which were intended to minimize inter-bloc and inter-party friction. For example, the elite-cartel allocated considerable resources to parties of the Civic Bloc who, until 1967, were excluded from the governing coalitions. These allocations amounted to less than the strict proportional share according to their weight in the entire electorate. This was evident in the allocation of money received by the state from Germany in accordance with the Reparations agreement. By the same token, the politicians opted for maintaining the religious Status Quo Agreement, which prevented separation of state and religion and guaranteed religious practices, such as Kosher food in state agencies, including the Israel Defence Forces (the IDF), religious holidays and religious burials, marriages and divorces.

In many respects, the Israeli party system resembled contemporary party systems in Western European democracies. As in similar European countries, electoral participation was high (about 87 per cent in the 1949 elections, dropping to 75 per cent in 1951; rising again to 83 per cent in the 1959 elections; more than 80 per cent in 1959, 1961, 1965 and 1969; and a bit less than 80 per cent in all elections since 1973). Thus, it was comparable to participation rates in countries such as Denmark, Germany, Italy and Sweden.

As can be expected in a highly politicized and ideological polity, the system was considerably fractionalized. The first indicator of fractionalization was that on average the number of parties represented in the Knesset was around 12. As far as the second indicator of fractionalization was concerned (that is, the power of the smaller parties), small parties enjoyed considerable political clout, whether they participated in governmental coalitions or not. This factor and the fact that the predominant party, Mapai/Ma'arach/Labour, never controlled a majority in the Knesset, which would have allowed it to establish a government on its own, (in 1949 Mapai had 46 seats in the Knesset; in 1951 it had 45; in 1955 – 40; in 1959 – 47; in 1961 – 42; in 1965 – 45 seats in the Knesset; in 1969 – 56; and in 1973 – 51), contributed to a continuous need to establish coalition governments. In turn, this constant need for coalition partners, contributed in more than one way to the smaller parties' influence and to the elites' determination to maintain their firm control over the entire system and especially over their parties.

The polarization of the party system was closely related to the bloc structure. That is, inter-bloc polarization was more meaningful than intra-bloc polarization. That polarization and the ideological distances within the blocs, determined the composition of the coalitions and in turn the policies that the ruling governments eventually adopted. Finally, because of voter loyalty (thus, for example, in the 1965 and 1969 elections, 74 per cent of all voters declared that they were voting for the same parties. Only after the 1973 elections did loyalty to the parties substantially decreased),[19] because of discipline (until the 1977 critical elections, the main change in voters' shifts occurred within the blocs) and self-interest and because of bloc and party elites firm control over members, voter volatility was quite insignificant in the actual conduct of the parties' affairs.

Thus, the various consociational operational arrangements, which were a response to social needs, were an essential contributing factor to Israel's political development after 1948.[20] To balance this emphasis on stability and lack of change, a view that has been shared by other writers who do not subscribe to the consociational explanation,[21] one must mention again the 'dynamic conservatism' that characterized the polity. That is, political development through careful adaptation to changing circumstances within relatively rigid structures.

In any event, the consociational arrangement allowed successive Israeli coalition governments, led by the Mapai/Ma'arach elite, to formulate and implement hard-line policies concerning the Arab–Israeli conflict and the Israeli Palestinians, to pursue a non-selective immigration policy, to implement a state sponsored social integrationist policy (that is, a melting pot strategy) for the incoming Jewish immigrants, to promote the gradual emergence of state-capitalism and to simultaneously implement expansionist economic policies and a policy of providing of generous universal welfare services.

As in other similar democracies, such as the Netherlands and Austria, the very success of the consociational arrangements in the Jewish sector led to their gradual decline.[22] Progressively, the integrative policies that successive Labour governments had pursued, coupled with the etatist ethos, narrowed, but by no means eliminated, the social and ideological gaps that had existed between the three blocs. This process began to have marked effects on the Israeli society and polity, especially after the 1967 War. Moreover, as larger groups – especially of Jewish immigrants from the Middle East and North Africa who had arrived in the late 1940s and the early 1950s – became better acquainted with the Israeli social and economic systems and accustomed to the political arrangements prevailing in the Jewish state, they replaced their dependence on the old ideological blocs and parties with reliance on the government and its expanding bureaucracy.

Consequently, members began to defect from the blocs and parties that had facilitated their immigration and initial integration. In the long run, it turned out that the main loser in this gradual process was the Labour bloc. These processes enhanced popular support for the rightist, nationalist and religious parties. This explains why the previously hegemonic Ma'arach lost so many votes mainly to Likud. In 1977 the Ma'arach gained only 32 seats in the Knesset. After a short revival that resulted in 47 seats in the 1981 elections and 41 seats in 1984, the party dropped to 39 seats in 1988, rose again to 44 in 1992, dropped dramatically to 34 in 1996; and in 1999 (now under the name One Israel), won only 26 seats in the Knesset. In an encapsulated manner, this is the story of the decline of the established parties.

The late 1960s and especially the 1970s, saw the equally gradual process of economic liberalization. This resulted from the rapid economic development in the wake of the 1967 War and from determined attempts by successive Israeli governments to integrate into the emerging global economy and to actively participate in various international economic organizations and regimes, such as GATT and the emerging European Union. The Israeli economic and political elites intended also to benefit from the support of the World Bank and IMF, which demanded such liberalization.

Political and economic liberalization had some ripple effects beyond the Jewish sector. Thus, on the eve of the 1967 War, the Israeli government eased the severe limitations that had been imposed on the Israeli-Palestinian sector. A major step in this direction was the elimination of the oppressive military government that had controlled all aspects of life of the Israeli-Palestinian community. This marked the beginning of a gradual change in the status of this sector, for as noted, until then consociationalism had a very limited effect on this sector. As a result of the late 1960s reform, the Israeli-Palestinian community began its long and arduous road toward a more substantive political and economic, but not social, integration into the Israeli system. Gradually, the Israeli-Palestinians benefitted from the prevailing power sharing arrangements. It has been almost natural that the Israeli-Palestinian parties have supported leftist coalitions. Consequently, the Israeli-Palestinian sector benefitted from this bloc's support, especially in terms of resource allocation.

CORPORATIST ARRANGEMENTS IN ISRAEL

As noted above, it was not surprising that in Israel, too, the consociational arrangements were gradually and to an extent replaced by liberal-corporatist patterns. This change occurred despite the fact that basically, even, until the 1999 elections, the old social ideological cleavages have not been eradicated. Until those elections, recurrent public opinion polls and voting patterns indicated that the relative electoral strength of the three loosely organized ideological blocs have only gradually altered. Thus, the religious bloc continued to control about 20 per cent of the voters (A change did occur in the 1999 elections – as a result of the increase in the power of the Sephardi ultra orthodox Shas party, the ultra religious bloc increased its share of seats in the Knesset from 14 in 1996 to 22 in 1999. The entire religious bloc – that is, the ultra religious parties and the religious Zionist party, the National Religious Party – increased its representation in the Knesset from 23 seats in 1996 to 27 seats in 1999) and each of the larger camps, the Labour and Civic blocs, controlled about 40 per cent. While not all cleavages disappeared, some were moderated, as is the case with the 'ethnic' (that is, Ashkenazi–Sephardi) cleavage and with the Right–Left differences in regard to liberalization and privatization.

Several factors influenced the gradual shift that began in the late 1960s. The first was the inclination of rank and file to alter their political reliance and allegiance. 'The man in the street' began to rely on political interest groups to promote his goals, rather than on traditional social-political blocs, the old parties or state agencies. This meant that more Israelis rescinded their old one-dimensional political loyalties and began to form new multi-dimensional allegiances. Second, society and politics were gradually freed from the firm control of the traditional ideological blocs. Third, these two developments were followed by a marked decrease in the parties' clout over their members and followers and simultaneously by the relaxation of the highly centralized Israeli power structure, especially that of the Israeli executive branch. Gradually, the decentralization of policy making, through the inclusion of new 'actors' such as industrialists, bankers, mayors and lawyers and the elaboration of the patterns of consultation with these new groups, was accompanied by the emergence of 'the new elites'.

These developments had various ramifications: the polity turned to the 'logical' extension, or rather to the substitute, of the consociational power-sharing model. As was the case in other consociational small states, such as the Netherlands, Belgium and Austria, the closest arrangement that could replace consociationalism and satisfy all actors was liberal corporatism.[23] As a result of the gradual political and economic liberalization that began in the late 1960s, as well as the further weakening of the blocs and parties, the Israelis turned to existing and new interest groups. Eventually, more Israelis either joined or established such groups with the hope that they would promote their well-being and protect their interests. Indeed, single-issue and multi-purpose interest groups have increased in number and significance.[24]

The further deterioration of the traditional political blocs and parties and the rapid expansion of interest groups that were engaged in articulation, aggregation and representation of the views and interests of various social groups, pointed to the substantial growing role of 'peak organizations', such as those of the industrialists, bankers, large commercial firms, organized labour and professionals. The volume, scope and intensity of regional and local interest groups, at what is known as the mezzo-corporatist level, have also increased. As in other liberal corporatist democracies, such as Germany, Sweden, Norway and Denmark, in Israel, too, peak, regional and local interest groups became indispensable partners in public policy making. Because of the executive's previous predominance in policy making at the national level, for a while the executive branch remained the senior partner in public policy making, but its power began to dwindle. In all of these developments, Israel has shown great similarity to other former consociational democracies where liberal arrangements have been instituted, such as Holland and Austria.

The further weakening grip of the state and especially of the executive branch, over social developments, combined with further economic liberalization, enhanced the power of individuals and of the private sector. Consequently there emerged a system in which new elites and rank and file involvement in public affairs increased considerably. The result has been that increasingly functionally differentiated and hierarchically organized bodies have represented the most significant interests in the Israeli society. The government formally and informally recognized these associations as legitimate partners in various spheres of public policy making. Each of these corporations maintained, or acquired, representational monopolies in its particular sphere. The heads of the large banks, for example, formed an informal group, or a 'cartel', that enjoyed disproportionate influence in social and economic policy making. The peak organizations of the industrialist, commercial and professional associations maintained federal structures. While these groups recognized the 'first among equals' position of the central government in the public policy making process, they gradually limited governmental veto power and its ability to mediate between the capitalists and labour. Moreover, each of these organizations learned to formulate and implement policies on its own, that is, without prior consultation with other corporations.[25] In short, under the emerging Israeli liberal arrangement, involvement in national level policy making reflected the relative strength of those corporations.

Since the late 1960s, Israeli political arrangements accurately reflected an early description of the main traits of liberal corporatism. According to this description/analysis, the arrangement is:

more than a peculiar pattern of articulation of interests. Rather it is an institutionalized pattern of policy-formation in which large interest organizations co-operate with each other and with public authorities not only in the articulation (or even 'intermediation' of interests), but in its developed forms – in the authoritative allocation of values and in the implementation of such policies. It is precisely because of the intimate mutual penetration of state bureaucracies and large interest organizations [that] we are dealing with an integrated system of 'societal guidance'.[26]

Until the late 1980s, the party system did not change in a drastic manner. Electoral participation remained at its previous level, that is, around 80 per cent. Until the mid-1990s, fractionalization did not grow in a dramatic fashion. For the second time in Israel's short history (the first time was in 1988), in the 1999 elections did the number of parties that gained seats in the Knesset rise to 15. Again, up until the 1999 elections, systemic polarization somewhat increased. With the exception of the Sephardi, ultra orthodox Shas, the established parties' connections to established social camps and class have continued to diminish. But voter volatility further increased and peaked in the 1999 elections.[27] This trend reflected the increasing inclination of the rank and file to reduce their loyalty to the traditional political camps and parties. From 1969 to 1996, party membership declined from around 18 per cent to less than 10 per cent.[28]

During the 1980s, the parties continued to lose power and status. Most notably, they ceased to be a channel for the dissemination of national resources to their members, especially in the geographical, social and political peripheries. More importantly, the parties were losing the last vestiges of their influence on policy making at the national level. The organizational structure of most established parties was rapidly changing, too, as they continued to shore off their traditional, or classical, functions. Thus, since the late 1960s, there has been a marked decline in the activities of the parties' branches. Many branches were closed down and activities at the regional and local levels diminished. When they were in government, national leaders became even less inclined to regard their own parties' inputs into the policy making process. The parties further withdrew from performing their 'classical' functions. Thus the parties lost their previous role in social and political socialization (for example, Labour and Likud closed down their cadre training centres and facilities). Because of the emerging liberal corporatist arrangements, the parties further lost their role in interest articulation and aggregation. These were 'usurped' by local, regional and national interest groups. The parties barely maintained some of their previous functions: mobilization of members and voters, representation of voters in legislative and executive political bodies and the mobilization, selection and promotion of leaders. The formulation of the party platforms (which, in turn, also became less important in recruiting members and voters) and policy making, remained almost the exclusive prerogative of the leadership. Furthermore, during this period, the parties lost the remnants of their previous role as channels for information dissemination, resource transfer from the centre to the peripheries and feedback from the rank and file.

During this interim period, the two large parties, Likud and Labour, were acquiring clear features of the catchall party model.[29] That is, as if in accordance with this model, in most Israeli parties strong top leaders have appeared that have further concentrated the power of decision-making in their hands. These leaders have been promoted not so much because of their ideological, or inspirational qualities, but rather because of the quality of their appearance in the media and because of their technical and managerial prowess. The marginalization of party members resulted in stagnation in party size, an increased reliance on mass media during campaigns and in the use of professionals in these campaigns. These parties aimed their campaigns at the centre, hoping to catch their voters there. In turn, this inclination resulted in further dilution of the parties' ideological platforms as a means for recruiting members and voters. The responsibility for recruitment of voters rested on the leaders. This emphasis on the leaders and their performance in the media reached its peak in the 1996 and especially in the 1999, elections.

Other parties, including the religious, the Israeli-Palestinian and the more 'leftist' parties, such as Meretz, maintained the essential features of the mass party model. Yet, new parties that were formed during the 1980s and especially during the 1990s and that directed their activities mainly toward the centre, such as Shinui, Dash and, later, the Third Way, exhibited clear characteristics of the electoral party model.[30] These parties reflected the general trend in the Israeli society toward the legitimization of pluralism. In fact, some of these parties that originated in interest groups have championed the transition to pluralism in the country. Accordingly, the parties' main concerns have been to structure voting patterns and voter behaviour, mainly on election day. Namely, these parties mainly attempted to mobilize centrist voters around a recognizable label or the personality of their leader or leaders. Usually these parties' ideologies and platforms were cast in general and ambiguous terms. Some of these parties, such as Dash and the Centre Party, in the 1999 elections, issued just a few 'points' that indicated their main goals and policies. By the same token, these parties were responsive to their perceived voters' needs and inclinations, were almost utterly pragmatic and were intended to attract voters rather than to launch in-depth debate or discourse about major ideological public issues. These parties have been characterized by a loose and flexible organization that is geared toward and capable of intensive activities during election campaigns. The relatively few party members, supporters and voters had only very limited influence on party policy, or on the manoeuvres of their leaders. Until the 1977 critical elections, the main change in voting patterns occurred within the blocs.

The net result of these developments was that during the period after the 1967 War, the organizational and behavioural patterns of various parties became more diversified. This diversity reflected the increasing social and political pluralism in Israel and the liberal corporatist arrangements that were introduced in the 1970s and 1980s.

Like the consociational arrangement that had characterized the Israeli polity until the late 1960s, the main purposes of the liberal corporatist arrangement were to achieve social and political stability, a degree of social integration and efficient political performance in an otherwise potentially unstable polity, which was still functioning in hostile external environments. At the national level, the main purpose of the parties' leaders was to attain a reasonable degree of consensus concerning pressing social and, especially, economic policies. As in the previous arrangement, consensus building was attempted chiefly at the elite level, which included the leaders of both old and new parties and new peak associations. As in the politics of the 'elite-cartel' during the consociational arrangement phase, these elites were keen on maintaining their autonomy and freedom of action.

The main decision making pattern at the national level has been that of bargaining, leading to business-like compromise agreements, especially in the economic sphere. These policy making patterns have not been limited to such spheres as wages and employment, but have had direct and spill-over influences on welfare policies, municipal matters and even military industries, as in the case of the scraping of the Lavie aircraft project (Israel's plan to produce an advanced fighter plane).

THE CURRENT SITUATION

The changes that began in the 1970s with the movement from the consociational to the liberal corporatist arrangement have continued to reverberate during the 1990s. Toward the end of this decade, it seems that liberal corporatism in Israel has been only a temporary, interim arrangement. In retrospect, the great contribution of corporatism has been that it has facilitated further change. Thus, it has affected the style of social action, leadership formation, leadership style and performance, the style of national-level policy making and reforms in the electoral system.

Israel, therefore, is now in the midst of its second political transition period. Essentially, the cleavage system that existed during the earlier corporatist interim period has not been substantially altered, yet it has been clarified. In the late 1990s, there are three social-ideological cleavages: those between religious and secular Jews, between Jews and Israeli Palestinians and between veterans and immigrants, especially from the former Soviet Union and Ethiopia. Although other previous cleavages, such as the social-economic and the Ashkenazi–Sephardi divides, have substantively lost their severity, they still linger. Occasionally, they cause unexpected internal conflicts, but even these are less damaging.[31]

In the Jewish secular sector, a gradual weakening of collective identities and loyalties have accompanied the slow amelioration of old 'ethnic' (that is, between various groups whose origins are in various Jewish Diaspora communities) and class differences. Thus, identification with large collectives, such as the old ideological blocs and parties, or the Kibbutz and Moshav movements, has waned. Instead, loyalty is further shifting to smaller, particularistic and local occupational interest groups. Indeed, Israelis increasingly join specialized voluntary associations and identify with them. This process has accelerated since the late 1980s.[32]

The trend among the religious, the ultra-religious, oriental Jews and certain Russian Jewish immigrants is in the opposite direction. Because of either defensive or offensive considerations, the main trend in these sectors is toward the fortification of traditional social and political institutions, that is, religious communities and factions, family, 'clan' and immigrant associations. Naturally, the leaders of these factions encourage this trend and invest considerable efforts and resources in strengthening their followers' loyalties.

Nevertheless, according to consistent public opinion polls and to the results of the 1999 elections, the most significant schism in the Israeli society is the attitudinal one. This cleavage that superseded all other divides pertains to four basic issues: the 'who is a Jew?' controversy; the relationship between state, civic society and religion; to a lesser extent the future of the occupied territories; and, especially, the existence in a post-modernist environment. The overlapping approaches to these issues create two large camps – Israeli-style 'nationalist/ conservative/rightist' and 'moderate/liberal/leftist' camps.[33] In his recent book, *New York Times* journalist Thomas Friedman calls such rifts – the rift between 'the Lexus' and the 'the olive tree'.[34] These trends and cleavages explain why only a few Israelis seriously believe in such notions as 'one integrated society', 'homogeneous culture' and 'mutual responsibility and tolerance'. While they may pay lip service and extol these traits, many Israelis are aware of the inapplicability and irrelevance of these notions. If it exists at all, the 'Israeli Personality' is a very strange mix of attributes – nationalistic, religious, xenophobic and aggressive on the one hand and liberal, humanitarian, tolerant and individualistic on the other.

The waning of collective identities has resulted in a marked decline in ideological political commitments, orthodox and ultra-religious Jews being the exception. In any event, as shown in the 1992 and 1996 elections, none of the emerging 'new ideologies', such as Milton Freedman-style economic liberalism, libertarianism, dedicated 'dark-green environmentalism' and feminism, has become a significant rallying factor for massive popular mobilization. In other words, as yet the majority of the Israelis have not developed post-materialist views. Hence, 'new politics', as well as civil society, are still in an embryonic stage.[35] In the meantime, there is considerable confusion among Israeli voters. Public opinion polls consistently show a large group of 'undecided' and 'floating' voters.[36]

The dwindling of old ideological commitments and communal loyalties have enhanced processes of individuation and, consequently, have promoted political fragmentation. Instead of the traditional ideological political camps, new 'normal' and mostly single-issue interest groups, such as parents', ecological, occupational, civil and personal rights, consumer and even religious associations, have proliferated. The net result is the emergence of an unstructured, almost chaotic, political pluralism, with strong inclinations toward individual preferences and also a certain degree of apathy. This apathy is not necessarily shown in the turn out on election day, but rather on a daily basis.

The Israeli 'new elites' have gained a certain influence over economic and political developments. Prominent members of these elites get attention in the mass media, attract followers, have direct access to senior policy makers and, thus, accumulate economic and political power. On the other hand, the traditional political elites, who were connected to the parties, are further losing their clout over Israeli politics and especially over the parties and the party system. Judging from the current ongoing processes in this sphere, some traditional political elites are bound to disappear almost altogether. This, for example, may be the fate of the Histadrut's elite, which has been replaced by powerful chairpersons of the large trade unions. This is also the case with the old parties' elites. Generally speaking, new and younger leaders replace veteran ones. Thus, for example, new young pacesetters appear in the cultural sphere, in the electronic and written media and in industry, particularly high tech.[37]

At the other end of the social ladder, that is, at the grass-roots level, more Israelis are becoming aware of their new social and political freedoms and autonomy. Not surprisingly, these persons are groping for additional empowerment. Regardless of their 'ethnic' (as noted earlier in this article this means groups of the same country of origin) or social economic background, the trend among young secular Israelis is toward greater emphasis on individualism and personal fulfilment. It is difficult to determine the exact size of this group of Israelis, but by any yardstick it is growing. The cumulative result of these trends is that the political culture of the secular sector is gradually losing its previous parochial and 'servile' characteristics, while acquiring new Western-style liberal and even post-materialist features.

This development is connected with a striking transformation that has occurred in the economy, which is in the midst of rapid liberalization and somewhat slower privatization. Except for some small parties – such as the Israeli-Palestinian Hadash party, the trade union's One Nation party and the party that was established by senior citizens but did not win any seats in the 1999 elections – there is a wide consensus among most parties that state intervention in the economy must be reduced to a minimum and that further liberalization and privatization should be carried out. The fact that the Histadrut, the Israeli trade union movement, has experienced a continuous crisis – and its present leadership shares the consensus on liberalization and privatization – has enhanced the political role of the private sector and its leaders. While during earlier periods Labour governments and the Histadrut were senior partners in public policy making, now economic policy is negotiated mainly between the government and the chiefs of the private sector. Usually, the results of such exchanges are package deals, which benefit the government and special interests. An example of this trend is the participation by the economic elite in the peace talks with Jordan and in the convoluted negotiations with the Palestinians during the reign of the Yitzhak Rabin government (1992–96). Partly through personal acquaintance and partly on the basis of their mounting contributions to political candidates and parties, industrialists, brokers, bankers and lawyers have established close relations with senior politicians and consequently gained access to senior policy makers. Thus, leaders of both Likud and Labour (it applies equally to the late Yitzhak Rabin, Shimon Peres, Binyamin Netanyahu and Ehud Barak) have been known for their close contacts with wealthy Jews in Israel and the Diaspora and with other members of the economic, commercial and financial elites.

The cumulative result of all the above is the weakening of the state.[38] Yet, not all state institutions are losing power at the same pace and to the same degree. Even if certain institutions do not gain additional prestige, some gain additional power. With the further decline of the parties and the Knesset and the weakening of the executive branch, the centrality of the judiciary has increased considerably. Consequently, the general trend toward the weakening of the state has become very evident and political power is shifting to the intermediate levels of the political system – to smaller, mostly local, promoting and protecting interest groups, to trade unions of workers in large strategic industries and to other small powerful voluntary associations. Meanwhile, veteran power brokers –

that is, mainly the parties' aparatchikis and members of Knesset – fight hard to maintain the vestiges of their prestige and power.

These developments both feed on and are influenced by new trends at the grassroots level, where there is a growing feeling that the 'man in the street' can affect – mainly through the media, courts and interest groups – certain political processes, public policies and their outcomes. For instance, it seems that continued grassroots protests, especially by women (among others, the Four Mothers Movement and Women in Black), against Israel's continued presence in south Lebanon have had an effect on the Israeli government's decision to withdraw from the Israeli controlled security zone.

Also, many members of these movements who had voted for former Prime Minister Netanyahu, or for his party, emphasized that their vote had been conditional. The same applies to those who voted for the Labour's Barak in the 1999 elections. Moreover, Israelis are increasingly willing to confront the government, especially through the courts, interest groups and the media.

However paradoxical it may sound, the reform in the Israeli electoral system introducing direct elections of the Prime Minister has further diminished the government's control over society, politics and the economy. The combination of pragmatism, reduced loyalty to parties and the enhanced power to select between individual leaders, leads Israelis to shift their support from one leader and party to another. These developments complement the political transformation mentioned above – power shifts to single issue as well as special interest groups and to individuals who can support the formal candidates and other contenders for top positions in the political system. The results of the 1999 elections serve as a very clear illustration of this process. Just as a reminder: as a result of these elections, the Labour party lost eight seats, the Likud lost 13 seats, the National Religious Party lost four seats and Hadash lost one seat. Moreover, the combined results of these social and political processes resulted in a growing fractionalization of the party system. As noted, in the 1999 elections 15 parties have won seats in the Knesset.

In the early 1990s, the two large parties – Likud and Labour – introduced closed primaries in order to cope with the changing patterns of political participation, For a while, the introduction of this mechanism infused hopes among the rank and file that they might be able to influence party politics and especially party policy making and policies. These very partial internal reforms indeed helped to increase membership in these parties. They created an impression that the parties were heading toward democratization. It even seemed that, following the example set by the major parties, certain smaller parties may introduce primaries too. However, soon afterwards, the leaders of the Likud reverted to the old oligarchic patterns of control over the party and reintroduced leadership elections in the party's central committee. The new 'centre parties', such as The Third Way, the Centre Party, Shinui and the Russian Immigrants' party have not introduced primaries at all.

The rapid reversal in internal organization and patterns of activity in the Likud, alienated party members, who were waiting for a dramatic change in this sphere. In the 1999 elections, these members defected from the Likud and pledged allegiance to other parties, especially to Shas. On the other hand, veteran activists in both the Likud and Labour resumed their attempts to regain power in their respective parties. Their main demand has been to abolish the primaries all together and to restore the power of the central committees. Party leaders have demonstrated ambivalence toward these demands and therefore the controversy over this issue lingers on.

Encouraged by the introduction of direct election of the Prime Minister, the leaders of the two large parties tried to flex their muscles *vis-à-vis* the parties' aparatchikis and bureaucracies. The formal argument for firing and replacing old hands was their wish to economize on expenses and to streamline the parties' bureaucracies. Actually, the purpose was to increase and ensure the leaders' control over these much weakened parties. These attempts resulted in new internal struggles. On the whole, the parties' leaders have been only partially successful in these exchanges and manipulations. The leaders learned the hard way that party aparatchiciks and activists were able to maintain their positions and power in these organizations. The leaders' solution was the compartmentalization and the creation of parallel mechanisms, especially for conducting election campaigns. This was very clearly evident in the internal developments in Labour and Likud on the eve of the 1999 elections. These developments, which began during the corporatist stage, continue after the 1999 elections. Similarly, most of the smaller parties have maintained the organizational structures, members to voters ratio and have considerably reduced the functions that characterized these parties during the interim corporatist period.

The main new feature of the party system is the solidification of systemic bi-polarity, referred to above as the divide between the Lexus and the Olive Tree. Reflecting the 'left/liberal/moderate'–'right/ nationalist/conservative' political ideological schism in the electorate, after the 1999 elections, the party system consists of two major camps. The Likud (19 seats in the Knesset), the NRP (five seats), the two ultra-orthodox parties – Shas (17 seats) and the United Torah Front (five seats) and Israel is Our Home (four seats) form the 'rightist/nationalist/ conservative camp'. One Israel (Labour with 26 seats), Meretz (10 seats), the Israeli-Palestinian parties (10 seats) and One Nation (two seats) form the 'left camp'. The 'centre' parties, the Russian immigrants' Israel Be-aliya (six seats), Centre Party (six seats) and Shinui (six seats) are far from being classical centre parties. Despite certain analytical difficulties, these parties should be regarded as part of the 'left/liberal/moderate' camp. Hence, Israel still lacks solid centre parties. These developments are reflected in public opinion polls taken before and after the 1999 elections. For example, the Tami Steinmetz Centre's Peace Index taken in May 1999, found that 40 per cent of the Israeli public thinks that the above mentioned schism has been maintained, 28 per cent responded that the schism has worsened and only 24 per cent felt that the divide has been narrowed. The authors of this index concluded that this schism has also been reflected in attitudes towards the peace process. Since the 1999 elections, the public positions have not changed in comparison to previous polls (67 per cent support the peace process).[39]

Finally, the re-emergence of strong nationalist, communal and religious fundamentalist loyalties in the Israeli society are reflected in the appearance of 'party-movements'. The ultra-orthodox parties follow this model. This development adds to the growing variety of party models that coexist in Israel. The chaotic situation in the twenty-first century, which is a result of the social and political structural change, makes the Israeli parties and party-system more 'normal' and similar to other Western polities.

THE COMPARABILITY OF THE ISRAELI CASE

As noted above, the analysis here is premised on the argument, presented in a number of recent publications, that despite the continuation of the Arab–Israeli conflict, in many respects, Israel is becoming a 'normal' Western-like state. Therefore, the Israeli political experience can serve as a comparative and theoretical case in various sub-fields of political science.[40] In this vein, there are similarities between the general trends of change in the political systems, party-systems and parties in Western Europe and Israel. The following comparison, which indicates such similarities, is based on analyses of changes that have occurred in Western Europe on the one hand and on the analysis presented in this paper on the other hand.[41]

Thus, the transformation of the European and Israeli party systems and parties results from new social and especially, political openness. Old cumbersome political arrangements dissipate and grassroots geographical and social and economic mobility in their homelands and host countries increases. This change is related to a marked weakening of allegiances and loyalties to political camps, blocs, parties and other collectives, including states. These two interwoven processes, which occur in certain sectors in Europe and Israel, lead to a more homogeneous citizenry in the sense that assertive individualism is more widely accepted and adhered to. Citizens are less dependent on old political institutions and thus can reduce their identification with such collective entities. Therefore, the successful establishment of new parties and the maintenance of veteran ones depend on the satisfaction of the needs and tastes of individual citizens and special interest groups.

The weakened parties have lost much of their capacity to create tightly controlled, isolated and self-contained political entities. As noted, this has also been reflected in a sharp decline in the number of party members. Those who become members are less involved in party organization and activities. Moreover, they lack actual influence on party policies.

Israeli and European parties rely mainly on state financing and on contributions of wealthy supporters, who have clear economic and political interests that can be promoted through their connections with the 'new political elites'. The parties now have only scant relations with traditional associations, such as the European Trade Unions or the Kibbutz movements in the Israeli case.

To balance the losses that the parties suffered as a result of the decrease in the number of registered members, the parties gained in their ability to conduct more diverse and flexible strategies in the campaigns. Thus, for example, parties can use aggressive propaganda directed at voters whose foremost concern is their own private interests. Similarly, parties relatively easily swap coalitions. As part of this strategic and tactical flexibility, various parties mobilize financial support from outside their traditional constituencies, even from foreign governments or interest groups.

Voter behaviour has become more particularistic, volatile and conditional. Therefore, most parties compete for voter support, practically regardless of the voters' social affiliation. Hence, voting has become a matter of expressing views and attitudes, especially about incumbent and competing leaders and, to a lesser extent, parties. The result is that most parties lack a particular social profile. Their social and economic platforms have become similar and almost identical. The party systems are characterized by the emergence of party-movements, which cater to specific interests. Most parties emphasize the use of the mass media for mobilizing voters. Under the combined influence of all of these factors, politics has become a profession and like other professionals, political leaders are mainly interested in prolonging their tenure in office and while in office tend to largely disregard their followers. They approach them again during election campaigns. Generally, the main functions that the parties perform are leadership selection and promotion and establishing governments.

Finally, in Europe and Israel there is a revival of religious and rightist parties that oppose political liberalism and tolerance, parties that espouse theocratic ideas, xenophobia and nationalism.

THE IMPLICATIONS

If, indeed, Western European and the Israeli political and party systems have changed according to the patterns suggested in the previous section, then the following are the main comparative and theoretical implications of the analysis in this article.

Like the European party system, the Israeli system has been going through advanced stages of 'systemic transformation'.[42] This transformation has been influenced by long term changes in social stratification and trends toward individualization, in general and in the cleavage systems, in particular. These long-term transformations influence changes in the political systems.

Therefore, the transformations of the party system and of individual parties are closely related to the political changes that have occurred over the last two decades both in some European states and in Israel. In other words, political change influences the transformation of the party system and specific parties and vice versa. Unlike intra-party politics, the change in citizens' political behaviour is a meaningful factor in party system transformation. Crosscutting patterns of citizens' political inclinations tend to create chaotic political systems.

The chaotic nature of the political system influences the main characteristic of the parties. Thus, party systems consist of a variety of party organizational models – catchall parties co-exist with mass, electoral and cartel parties.

Most parties have ceased to perform various traditional functions, especially political socialization, aggregation and definition of voter interests and participation in public policy making. Membership in parties has further declined as citizens turn to interest groups. As a result of the citizens' strong preference for interest associations over parties, religious and 'ethnic' parties, which are based on strong affinities and loyalties, have re-structured their organization and turned themselves into party-movements. These party-movements are designed to supply a variety of services to their members and thus to further increase their dependence and loyalty.

Meteoric leaders have become more prominent in all types of parties. These leaders concentrate considerable power within the parties and shape the main patterns of behaviour that are mainly intended to facilitate their own election and re-election. Consequently, political activists and party functionaries have become junior partners in the conduct of affairs in these entities.

NOTES

1. Dan Horowitz and Moshe Lissak, *Trouble in Utopia: The Overburdened Polity of Israel*, Albany: State University of New York Press, 1989.
2. For a similar approach see, for example, Reuven Y. Hazan, 'Party System Change in Israel 1948–98: A Conceptual and Topological Border-Stretching of Europe?' in P. Pennings and J.-E. Lane (eds.), *Comparing Party System Change*, London: Routledge, 1998, pp.151–166.
3. For an earlier and a shorter version of this section see, Gabriel Sheffer, 'Structural Change and Leadership Transformation', in David Levi-Faur, Gabriel Sheffer and David Vogel (eds.), *Political Change: Israel in a Comparative Perspective*, London: Frank Cass, 1999, pp.55–72.
4. Shmuel Noah Eisenstadt, *The Transformation of Israeli Society*, London: Weidenfeld and Nicolson, 1985.
5. Ehud Sprinzak and Larry Diamond (eds.), *Israeli Democracy under Stress*, Boulder: Lynne Reinner, 1993, pp.21–43; Avner Yaniv, *National Security and Democracy in Israel*, Boulder: Lynne Reinner, 1993, pp.1–10, 227–233.
6. Alan Dowty, 'Israel's First Decade: Building a Civil State', in Ilan Troen and Noah Lucas (eds.), *Israel: The First Decade of Independence*, Albany, State University of New York Press, 1995, pp. 31–50; Alan Dowty, *The Jewish State, A Century Later*, Berkeley: California State University Press, 1998, part I.
7. See especially, Sammy Smooha, 'Ethnic Democracy: Israel as an Archetype,' *Israel Studies*, Vol. 2, No. 2, 1997.
8. See for example, Avraham Brichta, 'The New Premier-Parliamentary System in Israel', in *Annals*, AAPSS, 555, January 1998.
9. Michael Barnett (ed.), *Israel in Comparative Perspective*, Albany: State University of New York Press, 1996; Levi-Faur, Sheffer and Vogel, *Political Change*.
10. For a similar analysis see, for example, Horowitz and Lissak, *Trouble in Utopia*; and Sheffer, 'Structural Change and Leadership Transformation'.
11. Shmuel Noah Eisenstadt, *Israeli Society*, Jerusalem: Magnes Press, 1967; Dan Horowitz and Moshe Lissak, *Origins of the Israeli Polity*, Chicago: Chicago University Press, 1978; Dowty, *The Jewish State*.
12. On the debate about the applicability of the consociational model to the Israeli case, see Emanuel Gutmann, 'Parties and Camps – Stability and Change', in Moshe Lissak and Emanuel Gutmann (eds.), *Ha-maarechet Ha-politit Ha-Israelit (The Israeli Political System)*, Tel Aviv: Am Oved, 1977; Gabriel Sheffer, 'Elite Cartel, Vertical Domination and Grassroots Discontent in Israel', in Sidney Tarrow, et. al. (eds.), *Territorial Politics in Industrial States*, New York: Praeger, 1978; Horowitz and Lissak, *Trouble in Utopia*; Peter Medding, *The Founding of Israeli Democracy 1948–1967*, New York: Oxford University Press, 1990; Arend Lijphart, 'Israeli Democracy and Democratic Reform in Comparative Perspective', in Sprinzak and Diamond, *Israeli Democracy under Stress*, pp.107–123; Alan Dowty, 'Israel's First Decade'; and see Reuven Y. Hazan's and Peter Y. Medding's articles in this volume.
13. Ian Lustick, *Arabs in the Jewish State: Israel's Control of a National Minority*, Austin: Texas University Press, 1980; Ian Lustick, 'The Changing Political Role of Israeli Arabs', in Asher Arian and Michal Shamir (eds.), *The Elections in Israel 1988*, Boulder: Lynne Reinner, 1990, pp.115–131; Jacob Landau, *The Arabs in Israel: A Political Study*, Oxford: Oxford University Press, 1969; Jacob Landau, *The Arab Minority in Israel, 1967–1991*, Oxford: Oxford University Press, 1993; Uzi Benziman and Atallah Mansur, *Dayarei Mishne (Subtenants)*, Jerusalem: Keter, 1992.
14. Peter Y. Medding, *Mapai in Israel: Political Organization and Government in a New Society*, Cambridge: Cambridge University Press, 1972; Medding, *The Founding of Israeli Democracy*.
15. For additional data see, for example, Asher Arian, *Ha-republika Ha-Israelit Ha-shnia (The Second Republic: Politics in Israel)*, Tel Aviv: Zmora Beitan, chapter 8.
16. Gerhard Lehmbruch, 'Consociational Democracy, Class Conflict and the New Corporatism', Paper Presented at IPSA Round Table on Political Integration, 1974; Gerhard Lehmbruch, 'Liberal Corporatism and Party Government', *Comparative Political Studies*, Vol. 10, No. 1, 1977.

17. For a discussion of the general phenomenon see, Eric Nordlinger, *Conflict Regulation in Divided Societies*, Cambridge: Harvard University Press, 1972; and for its application to the Israeli case see, Gabriel Sheffer, 'Elite Cartel, Vertical Domination and Grassroots Discontent in Israel'.

18. This view of mass parties conforms with Michels' analysis, Robert Michels, *Political Parties: A Sociological Study of the Oligarchical Tendencies of Modern Democracies*, New York: The Free Press, 1962; on this aspect in Israel see, for example, Arian, *The Second Republic*, chapter 6.

19. Arian, *The Second Republic*, chapter 8.

20. For a similar observation see, for example, Dowty, 'Israel's First Decade'.

21. See, for example, Itzhak Galnoor, 'The Crisis in the Israeli Political System: The Parties as a Central Factor', in Moshe Lissak and Baruch Knei-Paz (eds.), *Israel Likrat Shnat 2000: Hevra, Politika Ve-tarbut (Israel Toward the Year 2000: Society, Politics and Culture)*, Jerusalem: The Magnes Press, 1996.

22. For a general explanation of this phenomenon see, Gerhard Lehmbruch, 'Liberal Corporatism'.

23. Gerhard Lehmbruch, 'Liberal Corporatism'; Peter Schmitter, 'Modes of Interest Intermediation and Models of Societal Change in Western Europe', *Comparative Political Studies*, Vol. 10, No. 1, 1977.

24. Yael Yishai, *Kvutzot Interes Be-Israel (Interest Groups in Israel)*, Tel Aviv: Am Oved, 1987.

25. For a discussion of some of these developments see, Michael Shalev, *Labour and the Political Economy in Israel*. New York: Oxford University Press, 1992.

26. Gerhard Lehmbruch, 'Liberal Corporatism', p.94.

27. Shalev, *Labor and the Political Economy in Israel*; and see Arian's discussion of the floating vote in Arian, *The Second Republic*, chapter 8.

28. See, for example, Arian, *The Second Republic*, pp.152–155.

29. Otto Kirchheimer, 'The Waning of Opposition', in Roy Macridis and Bernard Brown (eds.), *Comparative Politics*, Chicago: Chicago University Press, 1986; Otto Kirchheimer, 'The Transformation of Western European Party System', in Joseph LaPalombara and Myron Weiner (eds.), *Political Parties and Political Development*, Princeton: Princeton University Press, 1966, pp.177–200.

30. Leon Epstein, *Political Parties in Western Democracies*, New Brunswick: Transactions, 1980.

31. Horowitz and Lissak, *Trouble in Utopia*.

32. Yishai, *Interest Groups in Israel*.

33. This is reflected, for example, in the monthly public opinion surveys published in *Ha'aretz* by the Tami Steinmetz Institute for Peace Research at Tel Aviv University.

34. Thomas Friedman, *The Lexus and the Olive Tree*, New York: Harper Collins, 1999.

35. Yaron Ezrahi, 'Democratic Politics and Culture in Modern Israel: Recent Trends', in Sprinzak and Diamond, *Israeli Democracy Under Stress*, pp.255–272.

36. For data on this aspect see, for example, Arian, *The Second Republic*, pp.210–216.

37. Eva Etzioni-Halevy, *Makom Ba-tzameret: Elitot Ve-elitism Be-Israel (A Place at the Top: Elites and Elitism in Israel)*, Tel Aviv: Tcherikover, 1997.

38 Ephraim Kleiman, 'The Waning of Israeli Etatism', *Israel Studies*, Vol. 2, No.2, 1997.

39 Tamar Hermann and Ephraim Yaar, 'The Peace Index – May 1999', *Ha-aretz*, 3 June 1999.

40 Barnett, *Israel in Comparative Perspective*; Levi-Faur, Sheffer and Vogel, *Political Change*.

41 Peter Mair, *Party System Change: Approaches and Interpretations*, Oxford: Oxford University Press, 1997; Peter Mair, 'Western Europe: The Dangers of Apathy', in Danny Korn (ed.), *Ketz Ha-miflagot (The Demise of Parties in Israel)*, Tel Aviv, Ha-kibbutz Ha-meuhad, 1998, pp.23–32; Stefano Bartolini and Peter Mair, *Identity, Competition and Electoral Volatility: The Stabilization of European Electorates 1885–1985*, Cambridge: Cambridge University Press, 1990.

42 In the sense suggested in Gordon Smith, 'A System Perspective on Party System Change', *Journal of Theoretical Politics*, Vol. 1, No. 3, 1989.

From Government by Party to Government Despite Party

PETER Y. MEDDING

This essay uses Lijphart's models of consensus and majoritarian democracy to analyze the evolution of the Israeli political system since 1948. Whilst taking account of societal divisions, issue differences and the electoral system, it focuses on the nexus between party, party system and government, and especially on changes in the pattern of party government. The explanation offered here challenges not only the conventional wisdom, but also, paradoxically, Lijphart's analysis of the Israeli case. Thus, while Lijphart's categories are used, radically different conclusions are reached.

The conventional wisdom about the development of the Israeli political system can be briefly summarized, as follows. First, Israel broadly fitted the consociational model, especially as regards the pattern of accommodation reached with the religious parties on certain fundamental matters: the application of religious law to issues of personal status; guarantees of autonomy for religious education; and acceptance of broad principles of freedom of religion and freedom from religion. For the first two or three decades after the establishment of the state, that pattern of accommodation seemed to work, albeit with ongoing tensions and intermittent crises, to facilitate the management of conflict (not its resolution).[1] In recent decades, however, the earlier pattern of accommodation seems to have broken down – attempts to alter it by the use of political power have become more frequent, readiness to compromise has declined and tensions over religious issues have intensified. Leaving aside reservations as to whether it offers an adequate explanation of the workings of the Israeli political system in the past, clearly, the consociational approach is not relevant to Israel today.

Second, the party system until 1977 is portrayed as a multi-party system whose extreme fractionalization, as well as its polarization and volatility were held in check by the existence of three or four major ideological blocs or camps. Throughout, the political system was dominated overall by Mapai (or a successor party), which received the

Peter Y. Medding is Dr Israel Goldstein Professor of the History of Zionism and the State of Israel at the Hebrew University of Jerusalem.

most seats in the Knesset and headed every government in Israel between 1948 and 1977.[2] Its loss, after the 1977 elections, of the capacity to dominate the system and control government, signals the transition to 'imperfect two-partism in a polarized multi-party system'.[3]

Third, it is common to regard this transition to a two-bloc or a virtual two-party system as being abetted by the fundamental transformation in Israeli party organization from mass-membership and ideological parties to electoral or professional-electoral parties.[4]

Fourth, Lijphart found that Israel never wholly fitted either the consensus or the majoritarian model of democracy, but was both. That is to say, on the executive-parties dimension – a set of characteristics relating to the party and electoral systems, issue divisions and the arrangement of executive power – Israel registered a high consensus democracy score. However, on the federal-unitary dimension – a cluster of elements relating to the centralization of government, constitutional limitations upon government and the type of legislative structure – Israel's score reflected a high level of majoritarian democracy. Thus, when Lijphart plotted his twenty-five democratic regimes on these two dimensions, only one country, Israel, had this hybrid pattern – a high consensus score on the executive-parties dimension and a high majoritarian score on the centralization dimension. 'Compared with the other twenty-four democratic systems', Lijphart concludes, 'this is certainly an unusual – both an 'abnormal' and 'lonely' – position'. In his view, however, 'Israel's degree of abnormality should not be exaggerated'.[5]

Lijphart's original analysis covered the 1948–1980 period. Later, he examined the 1948–1967 and 1967–1990 periods separately and found that Israel's consensus score on the executive-parties dimension was highest before 1967, but subsequently declined. This he took as evidence of the Israeli political system's movement from a predominantly consensual multi-party pattern to a predominantly majoritarian two-partyish or two-bloc pattern. Moreover, he argued, that trend would be reinforced by direct elections for Prime Minister, which would turn 'the election for the country's most important and powerful position into an all-or-nothing contest or zero-sum game'.[6] Despite the demand that the Prime Minister gain parliamentary approval for the new government and the possibility of being removed from office by a vote of no-confidence, (a clear limitation upon the direct popular electoral majority), the 'divisive potential of the winner-take-all majoritarian government' would remain high, Lijphart predicted, because parliament was likely to be reluctant to do so at the cost of terminating its own mandate and having to face new elections.

There seems to be considerable empirical support for the claims that after 1967 the majoritarian aspects of Israeli democracy strengthened and that a two-party or two-bloc pattern developed within what was still a polarized multi-party system. To begin with, during the first six Knessets (1949–1965) the sum of the two biggest parties averaged 63 MKs, but during the next seven Knessets (1969–1992) that figure rose to 82 MKs, with a high in 1981 of 95 MKS (79 per cent). Second, from 1949–1965 the largest party was on average 2.15 times larger than its nearest rival, but from 1969–1992 it was only 1.27 times as large. Third, whereas only one party could form and lead the government until 1977, from then on, the two largest parties competed virtually neck and neck to attain a parliamentary majority and in fact alternated in coalition formation and leadership of the government. Fourth, various minor parties were fairly stably aligned with one or other of the two larger parties, thus leading to the establishment of pre-election and post-election blocs that operated in concert in coalition negotiations. The degree of commitment of the various parties to those blocs varied, however, thus affecting their cohesion and bargaining power and from time to time parties hitherto aligned with one of the major parties entered coalitions headed by the other. Fifth, polarization was increased perceptibly by the heightened intensity of issue and group differences, especially when these overlapped with the major party blocs.

In what follows, I shall endeavour to show that contrary to the above, since 1948 the Israeli political system has moved from a predominantly majoritarian democracy to a predominantly consensus democracy, rather than vice versa. More specifically, until 1967, despite the presence of powerful consensus elements, Israel's executive power was both structurally-centralized, controlled and directed in a highly majoritarian manner by a strong form of party government. After 1967, however, Israel's executive power remained highly structurally-centralized, yet was operated by a far weaker form of party government in a less majoritarian manner, that is to say, more in accordance with Lijphart's model of consensus democracy and increasingly so as time went on. Initially, the strengthening of the consensus elements on the executive-parties dimension was due to underlying social processes that altered the relative weights of, and dynamics of competition between, the major political actors and forces. As a result, the balance in the political system between the majoritarian and the consensus elements swung steadily toward the latter. While in some regards, the introduction into the parties-elections dimension of a powerful majority-strengthening structural element – direct elections for Prime Minister – had the predicted effects, in other regards, paradoxically, it further weakened the majoritarian elements whilst simultaneously boosting the consensus elements, thus tipping the overall balance further in favour of the latter. As a result, in Israel today, party government, although not entirely absent, is weaker than ever before.

SOME CONCEPTUAL CLARIFICATIONS

In demonstrating how these conclusions have been arrived at, I shall focus on the two measures in Lijphart's executive-parties dimension that determine the actual operation of party government – concentration of executive power versus executive power sharing; and executive dominance versus executive-legislative balance. (His analysis of Israel's majoritarianism and structural centralization on the federal-unitary dimension both before and after 1967 is taken as correct and needs no further discussion.)

According to Lijphart, the 'concentration of executive power' – the majoritarian element – is typified by the 'one-party, bare-majority cabinet', whereas 'executive power sharing' – the consensus element – is typified by 'a coalition consisting of all major parties in the legislature'. Thus, the smaller the size of the coalition, in terms of the number of partners (party, parliamentary or ideological), the greater the concentration of executive power and, conversely, the bigger the coalition, the higher the degree of executive power sharing. That is to say, unlike single-party majority governments, coalition governments are inherently constrained by the necessity of attaining agreement among the partners in order to establish the parliamentary support underpinning the government in which executive power is vested and to maintain that agreement over time, both of which make it necessary, prudent or desirable to take into account what its partners want.

By definition, therefore, coalition government consisting of a number of parties is a sharing out of executive power among the various partners. It thus limits the capacity of the senior coalition party – the managing partner, as it were – to exercise executive power according to its own policies and understanding. Rather, it must meet the concerns and satisfy the demands of other coalition partners if it is to obtain and retain the support of the parliamentary majority. Lijphart's test for the degree of concentration of executive power or power sharing combines cabinet composition with size – the former is at its height in a minimum winning coalition, the prime example being a single-party cabinet, namely, one in which the Prime Minister and all ministers belong to the same party.

In the second dimension – executive dominance – the majoritarian element is manifested in effective formal executive control of the legislature, whereas, conversely, the consensus element is manifested in executive-legislative balance, that is to say, in the absence of such executive control and the consequent need therefore to obtain and maintain legislative approval of the executive's establishment, composition, policies and activities. When formal executive control of the legislature is backed up by a solid and stable party majority in the legislature, the majoritarian element is doubly enhanced. Conversely, where a formally dominant coalition executive, based on a sharing of power, is further limited in exercising its authority by the fragility, fluidity and instability of its multi-party parliamentary majority and thus constantly constrained by legislative capacity and willingness to remove it from office, the consensus element is doubly enhanced. And in keeping with these assumptions, Lijphart's measure of these elements is cabinet durability – the government's capacity to stay in office by ensuring that it cannot be removed.

As it stands, Lijphart's analysis is incomplete. To begin with, his concepts and definitions are not sufficiently differentiated. As a result, it is first assumed that concentrated executive power and executive dominance, on the one hand, and executive power-sharing and legislative-executive balance, on the other, are virtually synonymous and always go together. Second, following on from this, it is assumed that concentrated executive power and executive dominance are invariably associated with single-party majority governments and likewise, executive power-sharing and legislative-executive balance with multi-party coalition governments. Contrary to those assumptions, however, in neither case do these invariable relationships and firm distinctions hold up theoretically or empirically. (But given the focus on Israel, here only the coalition case is discussed.)

The theoretical problem with Lijphart's schema is that the two fundamental criteria underlying his opposing models of democracy – majoritarian and consensus – are not the polar opposite concepts that they are intended to be, but rather, are necessarily mutually-reinforcing. That is to say, conceptually, each contains and rests upon elements of the other. Indeed, Lijphart himself recognizes this by emphasizing that consensus government implies limitations over the power of a popularly elected majority executive power, whether constitutionally by judicial review, or structurally by multi-cameral legislative bodies and separation of powers requiring executive-legislative agreement. While these may, but do not necessarily, amount to minority veto (the problem being that both the executive and the legislature represent electoral majorities, albeit different ones), this is not so in the case of other majority-limiting devices such as coalition governments. But, here, in fact, the limitation upon majority rule is the requirement for more than a simple majority. To that extent, consensus government is inherently majoritarian, if not super-majoritarian. These conceptual difficulties are compounded and highlighted by the nature and realities of parliamentary systems in which coalition governments based on power-sharing (a consensus characteristic) may operate on the basis of executive dominance of the legislature (a majoritarian characteristic.) What is more, the larger the coalition size (a consensus variable) the greater its parliamentary majority and hence the greater its capacity for dominance over the legislative body, provided, of course, that it can maintain a stable parliamentary base of support. All in all, which characteristics belong to the majoritarian model and which to the consensus model is far from clear.

Moreover, Lijphart's second assumption (single-party majority government/concentrated executive power/executive dominance – multi-party coalition government/executive power-sharing/legislative-executive balance) excludes the empirical possibility that multi-party coalition governments can develop mechanisms for generating sufficient internal cohesion and coherence to enable them to function more in a majoritarian fashion with concentrated executive power than in a consensus fashion where executive power is cut up and parcelled out in segments to coalition partners who, in the absence of a coherent and agreed overall governmental policy, wield it in accordance with partisan or personal considerations. In short, the type of democratic government depends not only on the structure and party composition of executive power – whether it is concentrated or shared – but also on the dynamics of executive power – whether those party actors operate it cohesively and coherently, despite the structural constraints.

A more satisfactory approach is to distinguish between the structural and dynamic dimensions of executive power. The structural dimension relates to whether executive power is concentrated or shared as determined by the number of parties in government. The dynamic dimension relates to whether executive power is operated by the party or parties in government in a cohesive and coherent, or in a divided and non-integrated manner, as determined by three criteria: policy integration – a coherent overall governmental programme; administrative co-ordination – ministers and ministries act in concert and their various undertakings are planned and co-ordinated from above and implemented on the ground according to agreed collective guidelines; and personal cohesion – ministers are bound by collective decisions and act as a collective unit.

When the structural and the operational dimensions of executive power are thus separated, the wielding of concentrated executive power in a divided and non-integrated manner and the operation of shared executive power coherently and cohesively are no longer foreclosed by definition. Rather, they become real possibilities, the actual presence, extent and facilitating conditions of which are to be determined empirically, as are their implications for the other majoritarian and consensus variables in Lijphart's models.

1948–1967: GOVERNMENT BY PARTY, DOMINATED MULTI-PARTY
SYSTEM, MAJORITARIAN-LIKE EXECUTIVE POWER

Applying these amended criteria to Israel between 1948–1967 reveals
that it was more majoritarian during this period than Lijphart and others
have suggested. Indeed, despite the obvious similarities with Switzerland,
the Fourth French Republic and Italy, on such major consensus variables
as multiple issue dimensions, a fractionalized multi-party system and
elections by proportional representation, Israel's overall pattern of
government was closer to the most highly-majoritarian democracies
(New Zealand and Britain) than to the former.[7]

As indicated above, the key to understanding the majoritarian reality
of party government in Israel before 1967 lies in effective executive
control, or as it was termed above, cohesive executive power and its
coherent operation. This was made possible and was actively pursued
and effectively realized in the following conditions:

1.   Post-election coalitions were the norm.
2.   Effectively, one party, Mapai, was the only possible coalition
     formateur throughout. It was not only by far the largest party in the
     legislature, but occupied a central and bridging position on all
     relevant issue continua, which enabled it to seek partners from all
     sides of the political spectrum and establish ideologically-balanced
     coalitions.
3.   Mapai set the conditions for entry into the coalition along lines that
     broadly approximated its own policy platform and entry was
     determined by the willingness of the potential coalition partners to
     abide by the policies set by Mapai. By and large, Mapai made few
     policy compromises in order to get potential partners to join,
     especially in areas of cardinal importance, although it was prepared
     to accommodate the policies of other parties on less important issues
     where these did not conflict directly or diverge greatly from its own.
     Other parties rarely if ever succeeded in dictating to Mapai on
     matters of coalition policy or who would be members of the coalition.
4.   Mapai sought to establish ideologically-balanced and oversized
     cabinets and succeeded in doing so about 60 per cent of the time.
     Such cabinets served to counteract the blackmail potential and veto
     power of minor coalition partners, thereby enhancing the capacity
     for developing majoritarian-type concentrated executive power and
     limiting the impact of consensus-type power-sharing.
5.   From the outset, Mapai based cabinet operation on collective
     responsibility. Its principles were set down in Basic Laws and were
     applied strictly and effectively by Mapai prime ministers to
     maintain cabinet cohesion and coalition discipline.

6. Mapai ensured that it had an absolute majority in the cabinet.
7. Mapai occupied virtually all the most important ministries throughout the whole period.
8. Mapai's pattern of party organization enabled its ministers to operate on behalf of a large and institutionalized membership as a cohesive collective entity. For example, its ministers and leading officials met frequently to take policy decisions prior to cabinet meetings, they regularly consulted party bodies, both formally and informally and they regarded themselves as bound by agreed party policy. Most other major parties maintained similar patterns of party organization and operated as disciplined actors. This made the task of coalition formation and operation significantly easier and regulated inter-party competition.
9. Executive dominance was not only structurally mandated by the parliamentary system, but effectively the legislative body was completely controlled by the executive. Thus, of the 1366 laws passed between 1949 and 1968, 93 per cent were initiated by the government, 5.7 per cent by private members' bills and 1.7 per cent emanated from committees. Whatever Israel's relatively low score on cabinet durability indicates, it cannot be taken as evidence of executive–legislative balance or of the weakness of executive dominance.
10. These mechanisms for facilitating leadership cohesion, policy coherence and administrative integration enabled Mapai-led coalitions to control and direct policy making and implementation in a co-ordinated and centralized manner. At the governmental level, the Ministry of Finance played a crucial and effective role in bringing this about by determining the content of the annual legislation that set the budgetary and other economic guidelines within which all ministries (including those controlled by other parties) operated, by allocating resources accordingly and ensuring that these were expended on the intended purposes and by shaping the legislative and policy initiatives of other ministries in accordance with its overall economic plan.

This pattern of economic policy centralization was specifically reinforced by Mapai's control of all major economic portfolios: Finance, Labor and Agriculture for the whole period and Commerce and Industry and Development for most of it. Significantly, every major ministry that dealt with the production of economic goods and with the control of the allocation of resources was held by Mapai. This was reflected dramatically in the steadily rising proportion of the nation's already centralized budget at its disposal. Throughout, the proportion of the budget controlled by Mapai ministries was much greater than their percentage in the government. Thus, from 1951–1967, the proportion of the budget allocated to Mapai ministries increased steadily from 72 per cent to 90 per cent, whereas it never held more than 70 per cent of the ministerial portfolios.

More broadly, at the societal level, policy integration and coherence were greatly facilitated by Mapai's simultaneous control of other major institutional networks such as the Histadrut, many municipal and local government authorities, the Jewish Agency and so forth, which enabled it to co-ordinate the policies and activities of its representatives in each of them and to resolve the inevitable disagreements, disputes and conflicts between them within party institutions, ideally by reaching agreement on an overall policy to which all would be committed.

In sum, during the period from 1948–67, despite the presence of strong consensus elements such as multiple issues, a multi-party system, proportional representation and coalition government, the basic dynamics of Israeli party democracy were majoritarian rather than consensual and were characterized not only by executive dominance, but by a high degree of party-directed cohesive executive power and coherent executive operation. These were underpinned by the high degree of governmental and structural centralization in Israel as evidenced by Israel's strongly majoritarian score on Lijphart's unitary-federal dimension.

1967–1996: GOVERNMENT BY PARTY LEADERS, STALEMATED MULTI-PARTY SYSTEM, CONSENSUS-LIKE EXECUTIVE POWER

This pattern broke down after 1967 and from then on, as was suggested above, the balance in the operation of the Israeli political system moved increasingly away from the majoritarian pole in the direction of the consensus pole. Remarkably, this change was not the result of innovations or reforms in the rules ordering the structuring and operation of the major political institutions. Rather, the opposite was the case: structural innovations followed rather than preceded and in fact were not the cause of but the response to, those changes in the balance between the majoritarian and consensus elements. Thus, the structural reforms of the 1990s were intended to counter the tendency of strengthened consensus elements to prevent the development of coherent executive power. Specifically, grafting direct elections for Prime Minister onto a multi-party, multiple issue, proportional representation, coalition-led parliamentary system was designed to decisively weight the balance in its operation in a majoritarian direction. However, as we shall see, this is far from what happened in reality.

In order to demonstrate these claims, even if only sketchily, I shall examine first, how and in which ways the consensus elements in Israeli politics became strengthened; second, how this process interacted with developments in the realm of party organization; and, third, the impact of these changes on the operation of coherent executive power, in general and on party government, in particular. Finally, the structural changes of the 1990s will be examined and their impact assessed empirically.

Signs of disintegration in the majoritarian-like pattern of cohesive and coherent executive power first became evident prior to the Six Day War. On 3 June, 1967, to be precise, Mapai's minor coalition partners succeeded in doing what they had tried but never managed to do before: effectively to dictate basic coalition terms to Mapai. They made their agreement to participate in the coalition conditional both upon the removal of Eshkol, the Mapai Prime Minister from the Defence Ministry and his replacement by Dayan, then a leader of the Rafi party that had split bitterly from Mapai only two years earlier, and on the inclusion of the Herut party led by Begin, which had effectively been excluded from all previous coalitions since the state's establishment.

This gave rise to a grand coalition, the first in Israel's history, known as *memshelet likud le'umi*, the Government of National Cohesion. What is more, the inclusion of Dayan and Begin in the cabinet and the accession of their parties to the coalition, were immediately followed by what was widely perceived to be a major policy change and Israel's decision after weeks of indecision to engage in a lightning pre-emptive strike that launched the Six Day War and later turned out to have determined its outcome literally within minutes of its outbreak. Although that perception did not reflect the Israel Defence Force's readiness and detailed operational and contingency plans, the change of policy that led to dramatic victory was commonly attributed to the accession to the coalition of its new members.

A number of major precedents were set by these events. Dictation to the coalition *formateur* by potential minor coalition partners and the increasing willingness and necessity of the major coalition party and its leaders to accept such dictation, give ground and make concessions on policies and administrative co-ordination, even on major matters, increasingly became the norm. Thus, in 1974 Prime Minister Golda Meir (followed by her successor Yitzhak Rabin) accepted the Mafdal's demand for a referendum on the West Bank as the condition of its entry to the cabinet. More broadly, agreement of the coalition *formateur* to a long series of policy demands by minor coalition partners and a massive increase in the actual allocations of resources on a party and sectorial basis on a whole range of issues, but most blatantly in the sphere of religion, became the norm for all would-be coalition *formateurs*, both Likud and Labour, between 1977 and 1996.

Moreover, not only were grand coalitions established in 1984 and 1988, but since then these have been a permanent and real option in bargaining to establish coalitions after elections and in attempts to stabilize them between elections. There are four reasons for this. First, according to surveys, they are extremely popular with the public. Second, they represent an attempt to bridge differences and maximize support for difficult decisions (such as the tough economic measures that brought hyperinflation to an end in 1984–85, and peace negotiations that involve territorial withdrawal and the evacuation of Jewish settlements). Third, they freed the smaller potential coalition partners (especially the religious parties) from having to choose between coalitions led by one or other of the larger parties. Last, but not least, bringing their party into a grand coalition, even as the junior partner, bolstered the internal authority of the leaders of major parties who had failed electorally and staved off potential challenges to their leadership, by putting their colleagues (and possible rivals), as well as many party activists in public office and by generally enabling elected and appointed party representatives to control or direct the allocation of governmental resources.

If in 1967 the minor parties were able for the first time to determine who would be Defence Minister and which parties would join the government and under what conditions, the results of the 1977, 1981, 1984 and 1988 elections were such that one or a number of small parties could and did determine which of the leading parties would form the coalition and who would be Prime Minister. From this perspective, the situation after the 1992 elections which gave Rabin and the Labour party a blocking majority that neutralized the coalition-determining power of the small parties was something of an exception that recalled the pre-1967 pattern.

A major factor in the breakdown of the pre-1967 patterns of party government, executive dominance and cohesive and coherent executive power was the increasing personalization of politics at virtually every level. Probably its first manifestation was the organized public campaign of spontaneous demonstrations urging Mapai and the government to save the country from impending disaster by the personal appointment of Moshe Dayan as Defence Minister. As his party, Rafi, were outside the coalition, the only way in those days to accomplish this was by it formally joining the coalition. At the party level, it was further manifested in the ongoing personal contests for leadership in both the Labour party and the Likud, where the main mark of differentiation was not ideological or policy-oriented, but the personalities of the leader and his rivals and personal qualities – trust and promises replaced collective goals, party unity and group solidarity. It was further promoted at the ministerial level by the defection of Moshe Dayan from the Labour party parliamentary faction immediately after having been elected on its list at the 1977 elections and his acceptance of a personal appointment as Foreign Minister in the first-ever Likud government led by Menachem

Begin. The first structural change that both gave formal institutional expression to and further promoted the process of personalization was the Knesset's decision in the late 1970s to replace the familiar PR party list method in municipal elections with a split system, in which mayors and heads of local government authorities were chosen in direct personal elections requiring a 40 per cent plurality in the first round (and provisions for a second round) whilst the PR list system was retained for choosing their councils. This was followed in the 1980s by the personalization of internal party elections with the introduction of primaries (local and national) for choosing candidates for various public and party offices and eventually for party leader. Personalization at the party level was institutionalized in the 1980s by the adoption of some form of primaries for internal party elections for Knesset candidates and party leaders, one obvious and immediate effect of which was a severe decline in the capacity of party institutions to bind, direct and lend coherence to the activities of party representatives and leaders.

Eventually, the contest for attaining control of the executive power was further personalized at the end of the 1980s with the introduction by the two major parties of direct mass primaries for selecting their leaders (and candidates for Prime Minister), in response to the mounting public campaign for direct elections for Prime Minister, that eventuated in the Knesset legislating to that effect just prior to the 1992 elections to apply as from the 1996 elections. (One immediate effect was to turn the 1992 Knesset elections conducted on the basis of party list PR into a personal election contest between the incumbent Likud Prime Minister Shamir and the Labour Party leader Rabin.) Via the constant magnification of the personal by both the electronic and print media, the process of personalization has enveloped and affected every facet and every level of political life. Even in the Haredi parties – the bastions of traditionalism – full rein has been given to this essentially modern phenomenon, as evidenced by the highly personalized character of the outside leadership of religious political parties by charismatic rabbis wielding traditional religious authority, instantly and personally conveyed to the masses by satellite transmissions and further disseminated and preserved for posterity on video and compact disk.

A further manifestation was the personalization of the exercise of executive power at the highest levels. This initially became prominent in Rabin's first term of office (1974–1977), with the appointment of a staff of personal advisers, who although located in the Prime Minister's office, were neither career civil servants nor party representatives, beholden either to the professional ethos and standards of the first, or the shared collective goals of the second, but individuals who owed their appointment to their personal relationship with and the trust of the chief executive and over the years their numbers and responsibilities increased. In response to the 'primarization' of internal and external elections, candidates for high party and public office quickly became surrounded by personal campaign staff, personal policy and media advisers and personal pollsters. While in external elections these personal teams did not entirely replace party bodies, party policies, party campaign teams and party pollsters, they remained quite separate from, and ran independently of, the latter.

Moreover, the phenomenon of party candidates, and indeed of parties, running for office, not on the formal party label, but ostensibly on a more general, attractive and less partisan label (albeit supported by the party) became increasingly common. While manifesting itself first in municipal elections, it reached a new level in the Histadrut elections in 1993, when Haim Ramon, a young and influential minister in the Rabin government, ran for the position of Histadrut Secretary-General, on a hastily drawn-up personal list, against the incumbent Labour candidate who had recently won the internal party primary. After a whirlwind, highly personalized, media-saturated electoral campaign, Ramon's list received the highest percentage of votes and he became Histadrut Secretary-General and immediately established a broad coalition with the Labour party and a number of other lists, including Meretz and Shas. Yet, within less than two years, having presided over a radical restructuring and downsizing of the Histadrut, Ramon resigned and resumed his membership in the Labour party as if nothing had happened and was soon reappointed as a minister in the Labour-led coalition government.

Overall, these developments have reduced the role and influence of the party organizations that formerly had dominated political life in Israel. The major reference groups for party candidates for public office were now more likely to be the potential and actual voters and supporters in the electorate than party activists, party members and party institutions. Face to face activities, often of a local and pinpointed nature, by party leaders, spokesmen and rank and file members, aimed at maintaining the support of the faithful and of persuading others gave way to centralized and mass TV campaigning run on a purely business basis by professional advertising agencies, media consultants and political advisers (often from overseas). Moreover, the role of party volunteers in getting out the vote has largely been taken over by paid workers. Significantly, this radical decline in the level of party activity of all kinds has occurred despite increasingly generous public financing of party political and campaign activities.

Increasingly since the latter part of the 1970s, the role of the *formateur's* party institutions in the exercise of executive power has shrunk. During its nearly thirty years in opposition, Herut (later Gahal and Likud) had been a leader-dominated party, with party institutions taking second place behind Begin in policy determination on matters of major importance. His accession to power in 1977 at the head of a Likud-led coalition reinforced this bottom-down leadership control of the party. Begin's personal decision to go against the basic thrust of declared party policy as well as his own previous position and bring about Israeli territorial withdrawal from Egyptian territory in order to make a peace treaty with Egypt is entirely consistent with Herut's established pattern of policy-making. So, too, was the fact that Begin's Camp David agreements became government policy despite their rejection by a majority of Herut MKs and its authoritative internal party institutions.

Similarly, when Labour was in office during the 1980s and 1990s, the party institutions no longer played the initiating, determining or mediating role in the operation of executive power that had been the norm in Mapai before 1967. Unlike Herut, however, they did provide those exercising executive power with a floor of broad agreement and generalized support, as was strikingly demonstrated in the case of the Rabin government's agreement to recognize the PLO and to negotiate with it over the matter of Israeli withdrawals from territories to be handed over for rule by a Palestinian Authority, as expressed in the Oslo Accords. While these radical changes in the official position of the Israeli government had not been foreshadowed by Rabin or the party during the 1992 election campaign, they were consistent with the broad thrust of Labour party's platforms and with its leaders' views as enunciated during (and between) the election campaigns of the 1980s. Thus, despite the fact that the Oslo Accords came as a total surprise, from the outset, the peace process had, or soon won, the overwhelming support of the majority of Labour party members, activists, institutions and voters.

Thus, over the years, party activists and institutions have had far less of an active role to play in articulating interests and values and in contributing to policy-making in response to such concerns. Increasingly, the main test for what policies the party should strive to achieve and present to the electorate for support and authorization policies has not, or not only, been what party leaders, institutions and members believe should be done for the good of the county or the public, whatever that is, but how popular they are or will be with the public and whether they will help or hinder the candidate or the party to get elected. Such judgements tend to be made by candidates and their advisers on the basis of public opinion surveys, rather than by party institutions. At the same time, national party primaries to select parliamentary and prime ministerial candidates have heightened the influence of rank and file party members, taking away from party institutions what previously had been a major function and thus further narrowing the role of sub-leaders and activists.

Moreover, party representatives and leaders had little interest and encouragement to invest in and become part of a collective team and to act as a cohesive unit. To the contrary, they had a much greater incentive to emphasize their individuality and independence, to garner product recognition, to keep themselves in the public eye, to get attention and that, to a large extent, is contingent upon their being able to distinguish themselves from their colleagues. The higher up the political ladder one goes, the greater the stakes and the more powerful such incentives and thus members of Knesset and ministers are particularly affected.

Under such conditions, all political leaders, from the Prime Minister, through the ministers, the members of Knesset, the would-be members of Knesset, are permanent candidates for individual office. In short, so long as they stay in politics, they are never not running for office. The overall effect of such extreme personalization and individualization of political competition has been the radical disaggregation of party structure and functioning.

Further evidence of and contributing to a strengthening of the consensus elements, was the breakdown of the previous pattern of close-knit, disciplined, cohesive and highly institutionalized parties, capable of mandating their Knesset representatives to behave individually as delegates and collectively as a cohesive group dedicated to the pursuit of party policies and goals. One direct consequence was the whittling away of executive dominance in the sense of effective governmental control of the parliamentary agenda. Thus, in Knessets 8–12 (1974–1992) private members' bills constituted 25 per cent of an average 304 bills per Knesset (as against six per cent previously). But in the 13th Knesset (1992–1996) there was a dramatic absolute and relative increase in private members' bills: 53 per cent of its 468 bills were now private members' bills and 47 per cent, government bills. Moreover, of these 250 private members' bills, 33 per cent were sponsored solely by MKs from opposition (non-coalition) parties, 42 per cent by MKs from government (coalition) parties, whilst 24 per cent were sponsored jointly by both government and opposition MKs.[8]

These figures provide only a rough measure of the extent of the reduction in executive dominance and of policy coherence and do not provide conclusive evidence of legislative control over or capacity to dictate policy to the executive. Rather, it must be assumed that the government has the parliamentary majority to defeat any private members' bills it chooses, irrespective of whether the sponsors are opposition or government MKs, but that it chooses not to do so for a variety of reasons. Thus, the extent of control over the parliamentary agenda and the degree of reduction in executive dominance, depend upon the reasons for government inaction. Clearly, the implications of inaction due to lack of objection to the proposed legislation are very different from the implications of inaction when the government does in fact object, but is reluctant to arouse public ire or lose electoral appeal by enforcing coalition discipline to defeat proposals that are popular with the public or the media. Under such circumstances, the government's control over the parliamentary agenda, in general, and its capacity for policy coherence, in particular, are reduced most, but not only, by the passing of opposition private members' bills (especially if they benefit electorally). They are reduced also by independent parliamentary initiatives and activities on the part of government MKs, whether singly, in a group or in conjunction with opposition MKs, unless, as sometimes occurs, the former act as surrogates for the government.

However, while this stark increase in the number and proportion of private members' bills clearly reflected a significant transfer of parliamentary initiative to individual MKs from all parties, executive dominance was not completely eroded so long as the government was still able to use its parliamentary majority to pass any bills that were important to it – from the budget down – and to reject votes of no-confidence. Moreover, the success rate for private members' bills did not improve over this period. Thus, in the first 12 Knessets, only 12 per cent of all private members' bills introduced into the Knesset became law and in fact, in the 13th Knesset, that percentage was halved. The reason for this lower success rate, however, was not an attenuation of independent initiative and activity by MKs, but precisely the opposite – an exponential increase in the number of private members' bills introduced, from an average of 336 bills in the first 12 Knessets to 3523 (!) in the 13th Knesset. Clearly, the likelihood of legislative success is only one factor motivating legislators in their independent policy initiatives and proposals. At work, also, are other factors, such as the opportunity to demonstrate legislative diligence, suitability for higher office and so forth. Not least amongst these motivations, however, are the opportunity and desire to attract media attention to themselves personally and give them public and electoral exposure.

The disaggregation of party, both institutionally and at the parliamentary levels, has also contributed to the further disintegration of cohesive executive power and its coherent operation, or what should properly be termed the disaggregation of executive power, not executive power-sharing. This is most notable in the virtual lapsing into desuetude of the most powerful weapon of cohesive executive power – collective responsibility. The capacity of ministers in the Israeli cabinet to criticize government policy, blame other ministers or departments or both for various failings, to express their lack of faith in, loyalty to and regard for the Prime Minister, to publicly cast abuse at each other and at the Prime Minister, increased exponentially over the years and seemed to have known no bounds.

Before 1967, the development of majoritarian-like coherent executive power was facilitated by the nature, distribution and structuring of the multiple issues dividing the society and the parties.[9] Briefly, during the 1950s and 1960s differences between the parties on major issues that were wide at the outset narrowed steadily, the intensity of disagreements declined, the ideological distance between the major parties decreased and deep partisan divisions over defence and foreign policy and economic policy were resolved and not simply managed. The period since 1967, however, has been characterized by the development of new, intense, mutually reinforcing and virtually non-negotiable issue conflicts over questions of religion, ethnicity, security, territories, demography, economic priorities and resource distribution. Unlike the past, where the various issues were separate from each other, after 1967 they have become inextricably interwoven. For example, the major issue of the period – whether or not Israel should withdraw from the territories on the West Bank (or Judea and Samaria, with the name itself an ideological statement), under what conditions and to whom it should relinquish control – has religious, national, security, demographic, economic, regional and international dimensions, that are weighed and combined differently by the political actors. Moreover, whereas the main issue divisions before 1967 were *between* parties, since then, significant differences over issues have been manifest *within* parties, as well.

The intensity, inter-connectedness and internal divisiveness of these multiple issue differences further complicated the already difficult task of coalition formation and operation in the 1980s and 1990s. And as if this were not sufficient, these difficulties were further compounded by the strengthening of proto- or repressed anti-system parties and their participation in governmental coalitions. Anti-system parties – those that openly challenge the legitimacy of the basis upon which the state had been established, even if they accepted parliamentary democracy – are not a new phenomenon in Israeli politics, but have been present from the outset, participated in elections and gained Knesset representation. Initially, however, the anti-system elements such as Herut, which denied the right of any Israeli government to agree to the partition of Palestine and sought the dismantling of the Histadrut and the labour economy, and the Communist party, which denied the legitimacy of Israel as a Jewish and Zionist state in Palestine, were excluded from coalition participation. Significantly, only after it moved toward the centre and became reconciled with a status quo that hitherto it had vehemently rejected did Herut's exclusion come to an end.

Thus, what is new is the inclusion of anti-system elements in government. Despite non-acceptance of the legitimacy and basic principles of democracy and rejection of Zionism and a Zionist Jewish state as heresy and their espousal of an ideology that values rabbinic rule according to Halakha above democracy and majority rule, since 1977, Haredi parties have regularly been included within the governmental coalition and their representatives have held ministerial office. At most, their acceptance of democracy is limited and contingent: the democratic process and majority decisions may be followed so long as they do not conflict with Halakha as interpreted by the rabbinical authorities. Thus, although they regard Halakha and theocracy as the ultimate ideal, Haredi parties neither campaign on a platform urging the overthrow of the democratic system, or the erasure of the Zionist character of the Jewish state, nor act purposively towards these ends and thus are not regarded as representing 'a clear and present danger' to the maintenance of those fundamental values.

How far these parties were prepared to go in openly challenging the Zionist and democratic basis of the Israeli state was tested in the 1990s with the entrenchment of these principles in Basic Laws and the declaration by the Supreme Court that a constitutional revolution was under way. For the Haredi parties, the very possibility of an entrenched constitution that was accorded or claimed superiority and took precedence over religious law and was interpreted by an independent judicial body such as the Supreme Court over which they had little political influence, was particularly threatening. At times, their opposition to the Supreme Court and to the possibility of a constitution, verged on a general attack on the rule of law.

Joining coalition governments has thus created acute moral dilemmas for the Haredi parties over the extent to which they can accept political and collective responsibility as partners in a government that does not behave in accordance with, or even acts contrary to, Halakha, as was clearly demonstrated during the 1980s and 1990s over the vexed issue of 'Who is a Jew?' To date, they have tended to make distinctions between ministries held by others for which they are only indirectly responsible and their own ministries for which they are personally responsible. While non-halakhic government policies or decisions in the former do not generally oblige them to resign from government, this is not the case in their own ministries, where they have in fact resigned from office rather than obey a court order to implement a policy or decision that in their view is contrary to Halakha, although, even here, the party stayed in the coalition. The continued willingness of Haredi parties to reach such pragmatic accommodations at the practical level and to confine their ultimate rejection of the fundamental values of Israeli society to the abstract theoretical level, indicates that they are not prepared to push their anti-system tendencies to their logical conclusions and act purposively to attain them and for that reason they are here characterized as proto- or repressed anti-system parties.

The inclusion of these repressed anti-system parties in governmental coalitions had major consequences for coalition politics and party government. Essentially contested constitutional issues that in the past were kept off the coalition agenda or managed on an ad hoc basis, were now the focus of demands and counter-demands for their decisive resolution. The presence of deep-principled disagreements at the centre of vociferous and highly-publicized disputes between coalition partners diminished governmental effectiveness, undermined its authority and, in general, brought coalition government into considerable disrepute.

Moreover, the pattern set by Herut in the 1950s does not seem to apply to the Haredi parties three decades later. Rather than weaken their anti-system stance, as might have been expected, the inclusion of the Haredi parties in governmental coalitions during the 1980s and 1990s entrenched and intensified it. In short, the state generously funded an autonomous network of Haredi educational institutions that inculcated their anti-system values and discouraged integration into the major institutions of Israeli society and provided financial and other incentives and premiums that facilitated non-integration in practice. In so doing, the state has supplied the means to make their anti-system stance, social segregation and communal autonomy self-sustaining. If in the past, anti-system parties were forced to pay a price that over time dampened their anti-system tendencies, during the 1980s and 1990s that is no longer the case. Rather than being penalized politically for their anti-system stance, Haredi parties, it seems, are now rewarded for it.

The disaggregation of executive power and the loss of cohesion and coherence were strikingly evident in the distribution of the non-defence state budget between the parties. Whereas in the period 1950–1976 (and also 1992–1996), the percentage of the budget per MK was significantly higher in the larger parties than in the smaller parties, between 1977 and 1992, however, the opposite was the case: the budget percentage per MK was more than twice as high for the smaller parties than for the larger parties. Similarly, whereas from 1950–1974, the religious parties received less per MK than the non-religious parties, from 1977–1992, their budget percentage per MK was five times that for the non-religious parties.[10] More conclusive evidence of the parcelling out of budgetary resources, the disaggregation of executive power and the immense difficulties facing a Prime Minister who sought policy coherence would be hard to come by. (Further support for our argument above, that the 1992–1996 period with its blocking majority bears great resemblance to the pre-1967 period may also be found in the fact that the overall pattern of budgetary allocations is very similar.)

In sum, after 1967 and especially in the 1980s and 1990s, on virtually every count, the majoritarian elements in the structure and operation of executive power in the Israeli democracy became weaker and the consensus elements became stronger. Coherent and effective control of executive power gave way to the disaggregation of executive power. Policy and issue differences led to the parcelling out of executive power, not power sharing. Collective responsibility virtually disappeared. Executive dominance was challenged by every member of the legislature.

Contributing greatly to these developments was the steady disintegration of the previous pattern of party government. Internal party bodies engaged less and less in setting policy for their governmental representatives, leaving this to a small group of party ministers, but this did not bring about the cohesive and coherent exercise of executive power. Rather, the unity of that group was undermined by conflicting individual interests and policy approaches (often fanned by departmental differences and bureaucratic infighting) and by leadership challenges and rivalries at the top. As the latter tended to be exacerbated when parties lost elections, party leaders facing internal challenges had a considerable incentive to stifle them by joining the government coalition, even at the cost of otherwise unacceptable policy compromises and deferments. Such considerations were not insignificant in the establishment of the National Unity Governments in 1984 and 1988. Not only were these governments the antithesis of the cohesive and coherent operation of executive power, they further reduced the policy influence of the party ministers as a group in favour of the top leaders upon whose capacity to co-operate and reach agreement the effectiveness of government largely depended. The result was a striking example of elite accommodation – the paradigmatic mechanism of consociational democracy – whereby leaders at the peak broker agreements and bridge differences over the heads of sub-leaders and outside of regular party bodies and channels, to the further detriment of party government and majoritarian-like executive power.

Finally, the simultaneous empowerment of the rank and file by the introduction of primaries to select the party leader and parliamentary representatives further weakened party institutions and middle level leaders and activists, formerly the backbone of party strength and party government. In sum, by the mid-1990s, government by party had given way to government by party leaders.

POST-1996 – GOVERNMENT DESPITE PARTY, FLUID AND
EXTREME MULTI-PARTY SYSTEM, DISAGGREGATED
MAJORITARIAN EXECUTIVE POWER

For the first time in 1996 and then again in 1999, Israel simultaneously elected its Prime Minister by popular majority and its Knesset by PR. To date, despite the thin empirical base, four conclusions are incontrovertible. First, direct elections have successfully accomplished what they were intended to do – take the choice of Prime Minister away from the small political parties and thus reduce their veto and extortion power. However, in doing so, they have also taken that power away from the large parties as well. Second, there has been a marked increase in the number of party lists represented in the Knesset and an absolute and relative decrease in the strength of the larger parties. Thus, after peaking at 15 in 1984 and 1988, the number of parties in the Knesset declined to 10 (its lowest number ever), when the electoral threshold was raised from 1 per cent to 1.5 per cent in 1992. However, following the inception of direct elections, 13 parties attained Knesset representation in 1996 and 17 did so three years later.

Third, direct elections have resulted in a radical downsizing of the largest party in the Knesset – the most likely coalition *formateur*. For the first six Knesset elections until 1965 it averaged 44 MKs (range 40–47), rising over the next seven elections to 47 MKs (range 40–56). But, the largest party dropped to 34 MKs in 1996 and to 26 MKs in 1999. As a result, whereas from 1949–1992, the largest party needed at most only an additional 21 MKs to form a majority coalition, the number required was 27 MKs in 1996 and 35 MKs in 1999. Fourth, the direct elections in 1996 and 1999 had a marked impact on coalition formation and operation; coalition stability and governmental control over the legislative body; parties, party government and the party system; and issue differences and it is on these that the following analysis focuses.

Prior to the 1996 elections, the Likud candidate for Prime Minister, Binyamin Netanyahu, succeeded in persuading Rafael Eitan, leader of the Tsomet party and David Levy, leader of the Gesher party (a breakaway from the Likud) to withdraw their proposed candidacies for Prime Minister. This was of critical importance to Netanyahu as it was widely assumed that most of their support would come from potential Netanyahu voters. The upshot of Netanyahu's negotiations with them were agreements that gave their respective parties six of the top thirty-seven places on a new joint list. Personally, they were each promised a senior cabinet position and the rank of Deputy Prime Minister. As it turned out, in 1996, the combined Likud-Gesher-Tsomet list obtained 32 Knesset seats, of which the Likud's two partners each received 5 Knesset seats, leaving it with only 22 MKs, as compared with 32 MKs in 1992. In sum, Mr Netanyahu's pre-election agreements to remove rival candidates came at the expense of 10 Likud MKs.

Netanyahu's pre-election strategy was also marked by significant policy compromises to other parties and potential voters that entailed acceptance of views and positions that were inconsistent with those that he had hitherto espoused. Thus, in the case of Gesher, he agreed to adopt social welfare policies that would require him to compromise on the commitment to a free market that was at the centre of his economic platform. This section of his agreement with Gesher was later incorporated verbatim in the Basic Principles of Government Policy that he presented to the Knesset for approval together with his ministry.[11]

Similarly, for years Netanyahu had led a public campaign opposing the Oslo Accords. Yet, about six weeks before the election he declared that a future Likud government under his leadership would recognize as a *fait accompli* and not undo, steps already taken under the Oslo Accords, hastily and badly drawn up as these were. For him, what was now at issue were future agreements with the Palestinians, especially those relating to final status. He also intimated that 'he would consider meeting with Arafat if this was vital for Israel's security'. This unilateral public reversal of the Likud's official position, one intensely held by most of its leaders, members and voters, was not preceded by any decision of an authorized party institution or policy-making body, but came as a bolt out of the blue.[12] Over the following weeks, however, first, the joint Likud-Gesher-Tsomet list steering committee fell in line and formally adopted Netanyahu's position and it was then incorporated in the Likud's election platform made public in mid-May. Precisely what that reversal meant, however, was subsequently revealed on a popular TV discussion programme, *Popolitika*, by Likud MK Michael Eitan who stated in no uncertain terms that had Netanyahu not declared publicly that he accepted the Oslo Accords, he would not have been elected.

Netanyahu assiduously pursued the support of the religious parties and their supporters. He needed to do little in the case of the Mafdal that had served in Likud-led governments since 1977 and was aligned ideologically on territorial issues and settlement policies. It campaigned to the right of the Likud in 1992 (and stayed out of the Rabin-led Labour government) and had worked closely with Netanyahu and the Likud in the public campaign opposing the Oslo Accords. Not surprisingly, in 1996 the Mafdal came out strongly in support of Netanyahu and a Likud-led coalition, although in the event of a Peres victory, the Mafdal declared its willingness to serve in his government.

Netanyahu's problem with the Haredi parties was somewhat more complicated. Although their voters and most of their rabbinical authorities were thought to be solidly behind Netanyahu and the Likud and manifested a strong antipathy to Labour and its allies as a secular threat to their way of life and to Judaism, a few leading rabbis, particularly Rabbi Shach of Yahadut Ha-torah and Rabbi Ovadia Yosef of Shas, were known to be dovish on territorial issues. Just before the election, despite strenuous counter-efforts by Peres and Labour, Netanyahu gained the public endorsement of Rabbi Schach, an agreement from Rabbi Yosef not to direct his followers how to vote, the blessing of a centenarian Shas rabbi widely revered for his special spiritual and mystical powers, deriving from his mastery of the Kabbala, and the official support of Agudat Israel's Council of Torah Sages (*Moezet Gedolei Ha-torah*). Of no small significance in tipping the scales in Netanyahu's favour was that 'whatever Peres had promised their rabbis, Netanyahu promised more'.[13] And on election day, the Haredi voters kept their side of the bargain in massive proportions.

Overall, as a result of his written and oral pre-election agreements, Netanyahu had mortgaged six ministries (one third of the total), a deputy minister with effective ministerial responsibility, an array of parliamentary chairmanships and made far-reaching promises of financial support for the separate institutions and particular needs of the Haredi community. He thus had far less than a free hand to conduct coalition negotiations after his narrow election as Prime Minister.

Three aspects of the coalition that Netanyahu established quickly and easily stand out. First, it was based on broad ideological agreement and specific pre-election understandings with three established religious parties (which in 1996 increased their Knesset representation from 16 to 23 Knesset seats) and with a Russian immigrant party, Israel Be-aliya, competing for the first time, that won seven seats. The leaders of those four parties supported Netanyahu (whether openly or behind the scenes) and so too did the overwhelming majority of their followers. Indeed, to all intents and purposes, Netanyahu and these parties had operated in his election campaign as a team, thus making them his natural coalition partners. The outcome of his negotiations, therefore was an ideologically-concentrated right-wing coalition, with the two small centre parties, Israel Be-aliya and Ha-derech Ha-shlishit, also to the right on different aspects of the territorial and settlement issues.

Second, Netanyahu's coalition manifested a considerable degree of structural concentration. To begin with, it was numerically narrow, consisting in all of 66 MKs. In terms of party composition, the combined Likud-Gesher-Tsomet list with 48 per cent of the coalition's Knesset seats accounted for 61 per cent of the ministers (11 out of 18). Moreover, they held most key ministries – Prime Minister, Defence, Foreign Affairs, Finance, Justice and Infrastructure. In fact, all of these (excepting Foreign Affairs) were held by ministers from Netanyahu's own party, the Likud (or his personal appointee). Overall, for most of the time, the 22 Likud MKs (33 per cent of the parliamentary coalition) supplied at least 50 per cent of the ministers.

Third, despite these advantages, Netanyahu's coalition was beset by a number of fundamental structural weaknesses. Its Likud-Gesher-Tsomet core was at best a joint parliamentary faction loosely representing three independent parties rather than a cohesive single party. In all, therefore, his coalition was made up of eight separate parties. The theoretical implications of such a high number of parties are well-known – the more parties there are in a coalition, the more diverse and extensive the demands for policies, offices and resources that a coalition *formateur* is likely to have to satisfy in the course of obtaining and maintaining his majority. Finally, three parties – the Mafdal, Israel Be-aliya and Shas – could each bring down the government and precipitate new elections at any time. As a result, the Prime Minister was constantly exposed to considerable veto or blackmail power on policy issues, public office appointments and resource distribution.

As a result of these structural weaknesses the Netanyahu government led by a directly-elected Prime Minister lost its capacity to exercise effective control over the legislature, act as a collective unit and pursue integrated policies. That is to say, direct elections for Prime Minister (a powerful majoritarian device) did not stem the ongoing disaggregation of the structures, operation and goals of executive power in Israel and may even have accelerated these processes, as can be seen from the following examination of resource distribution; party leadership and solidarity; ministerial collectivity and *esprit de corps*; and legislative proposals.

As to the first, the data relating to the percentage of the national budget per MK in the first year of the Netanyahu government reveal a replication, if not intensification of the 1977–1992 pattern. In 1996, the percentage of the national budget per MK for the smaller coalition parties was four times greater than it had been in the Rabin era, whereas the large parties' percentage did not change. As a result, the smaller parties' percentage had now increased from twice to three and a half times that of the larger parties. Similarly, the religious parties' budget percentage per MK was three and a half times that of the non-religious parties.[14]

Second, Netanyahu's term in office was characterized by his distance from and loss of support of other major Likud leaders and parliamentarians. From the moment that he became the popularly elected Prime Minister, he virtually ceased to function as a party leader in conjunction with its institutions (which he in fact controlled) to integrate its parliamentary representatives, and as the spearhead of collective decision-making by its ministers. That pattern was clear from the very outset in the lack of consultation with other party leaders in the coalition-making process and the selection of ministers. The latter were kept on hold to the very last moment, although in some cases the final choice was imposed upon him by prospective ministers who made their acceptances contingent on the appointment to office of other fellow party leaders seemingly left out by Netanyahu. As a result many of the appointees and those left out were disgruntled from the outset.

This pattern continued throughout his term of office. Three senior Likud ministers resigned or were forced out, in each case giving voice to lack of confidence in Netanyahu as Prime Minister and party leader. Neither was Netanyahu able to maintain the confidence and loyalty of the Gesher MKs and of their leader, David Levy, Minister of Foreign Affairs. Eventually the loss of support of these ministers and their parliamentary followers undermined the Netanyahu government's majority. Nor did Netanyahu succeed in retaining the confidence and steady co-operation and support of ministers from other parties. All in all, Netanyahu failed to establish the basic solidarity and *esprit de corps* among either his party ministers or the government as a whole upon which the formal rules of collective responsibility rest. Collective responsibility without collective decision-making, willing co-operation, a sense of common purpose and unity, welded together by acceptance of the leadership of the Prime Minister, turned routine governmental and parliamentary decision-making into a chronic crisis of confidence, in which, whether formally or not, the stability of the parliamentary majority was always in doubt.

As Natan Sharansky, head of the Israel Be-aliya party and Netanyahu's Minister of Trade and Industry put it in a recent interview:

> Bibi has a lot of skills. I also think his government had important accomplishments. He brought the right into the centre so that the peace process belongs to the whole nation of Israel, not just to the left... But during his years in government I saw how petty politics eroded many of his talents. He didn't succeed in constructing systems that would work for him and he wasn't able to turn ministers into partners, friends. And the load on him was impossible. He lost perspective. One day there was a strategy, the next day not. Almost all the ministers felt that they didn't know where they stood.... But because there were so many pressures on him, it was impossible to know which pressure of which moment would be decisive. It's impossible to conduct any sort of policy like that.[15]

The erosion of concentrated executive power, the absence of collective responsibility in the substantive sense, the lack of cohesiveness and the incapacity to operate executive power coherently could not be put more aptly. Under such conditions, obviously, executive dominance – the capacity of the government to control the parliamentary agenda – was likely to prove even more difficult than before. Thus, despite direct elections, the more disunited Netanyahu's party, parliamentary list and government were, the less stable the government's parliamentary majority was, which increased the coalition partners' policy, office and resource demands and raised the level of concessions and payoffs needed to satisfy them, as was increasingly evident in the annual budgetary process.

Furthermore, as in the past, a constant stream of private members' bills continued to challenge government control over the parliamentary agenda and further eroded its capacity for coherent policy-making. Thus, a total of 271 bills were passed by the 14th Knesset (1996–99), 51 per cent of which were private members bills and 49 per cent government bills. As in the previous Knesset, the rate of success was quite low, with only 5.3 per cent of private members' bills being passed, but again this is a function of the large number of private bills introduced, 2599 to be precise. Put differently, in the 13th and 14th Knessets, on average between 850 and 900 private members' bills were introduced annually, or more than nine bills per MK per year for the hundred or so MKs who were not ministers or deputy ministers. Significantly, in the 14th Knesset, there was a 60 per cent increase in the proportion of opposition private members' bills passed. In all, 31 per cent of successful private members' bills were sponsored by government MKs, 14 per cent were jointly sponsored and 55 per cent solely by opposition MKs, which indicates that the challenge to executive dominance increased perceptibly during the period of the Netanyahu government.[16]

One of the opposition MKs private members' bills passed in the 14th Knesset called for its dissolution and the holding of early elections for Prime Minister and the 15th Knesset. These took place on May 17, 1999 and resulted in a decisive victory for Ehud Barak over Binyamin Netanyahu by a margin of 56 per cent to 44 per cent and to a Knesset in which 17 parties were represented. These results put paid to the conventional wisdom that the Israeli party system was divided into two tight and evenly-matched blocs, that guaranteed extremely close races in direct election contests for Prime Minister between their leaders (as had indeed occurred in 1996). At the same time, however, they further confirmed that direct elections for Prime Minister were the bane of larger (and generally more heterogeneous) parties and a boon for smaller (and generally ideologically, demographically, or socially homogeneous) parties, or as they are loosely known in Israel, sectorial or 'tribal' parties. Together, the Likud and Labour lost over a third of their representation in the 14th Knesset. The performance of the smaller lists varied: while Shas, the third-largest party increased its Knesset representation by 70 per cent to 17 MKs (narrowing the gap between it and the Likud to two seats), other smaller homogenous lists (Mafdal, Israel Be-aliya) lost seats (to new homogeneous lists that competed directly in the same defined population) while Ha-derekh Ha-shlishit and Tsomet won no seats at all. On the other hand, two new and probably more heterogeneous centre party lists – Mercaz and Shinui – received six Knesset seats each. In all, those parties that were members of the Netanyahu government and those to the right of it which were re-elected to the 15th Knesset (Likud, Shas, Yahadut Ha-torah, Mafdal, Israel Be-aliya, Israel Beteinu, Ihud Le'umi), had a net gain of one seat, whilst the parties that were in opposition to the Netanyahu coalition (Labour, Meretz, the Arab parties, Am Ehad) had a net loss of four seats, which is, of course, somewhat surprising given the size of Barak's majority.

Taken together, these election results indicate that parties and candidates do not move in tandem. Thus, whereas Barak's share of the vote in 1999 represented a 12 per cent relative increase over that of Peres in 1996, his predominantly Labour Israel Ahat list lost 24 per cent of its Knesset seats. In contrast, while Netanyahu's vote declined relatively by 12 per cent between 1996 and 1999, his Likud list lost 40 per cent of its Knesset seats.

The growth of the centre parties in the 15th Knesset (there were now 18 MKs representing centre parties, an increase of 54 per cent over the 14th Knesset) suggests that direct elections for Prime Minister – the ultimate majoritarian and two-bloc mechanism – further promoted the multi-issue, multi-party, multi-bloc and essentially consensus dynamic of Israeli democracy. Indeed, after the 1999 elections, there are now 5 distinct party blocs in the Knesset: Labour-left (38 seats); Likud-right (27 seats); religious (27 seats), centre (18 seats); Arab (10 seats) and this as we shall see, had a profound impact upon Barak's pre-election coalitions negotiations and on the formation of his post-election parliamentary majority and of his coalition government. In the absence of hard data, rough calculations based upon opinion polls, previous voting patterns and the publicly-declared positions of the various parties toward the candidates seem to indicate that about 62 per cent of Barak's vote came from the Labour-left and Arab blocs, 21 per cent from the Centre bloc, seven per cent from the religious bloc, six per cent from below threshold parties and nearly four per cent from the Likud-right bloc. Looked at another way, the support of all 670,484 Israel Ahat voters would have constituted only 37 per cent of Barak's total vote and any slippage would have reduced that even further to about one third. Similarly, in 1999, Netanyahu received only 33 per cent at most from Likud voters before slippage. (In 1996, by way of contrast, the best estimates would indicate that both Netanyahu and Peres received over half of their votes from supporters of their own parties and obviously the decline is due to the decreased support in the electorate for both their parties in 1999.)

Where elections are solely for the Knesset, the party and its candidate for Prime Minister – usually the party leader and the head of the Knesset list – have the same electoral interest – the more votes that the party receives, the greater are the candidate's chances of being elected Prime Minister. Similarly, the more popular and highly-regarded the party leader, the greater the benefit to the party. Both had an extremely strong incentive to work together as the more votes the party received, the greater would be its and its leader' legislative influence and share of executive power. The same electoral logic also meant that there was no advantage to either party or candidate in not working together and a particularly powerful disincentive for one to work against the other.

In the post-1996 system of dual elections, only in the unlikely situation that a single party receives more than half of the votes in the Knesset elections is its share of the vote likely to be decisive in elections for Prime Minister (provided, of course, that the party Knesset voters also support its prime ministerial candidate). The electoral logic of direct elections for Prime Minister, however, is that to win a candidate must get an absolute majority of 50 per cent plus one vote. The empirical experience of 13 Knessets shows that parties with as low as 33 per cent of the vote (40 seats) headed governmental coalitions (although the average was slightly higher). However, a would-be Prime Minister whose party had 33 per cent in the Knesset would have at most only two-thirds of the votes required for election. And if, as recently, the leading parties have won as few as 20 per cent of the Knesset seats, more than 60 per cent of the votes that their candidate requires for election as Prime Minister, must come from voters for other parties.

The different electoral logic of these two simultaneous elections has had a fundamental impact on the relationship between candidate and party, that is to say between party leader and party. While clearly apparent in 1996, that impact was much more marked in 1999. In essence, any party which fields a prime ministerial candidate has a strong incentive to campaign both for the candidate and for itself, but the incentive of the candidate to campaign strongly on behalf of his party is far weaker. A candidate for Prime Minister, going into an election requiring at least 40 per cent of his vote from voters for other parties, is likely to find it much easier to persuade them to vote only for him than to vote for him and his party and that trying to do the latter may well cost him their vote. The incentive not to discourage them from voting for other parties so long as they vote for him for Prime Minister is considerable. The electoral logic of the prime ministerial campaign therefore is 'so long as you vote for me, it doesn't matter which party you vote for', creates a clear disincentive for candidates to campaign wholeheartedly on behalf of their party, that is reinforced strongly to the extent that the party is or is believed to be negatively perceived by voters and his association with it are likely to dissuade them from voting for him.

Such calculations are likely to give further impetus to the already strong tendency of candidates in direct elections, especially at the national level, to distance themselves from the party by running an independent campaign conducted by outside advisers and professionals rather than by the party organization, to employ personal pollsters, media consultants and advertising agencies and not those used by the party, to become financially independent of the party and so forth and if necessary, to disguise, camouflage and generally de-emphasize the party name, image or connection. Such a campaign focusing on the single zero-sum goal of getting the candidate elected and limiting the involvement of other party leaders, institutions and of the party organization, will do little to actively assist the party's Knesset effort. The party, however, has little option but to accept such a state of affairs, on the grounds that being in the Knesset with a reduced number of seats and the party leader as Prime Minister is preferable to being in the Knesset with a reduced number of seats and the party leader at the head of the parliamentary opposition. In short, the electoral logic of pre-1996 Knesset elections – that the better the party does the better off its leader will be – no longer applies. Put differently, if split-ticket voting is a boon for smaller homogeneous parties and a bane for the larger heterogeneous parties, it is a mixed blessing for candidates for Prime Minister: while, on the one hand, it detaches them from many of the constraints and limitations of party, on the other hand, it deprives them of the loyal support of party MKs and the cushion of collective leadership.

Faced with rival candidates, Barak followed a very different strategy from that of Netanyahu in 1996. Long before the elections were called, he sought to persuade retiring Chief of Staff, Amnon Lipkin-Shahak, to join Labour and promised him a senior ministerial office. The latter declined, subsequently declaring his intention to run personally for Prime Minister on an anti-Netanyahu platform. During the campaign, Barak also made overtures to Yitzhak Mordechai, former Likud MK who had topped its primaries and had been Defence Minister until his abrupt dismissal by Netanyahu and was now running for Prime Minister at the head of the new Mercaz centre party list. Significantly, both Lipkin-Shahak and Mordechai rebuffed Barak's offers of senior government ministries on the grounds that only centre candidates could build a voting coalition with enough support to defeat Netanyahu. In their estimation, dislike of Labour was so strong and deep-rooted among large sections of the voters (haredim, sefardim, development towns, the middle classes) that Barak would go down to certain defeat, whereas if he withdrew in their favour and joined forces with them, the removal of Netanyahu from office was assured. As the elections approached, the polls indicated clearly that Mordechai's early support was dissipating and it became increasingly clear that his candidature was not viable. Its continuation, therefore, served only to reduce Barak's chances of defeating Netanyahu in the first round. Eventually, under tremendous pressure from his party colleagues, Mordechai withdrew on the very eve of the election and together with other Mercaz leaders strongly urged their supporters to vote for Barak.

From Barak's point of view, this outcome was optimal. Not only had he (and the public opinion polls) stared them down, but he had done so without a single pre-election coalition commitment, promise, compromise or pay-off. Moreover, he received the votes of their supporters at little or no cost, with the Mercaz party receiving only two rather minor ministries rather than the four (including the two senior ones) he had earlier offered them. For his part, Barak embarked on a bridging strategy to attract voters from sections of the electorate where antipathy to Labour was strong and to transcend social divisions by forming a new and even more heterogeneous list than before with the symbolically significant name of Israel Ahat – One Israel. Central to that strategy were agreements with the Gesher party led by David Levy which had recently cut its ties with Netanyahu and the Likud and saw itself as the tribune of the disadvantaged sectors in Israeli society (mainly sefardim in development towns and poor metropolitan areas). The other group brought under the party umbrella was Meimad, a modern-orthodox, liberal, highly-educated group, whose members were well integrated into all spheres of Israeli society. It first ran (unsuccessfully) in the 1988 elections and its leader, Rabbi Amital, had served as a minister in the Peres government in 1995–1996. Meimad strongly supported the peace process with the Palestinians and accepted the need for Israeli territorial withdrawal. It shared a common language and Zionist values with the secular segments of Israeli society and sought mutually satisfying compromises on issues of religion and state.

Symbolically and electorally these were major gains for Barak, opening bridges to sections of the electorate that had seemed closed to Labour and neutralized the criticism that Labour took a superior, overweening and elitist approach to sefardim and sephardi culture. Moreover, the adoption of an entirely new name – Israel Ahat – not only projected a new, positive, unifying and appealing public image, it virtually removed the name Labour from public view, creating the perception that Labour had vanished. Finally, Barak was able to include these groups at little cost: no policy compromises, the promise of one ministry for each group (in the case of Gesher and David Levy a senior ministry) and the allocation to each of one place in the first 20 on Israel Ahat's list and another in the next 15, which in the event deprived Labour of three MKs.

The fact that Barak was the new list's candidate for Prime Minister, was used as further justification (if any was needed), for establishing a personal and professional team to conduct an independent campaign on behalf of himself and of Israel Ahat, unencumbered by and significantly distanced from the Labour party and its negative image. In such a set-up, obviously, he and his personal staff, not some party body, or a set of party advisers, determined policy for his own race and this automatically became that of Israel Ahat. Clearly, Labour alone could not make policy for all three, the result being that Barak's personal campaign submerged, if not became, the party's campaign – deciding the message and choosing the electoral targets at which it was aimed. Although the Labour party was active in mobilizing support for the Knesset list, in effect its campaign did not exist independently of the Barak campaign, but, at best was a satellite.

Reinforced by his resounding personal victory with a 56 per cent popular majority and mandate, Barak's employed a similar approach in the post-election phase. His approach to and pattern of coalition formation can be stated briefly and clearly in terms of the criteria used above. First, coalition participation was made subject to others' acceptance of the policy guidelines laid out in his campaign programme and that of Israel Ahat. As a result, the Likud, which sought to alter those guidelines in accordance with its own policy preferences, did not make it past the preliminary negotiation stage. Similarly, in order to publicly demonstrate its commitment to the rule of law and its recognition of the authority of the courts, Shas was obliged not only to state this unequivocally, but also to drop its leader, Aryeh Deri – who had been convicted of accepting bribes and whose four-year prison sentence had been stayed pending appeal to the Supreme Court – and to effectively exclude him from involvement in coalition negotiations.

Second, Barak conducted these negotiations personally, aided not by other experienced Labour MKs but by his personal staff and a team of negotiators representing all components of Israel Ahat which he chose personally and whose main characteristic with one exception was no previous experience in coalition negotiations, if not of politics, in general.

Third, he established an oversized, heterogeneous and ideologically-balanced coalition of eight parties with 75 MKs – Yisrael Ahat (26 MKs), Meretz (10 MKs) on its left, Mercaz (6 MKs) and Israel Be-aliya (6 MKs), to its right, but in the centre and three religious parties Mafdal (5 MKs), Shas (17 MKs) and Yahadut Ha-torah (5 MKs), that during the 1980s and 1990s had been the bastions of the right. The resignation of no single party, with the possible exception of Shas, could deprive the government of its majority and even then the government could probably restore it by the co-opting other available partners.

Fourth, although Yisrael Ahat with only 26 Knesset seats constituted just over a third of the coalition parties' Knesset majority, from the outset Barak insisted on a Yisrael Ahat government majority. Significantly, his justification for such an imbalance in the MK/minister ratio (various other parties had ratios of approximately 5:1, 4:1 and 3:1, whereas Israel Ahat's ratio was approximately 2:1) was that 56 per cent of the vote was equivalent to nearly 70 Knesset seats and entitled him to such a majority in order to enable him to carry out his election promises and implement his policies in accordance with the decisive personal mandate he had received. Finally, Barak gave Israel Ahat all the key ministries: Prime Minister, Defence, Foreign Affairs, Finance, Justice and Internal Security.

Clearly this pattern of coalition formation is reminiscent of the major principles of coalition formation employed by Ben-Gurion and Mapai during the heyday of party government and majoritarian democracy before 1967. However, there are also some fundamental differences between the pre-1967 and the post-1996 patterns of coalition formation relating to the place of party in government and to the basic principles upon which the concentration of executive power and its cohesive and coherent operation are based. These differences are a direct result of the system of direct elections for Prime Minister that was adopted in Israel and, although clearly noticeable after the 1996 elections, they were particularly prominent in 1999. Prior to 1996, coalition negotiations had generally been between parties and conducted on their behalf by their leaders or officially designated negotiators and the agreements reached between the parties were submitted to their respective party bodies for approval. After 1996, however, coalition agreements were not between the elected Prime Minister's party and the other parties, but between the elected Prime Minister himself and the other parties.

With the change in the electoral law, the Prime Minister elect was charged personally with the responsibility of establishing a government and appointing its ministers as he saw fit. However, the government and its appointees required the support of a majority of the members of the Knesset. This had an anomalous outcome. On the one hand, after coalition negotiations that determined how many and which ministries each partner would receive, the latter each chose its own ministers, decided which ministry they would receive and handed this information on to the Prime Minister who acted upon it. In short, as in the past, the coalition partners chose their own ministers according to whatever internal party rules they had for ministerial selection and the Prime Minister had no say at all in the matter, despite the fact that by law the appointment of ministers was his prerogative and his alone. On the other hand, in one party and one party alone, the opposite was the case: the party had no say at all in the appointment of the ministers. This of course, was the Prime Minister's own party. There, he personally chose the ministers and allocated them to their respective ministries. In not consulting with party leaders and colleagues, in keeping them out of coalition negotiations and in calling in prospective ministers one by one to inform them whether they had been appointed and to which ministry (in the meantime keeping them waiting outside his office for their turn in the full blaze of television floodlights) Barak acted as if he and he alone was empowered to appoint ministers and as if the party was specifically precluded by law from having any say in these matters.

While formally, the decision to appoint all ministers and present them
to the Knesset is his by law, there is nothing in that law to prevent or
preclude a Prime Minister from consulting with party leaders, officials
and institutions, soliciting their advice and encouraging their input.
What is more, there may be good reason politically to do so, as the
united, co-operative and collective spirit of the ministry and of the party
are a potential resource and asset for Prime Ministers who know how to
mobilize and utilize them, whilst their absence may well undermine the
personal authority of the directly elected Prime Minister and turn out to
be a fatal flaw, as Netanyahu discovered. In sum, the empowerment of
the Prime Minister by direct elections has made his own party impotent,
while strengthening rival parties. Thus, while he can sack a minister
from his own party at will, he cannot do so to a minister from another
party, at least not without first consulting its leaders, unless he is
prepared to brook a possible coalition crisis.

The 1999 elections again provided evidence that the candidates for
Prime Minister, not their parties, made policy and enunciated it publicly
on all major questions – defence, security, foreign affairs, the peace
process, the economy, religion and state, social justice and so forth.
There were no, or only perfunctory, internal party discussions and
debates over policy proposals and obviously no authoritative agreement
on positions that bound the party and its representatives in government
and in the Knesset, as had been the case in the heyday of party
government, or even in drawing up broad and highly generalized party
platforms prior to elections, manifestations of which were still
discernible in the 1980s.

This function has been taken over by the party leaders who are
candidates for election and who subsequently serve as Prime Minister
and leader of the opposition respectively. As their parties in the Knesset
stand and fall by their success or failure, party leaders decide upon and
enunciate the platform on which they seek to be elected to office and the
party has little alternative but to fall in line and adopt the leader's
policies as its own. In the case of the other parties, however, the
situation is reversed. Dual elections have freed them of the need to make
policies on all major issues – as they did in the past when they all
competed with each other. In this regard, now all that is left to them is
to choose one of the two prime ministerial packages put before them.
This provides an electoral boost for those parties as it permits them to
concentrate on conveying their distinctive message and promoting the
particular concerns and interests of their constituents and to mobilize
them to both vote and vote for them in the elections, so as to maximize
their party's influence in the Knesset and to strengthen their bargaining
power in coalition negotiations. In short, there is no reason for these
voters to vote for the large parties with prime ministerial candidates, as

there was in the past and every reason to vote for the smaller parties without prime ministerial pretensions.

The changes in the election system in 1992 were a direct response to the breakdown of the previous pattern, indeed, a conscious attempt to counteract the profound destabilization of the system of parliamentary government that had occurred during the 1980s. Their purpose was to restabilize the system by taking the choice of Prime Minister out of the hands of party politicians and a few small parties which were portrayed as not always placing the interests of the whole and the good of the nation above their sectoral, partisan, particular and immediate interests. The assumption was that direct elections would replace the uncertainties of narrow, fluid and fickle parliamentary majorities with a decisive and unambiguous choice of the head of the executive power.

However, as noted above, the institution of direct elections for Prime Minister has to date had the opposite effect – in undermining large parties it increased the difficulty of establishing the stable parliamentary majority that supports of the Prime Minister's government coalition and enables it to exercise executive power. And the more that the stabilizing contribution of large parties to parliamentary government is undermined, the greater will be the reliance of governmental executive power on the stabilizing role of a directly elected Prime Minister. Yet at the same time, direct elections have also removed the structural foundations upon which rest the capacity of an elected Prime Minister to exercise executive power stably, cohesively, coherently – namely, collective responsibility and its party underpinnings.

The formal principles of collective responsibility and their legal ramifications were set out above and it was shown how these were reinforced by a coalition structure in which a single party had a majority of ministers and these operated as a collective unit in determining policy for the government as a whole by a majority vote, usually in line with party expectations, express party policies and not infrequently in conjunction with authoritative party bodies. Thus, party government and collective responsibility went hand in hand: the party in government operated as a collective unit, thus enabling the governmental coalition, by its nature a divided body, to act largely as if it were a collective unit.

The present system has retained the formal elements of collective responsibility while depriving it of its party core. But, as was noted above, there is nothing in the law to prevent or preclude a directly elected Prime Minister from mobilizing the support of his party parliamentarians and ministers and to operate executive power on the basis of collective decision-making and responsibility and thereby bolster his own political authority as well as the government's capacity to exercise executive power cohesively and coherently. Netanyahu did not do so and neither the approach adopted by Barak to date, as outlined above, nor his recently-unveiled plans to turn Yisrael Ahat into a new party (thereby bringing about the demise of the Labour party) indicate that this is his intention. Rather both dealt with their own party – including institutions and fellow party leaders and ministers – not as a resource and an asset, but as an encumbrance and a limitation upon their authority.

Why this is in fact so, given the obvious advantages of mobilizing the party for political support raises fascinating questions about the interaction between the conflicting logic of political structures and the personalities of political leaders. In short, the underlying principle of direct elections is to concentrate executive power by placing an individual at its head and locating responsibility for its operation in the hands of that individual. In such a system, all political appointees are directly or indirectly responsible to the head of the executive power and serve at his discretion. There is no collective responsibility and the principles of joint-decision making follow the principles of Lincoln's cabinet. Party, while not irrelevant, plays at best an auxiliary and supportive role, but effective executive power can be operated without it, although whether cohesively and coherently is a different matter.

The underlying principle of parliamentary government is a stable majority, usually supplied by one party or a coalition of parties. This provides the basis for the constitution of the executive power, executive dominance and its effective and coherent operation. The essence of such an executive power is collective decision-making and collective responsibility. Heading the executive power therefore is not an individual person, but a collective body of ministers, amongst whom the Prime Minister is *primus inter pares*. He may enjoy discretion to appoint, move and remove his party ministers, but, in the last resort he serves only so long as he enjoys the confidence of his ministry and his parliamentary party, which generally is the body that elects him and therefore has the power to vote him out of office at any time. That, of course, serves as a powerful constraint upon the Prime Minister and a powerful incentive to consult, seek the advice and be attuned to the wishes and views of his party, parliamentary and ministerial colleagues.

In making the electoral changes that it did in 1992, Israel adopted both of these inherently contradictory principles – in effect, pitting personal responsibility against collective responsibility, majoritarian electoral logic against the electoral logic of proportional representation, candidate against party, the fixed choice of direct elections against the uncertainties of parliamentary votes of confidence, Prime Minister against fellow ministers and the principle of Lincoln's cabinet against the principle of *primus inter pares*. Such structural contradictions allow the responsible political leaders to make choices, rather than dictate behaviour. What choices those politicians make, how they combine the conflicting elements, what weight they give to the respective structural constraints and possibilities, and to the conflicting demands of competing electoral logics, whether they serve to stabilize an inherently unstable situation involves a variety of complex considerations, not the least of which it seems are the personal qualities and goals, if not the personalities of the individual leaders.

Indeed, the empirical experience of those choices to date indicate not only the continuation and acceleration of the movement away from government by party toward government by party leaders to government despite party and in many regards to government against party. Moreover, executive power has been further concentrated formally by direct popular election of a Prime Minister with the power to appoint the majority of ministers, but the decline of large parties and party discipline have eroded executive dominance and the capacity of the executive power to control the legislative agenda. Stable coalitions with a parliamentary majority now rest on the support of a large number of small, homogeneous and distinctive parties. Whether and to what extent this has resulted in extensive policy compromises, budgetary allocations, ministerial and office payoffs that undermine the cohesive and coherent operation of executive power, depends, it so far seems, on the Prime Minister's strategy in pre-and post-election coalition negotiations. Finally, the ongoing fractionalization and fragmentation of the party system into many small party lists, differentiated along multiple and overlapping issue dimensions, would indicate that Israel is far indeed from a two-party or two bloc system and is much closer to an extreme and fluid multi-party and multi-bloc system, that in the recent past has not prevented it from manifesting the ideological distance, divisiveness and anti-system properties of polarized pluralism.

Paradoxically, while the zero-sum nature of direct elections for Prime Minister was predicted to increase divisiveness, polarization and further destabilization, in some regards, the fact that this structural element is not subject to the vagaries of bargaining between politicians gives it something of a fixed quality, if not a stabilizing capacity, especially when compared to the inherently fluid character of the other major structural elements in the new Israeli 'tribrid' – majoritarian and consensus parliamentary coalition government with a personally elected head of the executive power.

NOTES

1. For characteristic examples of this albeit limited application of the consociational model to Israel, see Emanuel Gutmann, 'Parties and Camps – Stability and Change', 'Religion in Israeli Politics – A Unifying and Dividing Factor' and Eliezer Don-Yehiya and Charles Liebman 'Separation between Religion and State – Slogan and Substance', all in Moshe Lissak and Emanuel Gutmann (eds.), *Ha-maarechet Ha-politit Ha-israelit (The Israeli Political System)*, Tel Aviv: Am Oved, 1979, pp.122–170, 397–410 and 373–396 respectively.

2. Emanuel Gutmann, 'Parties and Camps'.
3. Reuven Y. Hazan, 'Party System Change in Israel, 1948–98: A Conceptual and Typological Border-Stretching of Europe?' in Paul Pennings and Jan-Erik Lane, (eds.), *Comparing Party System Change*, Routledge: London, 1998, pp.151–166.
4. See for example, Benyamin Neuberger, *Ha-miflagot Be-Iisrael (Political Parties in Israel)*, Tel Aviv: Open University Press, 1991; and Giora Goldberg, *Miflagot Politiot Be-Israel: Mi-miflagot Hamon Le-miflagot Elektoraliot (Political Parties in Israel – From Mass Parties to Electoral Parties)*, Tel Aviv: Ramot Publishing, 1992.
5. Arend Lijphart, 'Israeli Democracy and Democratic Reform in Comparative Perspective', in Ehud Sprinzak and Larry Diamond, (eds.), *Israeli Democracy Under Stress*, Boulder: Lynne Rienner, 1993, p.110.
6. Lijphart, 'Israeli Democracy and Democratic Reform in Comparative Perspective', p.119.
7. The data and the argument in this section are based upon Peter Y. Medding, *The Founding of Israeli Democracy 1949–1967*, New York: Oxford University Press, 1990.
8. These figures are based on Reuven Y. Hazan, 'Executive–Legislative Relations in an Era of Accelerated Reform: Reshaping Government in Israel', *Legislative Studies Quarterly*, Vol. 22, No. 3 (1997).
9. Medding, *The Founding of Israeli Democracy*, pp.81–107.
10. See David Nachmias and Itai Sened, 'The Bias of Pluralism: The Redistributive Effects of the New Electoral Law in Israel's 1996 Election', in Asher Arian and Michal Shamir (eds.), *The Elections in Israel 1996*, Albany: State University of New York Press, 1999, pp.269–294.
11. In Avraham Diskin and Menachem Hofnung (eds.), *Ha-behirot La-Knesset Ula-rashut Ha-memshala – 1996: Leket Mekorot (The 1996 Knesset and Prime Ministerial Elections: Readings and Cases)*, Srigim: Nevo, 1997.
12. Keren Neubach, *Ha-meirutz, Behirot '96 (The Race, Elections '96)*, Tel Aviv: Yediot Aharonot, 1996, p.230.
13. Gideon Doron and Rebecca Kook, 'Religion and the Politics of Inclusion: The Success of the Ultra-Orthodox Parties', in Arian and Shamir, *The Elections in Israel 1996*, p.72.
14. Nachmias and Sened, 'The Bias of Pluralism'.
15. *Ha-aretz*, 30 July 1990, p.10.
16. My calculations are based on figures supplied by the Knesset Archives

Abstracts

Parties, Elections and Cleavages: Israel in Comparative and Theoretical Perspective
Moshe Maor and Reuven Y. Hazan

This chapter looks into the triangle of studies dealing with party system change, which consists of political parties, electoral systems and societal cleavages. It points out that the trigger for changes in party systems, and each of their components, might come from anywhere in the political system. Methodologically, this perspective implies that each of the aforementioned parts can be treated as either dependent or independent variables, depending on the questions asked. The chapter then outlines the dramatic electoral and political reforms that were adopted in Israel in the 1990s, and delineates the studies which make up the book.

The Party-Effects of Electoral Systems
Giovanni Sartori

This chapter refocuses the debate on the causal chain between electoral systems and party systems. It argues that the electoral systems 'cause' the party system, and challenges the prevailing view that electoral systems are not a fundamental causative factor in the development of party systems. The chapter concludes with an analysis of the new electoral system in Israel and its faults. It posits that Israel is the worst case of multidimensional competition, which has produced a dysfunctional system, and hence Israel cannot afford to maintain an electoral system that has misperformed. The chapter raises a provocative suggestion on how to improve the contemporary predicament in the Israeli party system.

Party Systems and Issue Dimensions: Israel and Thirty-Five Other Old and New Democracies Compared
Arend Lijphart, Peter J. Bowman and Reuven Y. Hazan

This chapter builds on Lijphart's previous work, and that of Taagepera and Grofman, on the relationship between the degree of multipartism and the number of issue dimensions. It extends the analysis to Israel and 35 other democracies during the period from the end of the Second

World War to the late 1990s. The chapter finds an extremely strong correlation between the two variables, and examines both the influence that the two variables have on each other and their link with the electoral system. Israel turns out to be a 'normal' case in one sense: Its number of parties and the issue dimensions of its party system are almost exactly in line with the broad comparative pattern. But it is highly unusual in the strength and persistence of one of the issue dimensions: foreign policy questions. Moreover, in the 1990s, the chapter finds that Israel has an especially high number of parties and, thus, more substantially defined issue dimensions than in any other time period. This increase, despite the electoral system variable being constant, is due to the direct election of the prime minister.

Changing Conditions of Party Competition: A New Model Party?
Gordon Smith

This chapter addresses, on theoretical terms, aspects of issue politics and examines Britain's New Labour as a test case – a significant transformation that is similar to the one currently taking place in the two major parties in Israel. Stressing the relative autonomy of political parties, it sketches the forces affecting the trend toward 'issue politics' in relation to the diversity of inputs and the changing balance among them. The chapter then discusses the various strategies available to parties in dealing with issues and elaborates on 'maverick issues' which have the greatest potential for a significant transformation of a party system. It argues that despite the increasing issue-basis of politics, the core parties still retain control of political power, which at the same time can lead to a decline in the legitimacy of the party state.

Religion and State in Europe and Israel
Benyamin Neuberger

This chapter delineates the main religion-state models and applies them to both Europe and Israel. It argues that there is a process of convergence of the various models. The two 'extreme' models, the established church model and the strict separation model, are becoming less pure, while most of Europe is converging towards two 'moderate' models, the recognized communities model and the endorsed church model. The chapter stresses the commonality of all four democratic models, and places Israel within the comparative context.

Conflict Management of Religious Issues: The Israeli Case in a Comparative Perspective
Eliezer Don-Yehiya

This chapter addresses the specific systems of conflict management in the religious area and elaborates these models by comparing the resolution of religious conflicts in Europe, the United States and Israel. It then expands this analysis by comparing the patterns of conflict management applied to religious issues in Israel with those that are applied to other controversial issues. The chapter outlines and compares the extent and circumstances of particular methods that are actually used in dealing with religious conflicts, and discusses the conditions for their effective and successful use.

Religion and Politics in Israel: The Rise and Fall of the Consociational Model
Reuven Y. Hazan

This chapter elaborates the presence and subsequent decline of the institutional mechanisms in Israel that have helped overcome religious conflicts. It places Israel within a comparative theoretical construct of consociational democracies, and argues that the literature has failed to classify Israel properly because the consociational methods have transformed over time. The focus of the chapter is the most central aspect of consociationalism in Israel, namely, the role of the parties and the party system. It discusses the impact of the recent electoral reforms in Israel on the methods of religious conflict management in the party system, and examines how the reforms have undermined the ability to produce agreements and successfully manage religious issues.

Rethinking De Swaan (1973): A Note on Closed Coalitions, Uni-dimensionality and the Role of Sectarian Political Parties
Abraham Diskin

This chapter addresses the trade-off faced by scholars of coalition formation, between their wish to develop simple and elegant models and the need to take into account the fact that few relatively weak parties can complicate such models. It examines de Swaan's famous coalition findings concerning 'closed coalition' theory and produces a considerable improvement in its predictive power. Whereas in the original model, 24 per cent of the formations examined by de Swaan are not closed, in the modified model presented in this article, only 2.5 per cent of the coalitions examined remain open. In the Israeli case, the number of open coalitions drops from 44 per cent to nil.

Political Change and Party System Transformation
Gabriel Sheffer

This chapter describes two systemic changes that have transformed Israeli politics since its creation and substantially influenced the party system. The first transformation occurred gradually, during the late 1960s and the 1970s, and was essentially a structural shift from consociational to corporatist political arrangements. This change took place against the background of changes in the social cleavage system. The second transformation is much less clear cut, and its direction is still to be seen. While traditional cleavages still linger, the waning of collective identities, on the one hand, and the absence of a developed 'new politics' alternative, on the other, imply the emergence of an unstructured and almost chaotic political pluralism, the weakening of the state and a shift of power toward single-issue groups, as well as special interest groups.

From Government by Party to Government Despite Party
Peter Y. Medding

This chapter uses Lijphart's models of consensus and majoritarian democracy to analyze the evolution of the Israeli political system via an analysis of changes in the pattern of party government, but arrives at radically different conclusions. According to Lijphart's seminal analysis, in the past 50 years Israel has moved toward majoritarian democracy and has become less clearly consensual. This chapter suggests that the Israeli political system has instead moved from majoritarian democracy to consensus democracy. It argues that since 1967, party government in Israel has presented a paradox: steady movement in the direction of consensus democracy toward a situation of government without party despite, and perhaps because of, the introduction into the system of a powerful majoritarian element – a directly-elected Prime Minister, yet one who remains subject to the confidence of a majority parliamentary coalition. As a result, party, and parliamentary, government, and collective responsibility have all been weakened fundamentally, whilst the power and authority of the Prime Minister have not been strengthened correspondingly.

Index

The letter 'n' after a page reference indicates a note on that page.

Other Titles in the Israeli History, Politics and Society Series

Israel: The First Hundred Years

Series Editor: **Efraim Karsh**, *King's College London*

A century after the First Zionist Congress in Basle, fifty years after the
establishment of the State of Israel, the Zionist saga remains as
controversial as ever. To its sympathizers, Israel represents a miraculous
story of regeneration and rebirth of Jewish statehood in their ancestral
homeland after millennia of exile and dispersion. To its detractors, it is
an artificial imperialist implant in a predominantly Arab region bearing
responsibility for its endemic violence. This five-volume series offers a
comprehensive evaluation of this controversial balance sheet by a
distinguished group of Israeli, European, and American scholars.

Israel's Transition from Community to State

The birth of the Zionist Movement, coming in the wake of Jewish
emancipation in Western Europe and at a time of intensified persecution
of Jewry in Eastern Europe, meant that for the first time since Jewish
dispersion, the possibility of the Jews discarding their minority status in
the lands they inhabited and creating their own vibrant home in their
ancestral homeland became a reality, however incomprehensible it may
have appeared in these early years. The next half-a-century saw great
strides in the economic, social and political life of the Yishuv that
culminated in the creation of the State of Israel. By way of doing so,
Zionism altered the relationship between Jews in Mandatory Palestine
and the Jewish communities of the Diaspora, between Jews and their
Palestinian-Arab contemporaries and ultimately between Jewry and the
British mandatory power. With contributions from some of the leading
scholars of Zionism and Israeli history, this volume addresses many of
the intellectual, social and political ramifications of Jewish settlement in
Eretz-Israel before the creation of the State of Israel.

264 pages 2000
0 7146 4963 5 cloth
0 7146 8024 9 paper
A special issue of the journal Israel Affairs
Israel: The First Hundred Years, Volume 1
Israeli History, Politics and Society Series

FRANK CASS PUBLISHERS
Newbury House, 900 Eastern Avenue, Ilford, Essex, IG2 7HH
Tel: +44 (0)20 8599 8866 Fax: +44 (0)20 8599 0984 E-mail: info@frankcass.com
NORTH AMERICA
5804 NE Hassalo Street, Portland, OR 97213 3644, USA
Tel: 800 944 6190 Fax: 503 280 8832 E-mail: cass@isbs.com
Website: www.frankcass.com

Israel: From War to Peace?

The end of the British mandate in Palestine heralded the birth of the new State of Israel. It also marked the end of one of the most tumultuous and momentous chapters in Jewish history. But the new state, born into a hostile environment and struggling with the manifold demands of sovereignty would have to face many post-Independence challenges to its existence, not least in the form of armed conflict and confrontation with its Arab neighbours. This volume examines the conflicts that from the 1948 until the 1967 Six Day War came to define the Israeli struggle for existence. In doing so contributors analyze the various military challenges to Israel from both the military and strategic perspective and in terms of the demands that these conflicts placed on Israeli society and political life. The final section addresses the recent peace process from the time of the Oslo Accords, while focusing on some of the key issues in any future settlement, most notably Jerusalem's future status.

288 pages 2000
0 7146 4962 7 cloth   0 7146 8023 0 paper
A special issue of the journal Israel Affairs
Israel: The First Hundred Years, Volume 2
Israeli History, Politics and Society Series

Revisiting the Yom Kippur War

P R Kumaraswamy, *The Hebrew University of Jerusalem* (Ed)
Preface by **Efraim Karsh**, *King's College London*

This book provides comprehensive and insiders' views of the Yom Kippur War 25 years after its outbreak in October 1973 and publication of the inquiry into it by the Agranat Commission in 1974. By looking at the political, military and intelligence components of the war, the volume offers new interpretations to Israel's conflict with the Arabs. The contributors, leading Israeli academics, some of them involved in the war, make a unique contribution to an understanding of this painful chapter in Israel's history. By making use of hitherto unpublished materials, including the recently declassified portions of the findings of the Agranat Commission that inquired into the intelligence failure, the volume contributes to a deeper understanding of the Yom Kippur War and its impact on Israeli society.

248 pages 2000
0 7146 5007 2 cloth   0 7146 8067 2 paper
A special issue of the journal Israel Affairs
Israeli History, Politics and Society Series

FRANK CASS PUBLISHERS
Newbury House, 900 Eastern Avenue, Ilford, Essex, IG2 7HH
Tel: +44 (0)20 8599 8866 Fax: +44 (0)20 8599 0984 E-mail: info@frankcass.com
NORTH AMERICA
5804 NE Hassalo Street, Portland, OR 97213 3644, USA
Tel: 800 944 6190 Fax: 503 280 8832 E-mail: cass@isbs.com
Website: www.frankcass.com

Israel: The Dynamics of Change and Continuity

David Levi-Faur, *University of Haifa*,
Gabriel Sheffer, *The Hebrew University of Jerusalem*, and
David Vogel, *University of California, Berkeley* (Eds)

The essays in this volume attempt to move beyond the question of
Israel's 'uniqueness' to examine the pace and direction of change of
Israel's political, social and economic institutions. Using the tools of
comparative analysis, scholars from Israel, the United States and Europe
describe the ways in which Israeli society is becoming more like other
democratic industrialized societies and in what dimensions Israeli
culture and institutions are slowing or resisting such convergence.

The contributions to this volume suggest that Israel is changing, even
converging with the global community in some ways but that the pace
and direction of change is uneven. In some areas, change is
evolutionary or glacial, slowed by tradition and entrenched institutions.

The topics explored include the Israeli judicial system, changes in
political leadership style, the effects of economic globalization on
Israel's political economy, the changing structure of interest group
politics, the relationship between the business sector and the
government, the evolution and future of Israel's ethnic divisions – both
within the Jewish community and between the Jewish and Arab
communities – and an analysis of the attempt to Americanize Israeli
abortion politics and Israeli environmental policy.

312 pages 1999
0 7146 5012 9 cloth
0 7146 8062 1 paper
A special issue of the journal Israel Affairs
Israeli History, Politics and Society Series

FRANK CASS PUBLISHERS
Newbury House, 900 Eastern Avenue, Ilford, Essex, IG2 7HH
Tel: +44 (0)20 8599 8866 Fax: +44 (0)20 8599 0984 E-mail: info@frankcass.com
NORTH AMERICA
5804 NE Hassalo Street, Portland, OR 97213 3644, USA
Tel: 800 944 6190 Fax: 503 280 8832 E-mail: cass@isbs.com
Website: www.frankcass.com

In Search of Identity
Jewish Aspects in Israeli Culture

Dan Urian, *Tel-Aviv University* and
Efraim Karsh, *King's College London* (Eds)

As Israel celebrated its fiftieth year of statehood, Israeli society faces a deepening crisis of identity. This is particularly evident in Israeli culture which, for quite some time, has been effectively disintegrating into several simultaneous sub-cultures. This process has gained momentum during the 1990s due to the relaxation of national cohesiveness following the Arab–Israeli peace negotiations, on the one hand, and the growing post-modern influences on Israeli culture, on the other. This, in turn, has brought to the fore a whole range of questions which have hitherto been ignored, not least the interrelationship between the Hebrew and Jewish aspects of Israeli culture. This study of Israeli culture affords a meaningful insight into a society in a state of transition.

296 pages 1999
0 1746 4889 2 cloth   0 1746 4440 4 paper
A special issue of the journal Israel Affairs
Israeli History, Politics and Society Series

US–Israeli Relations at the Crossroads

Gabriel Sheffer, *The Hebrew University of Jerusalem* (Ed)

'… a vital source of information on the complex nature of the special relationship between the US and Israel.'
Israeli Perspectives

The essays by distinguished American and Israeli scholars deal with, among other things, the general global setting and its implications for this relationship; with 'hard' strategic factors; and with less tangible aspects, such as American images of Israel, the attitudes of other American religious denominations, and the situation of the American Jewish community and the influence of public opinion and the media on American policy towards Israel.

256 pages 1997
0 7146 4747 0 cloth   0 7146 4305 X paper
A special issue of the journal Israel Affairs
Israeli History, Politics and Society Series

FRANK CASS PUBLISHERS
Newbury House, 900 Eastern Avenue, Ilford, Essex, IG2 7HH
Tel: +44 (0)20 8599 8866 Fax: +44 (0)20 8599 0984 E-mail: info@frankcass.com
NORTH AMERICA
5804 NE Hassalo Street, Portland, OR 97213 3644, USA
Tel: 800 944 6190 Fax: 503 280 8832 E-mail: cass@isbs.com
Website: www.frankcass.com